A GAME OF TWO HALVES

A GAME OF TWO HALVES

Famous Football Fans Meet Their Heroes

AMY RAPHAEL

ALLEN&UNWIN

First published in the United Kingdom by Allen & Unwin in 2019
Copyright © Amy Raphael 2019

'Refugees' © Brian Bilston, 2016,
is reproduced with the kind permission of the author

All photographs featured herein are the copyright of the contributors, with the exception of the photographs of Gary Lineker on p. 109 (© David Cannon/Getty Images), Jürgen Klopp on p. 155 (© Frm/DPA/PA Images), John McGlynn on p. 185 (© John Marsh/EMPICS Sport/PA Images) and Ian Wright on p. 281 (© Bob Thomas Sports Photography via Getty Images).

Allen & Unwin
c/o Atlantic Books
Ormond House
26–27 Boswell Street
London WC1N 3JZ

Phone: 020 7269 1610
Fax: 020 7430 0916
Email: UK@allenandunwin.com
Web: www.allenandunwin.com/uk

A CIP catalogue record for this book is available from the British Library.

Hardback ISBN 978 1 91163 003 6
E-Book ISBN 978 1 76063 656 2

Designed by Carrdesignstudio.com
Printed in Great Britain by CPI Group (UK) Ltd, Croydon CR0 4YY

10 9 8 7 6 5 4 3 2 1

Foreword by Raheem Sterling..ix

Foreword by Gary Lineker..xi

Introduction by Amy Raphael..1

David Morrissey & Steven Gerrard................................15

Romesh Ranganathan & Héctor Bellerín................................43

Clare Balding & Lucy Bronze................................79

Gary Lineker & Fahd Saleh................................109

Johnny Marr & Pep Guardiola................................127

John Bishop & Jürgen Klopp................................155

Val McDermid & John McGlynn................................185

Omid Djalili & Frank Lampard................................215

Rachel Riley & Rio Ferdinand................................251

Wretch 32 & Ian Wright................................281

Amy Raphael & Vivianne Miedema................................307

David Lammy & Eric Dier................................333

Acknowledgments................................367

Refugees

They have no need of our help

So do not tell me

These haggard faces could belong to you or me

Should life have dealt a different hand

We need to see them for who they really are

Chancers and scroungers

Layabouts and loungers

With bombs up their sleeves

Cut-throats and thieves

They are not

Welcome here

We should make them

Go back to where they came from

They cannot

Share our food

Share our homes

Share our countries

Instead let us

Build a wall to keep them out

It is not okay to say

These are people just like us

A place should only belong to those who are born there

Do not be so stupid to think that

The world can be looked at another way

(now read from bottom to top)

Brian Bilston

Foreword by Raheem Sterling

Technically, I, myself, am an immigrant...

And yet when it comes to pulling on a white shirt in front of 90,000 people, I am just as English as the other ten players on the pitch. Game in, game out, I give my all to this country that has offered me so much.

I moved to London from Jamaica when I was five. My mother had moved slightly earlier to secure qualifications, so that she could offer me and my sister a better life. She achieved that, but it wasn't without hard work and endless sacrifices. The integrity and work ethic she continues to show are part of the reason I have been invited to write this for you today – her values and mental strength are infectious. Throughout my life, my mother has been the definition of integrity. She has helped me grow into the man I am today, unafraid to use my voice to represent those who are very rarely heard.

The estate I settled in after moving to London is shadowed by Wembley Stadium – the home of English football. My home. The team bus drives through areas which hold so many of my childhood memories and I have to pinch myself. How did I get here?! They talk about the American dream; this is the English dream. This is what makes the country we live in so special – we are diverse, we are cultured, but most importantly we are one.

Laziness breeds stereotypes. Every single one of us brings something to the table and everyone deserves to have their voice heard. I urge you all to just stop. And listen. Ask questions. And get to know those around you. Understand their culture and their background because that level of knowledge is powerful. And with such power we can make real positive change.

Foreword by Gary Lineker

Imagine this: Leicester is bombed and completely destroyed. We are forced to flee elsewhere because our families are being persecuted. Our parents have been killed. We can only leave by boat. It is a risk for our young children, but it is probably their only chance of survival. The sea is freezing cold. The boats are unsteady and unsafe. More family members die on the journey. The lucky few make it to the shore of another country. We have risked our lives to get there, but we find we are not wanted.

As soon as I started reading refugees' stories a few years ago, my conscience kicked in. Most of those who flee their countries don't choose to leave; they are political or economic refugees who desperately miss home. Feeling empathy for fellow human beings who have been dealt a really rotten hand is not a weakness. Fearing the arrival of refugees in your country does not make you patriotic, it makes you mean-spirited.

I don't regret tweeting my support for refugees, but it's a shame that Twitter pigeonholes those of us who speak out. We are judged as being on the extreme left or right, whereas I think most of us are somewhere in the middle. I do occasionally offer my political thoughts, but I don't think the refugee situation is political, it's humanitarian.

Some of the treatment of young migrants arriving in the UK has been heartless. I, for one, don't want to live in that kind of fractured society. And, unfortunately, some of those attitudes have been spilling out into the stands of football grounds. As Raheem Sterling has discovered, one of the most straightforward ways to answer the abuse coming from a minority of fans is by scoring goals. He deserves every accolade that has come his way this season – and none of the abuse.

There are more than 3.5 billion football fans in the world. At its best, football is about a shared language, respect and the celebration of diversity, as the footballers and managers in this book illustrate. Football can bring people together and, in doing so, it can set a really good example. I do believe that football gives back to society by doing that and by lifting people's lives.

When approached to write the foreword to *A Game of Two Halves*, I didn't hesitate because we must all find a way to help our fellow human beings. We have to do more to help each other. Reminding people that refugees don't choose to leave their homes is important and if this book can do that in a small way, it's a good thing.

Interviewing Fahd Saleh, a former goalkeeper for a team in Homs, Syria, for this book was thought-provoking and inspiring. It was a reminder that some of us are lucky to have been born in a relatively safe place by the lottery of birth. I consider myself fortunate to have played football around the world, to have four healthy sons and to live in a country untouched by war. Lucky, yes. Complacent, never. Call me all the names under the sun. I will never stop being patriotic nor will I stop standing up for refugees. We cannot forget them. They are human too.

Introduction by Amy Raphael

I was in Italy when the news came that we were to leave Europe. I lay awake all night, staring at the polls in the blue light of my mobile. Time passed. Four in the morning. Five in the morning. There was no going back. The 52 per cent had had their say. I flung open the window in a futile attempt to make the world seem bigger. I stared at the mist hanging low over the fields, at the sky streaked pink. I felt untethered, as though Britain had cut the umbilical cord connecting it to Europe.

A few months later, in August 2016, I came across two news stories that stayed with me. The first was a series of photos of Syrian children in Aleppo using a bomb crater filled with rain water as a swimming pool; one image showed a fully dressed boy bellyflopping painfully into the small, craggy hole as his mates looked on. The second was drone footage of kids playing football in Aleppo's dusty, desolate ruins. Just two lads kicking a ball back and forth with not a single other person in view. I knew millions had fled Syria since the civil war started in 2011, but the empty streets of Aleppo made me wonder exactly how many. So I looked up some statistics.

Over 5.6 million people have fled Syria since 2011. (The pre-war population was around 22 million, so a quarter of Syrians have left their country.)

Millions more are displaced inside Syria.

Around the world, 57 per cent of refugees come from three countries – Syria, Afghanistan and South Sudan.

An unprecedented 70.8 million people are forcibly displaced worldwide, of which 25.9 million are refugees. Half of those are under eighteen. Ergo half of them are children.

Or, to put it in different terms, one person is forcibly displaced every two seconds.

Every two seconds.

And Britain had just voted – among other things – to tighten, if not shut, its borders.

I wanted, like so many, to find a way of keeping the conversation going about displaced people. Why? Because, put simply, Britain thrives on its diversity and multiculturalism. We have, I believe, a global responsibility to look after each other. We are better together.

I thought again of the kids in Aleppo jumping into the makeshift pool, of the boys kicking a ball about a city that used to be thriving. They were doing what children do – trying to bring some normality to their lives despite everything. I recalled footage of kids in refugee camps across the world playing football. Football is the most popular sport in Syria and, indeed, across the world. It's matched only by the Olympics in terms of its global reach; according to FIFA, the World Cup 2018 was watched by almost half the world's population. It's a global sport with a global language.

It's easy to criticize football because of the sheer amount of money involved in it these days, but it also has a developing sense of social responsibility. Since its inception in 2006, Soccer Aid, an annual televised game in which retired footballers play against celebrities, has raised over £35 million for UNICEF UK. Ten years later, in 2016, Amnesty International started their 'Football Welcomes' weekend to 'celebrate the contribution refugees make to the game'. (By 2019, the British clubs taking part in this initiative had trebled to 160, with free match tickets and stadium tours given to refugees and people seeking asylum.)

You don't need to look very far to find immigrants playing at the very highest level across the world. Zlatan Ibrahimović, the retired Swedish international who has played for teams including Ajax, Juventus, Barcelona, Milan, PSG, Manchester United and LA Galaxy, has a Bosnian father and a Croatian mother. Kylian Mbappé, the France and PSG striker, is the son of a Cameroonian father and Algerian mother. France, Switzerland and Belgium have teams built on the sons of immigrants – Romelu Lukaku and Vincent Kompany are just two Belgian players of Congolese descent.

As Raheem Sterling writes in his foreword to this book, he too was born outside England. And yet when he pulls on the white shirt emblazoned with three lions, there is no doubt where his allegiance lies.

�✿ ✿ ✿

Trying to work out a way to keep the conversation going about displaced people as we drift away from democracy, I came up with the idea of asking famous football fans to meet their heroes for a charity book that raises money for refugees. Those who agreed to be in the book wouldn't be given an agenda; if the subject of tightened borders came up, then great. If not, then the fan and the footballer or manager could chat about whatever took their fancy. It was clear, to me at least, that the conversations would never be too far away from politics.

Football is, by its very nature, political. Look at Henning Mankell's piece for a 2006 issue of *National Geographic*, in which the Kurt Wallander novelist wrote about visiting Angola in 1987: 'War could never kill soccer in Angola. The soccer fields were demilitarized zones, and the face-off between teams conducting an intense yet essentially friendly battle served as a defence against the horrors that raged all around. It is harder for people who play soccer together to go out and kill each other.'

In the same issue (devoted to 'why the world loves soccer'), author Courtney Angela Brkic wrote about a 1990 match between Zagreb's Dinamo and Belgrade's Red Star that is widely seen as marking 'the beginning of Croatia's war for independence'. And, of course, Diego Maradona's second goal against England in the 1986 World Cup is arguably the best ever scored on the global stage but will forever be overshadowed by the goal he scored four minutes earlier; the 'Hand of God' goal saw the dazzling Argentinian labelled a cheat exacting revenge for the Falklands War that England 'won' four years earlier. These stories illustrate how central football can be to people's way of life, even if lazy journalism all too often portrays the footballers themselves as abandoning their roots.

In the late 1990s, when I was sports editor of *Esquire*, I wrote two chapters for *Perfect Pitch*, a series of football books edited by Simon Kuper and Marcela Maro Y Araujo. In one chapter I asked

Liverpool midfielder Steve McManaman to give me a tour of the Liverpool he grew up in and, while doing so, he talked passionately about his support of the city's striking dockers. Meanwhile, his teammate Robbie Fowler was fined for showing a T-shirt supporting the sacked dockers after scoring against SK Brann. In the second chapter, I met former Arsenal manager George Graham in his London flat just after he'd become manager of Tottenham. We talked about tribalism; I'd watched Arsenal v Tottenham in a north London pub a few days earlier and an Arsenal fan had dismissed Graham as a 'fucking spiv'. By way of response, Graham said, 'I can understand the fan. But I think this hatred between clubs is sad. Can't you support one team without hating another?'

When I started work on *A Game of Two Halves*, I asked Simon Kuper – now a columnist for the *FT* and author of the award-winning book *Football Against the Enemy* – about football not only being tribal but also a unifying force. 'It's not uncommon for people to support a big club, a small club and a foreign club. Or to follow a player,' he told me. 'The whole scene, even in England, is more fluid than people imagine or admit to. Of course football is divisive, but it's also the only thing that unites people any more. Because of the way we now watch TV or listen to music, there is no longer any communal conversation in most modern nations. But when there's a big international football match, people will discuss it the following day at the bus stop, in the office, at school. There's nothing else like it. It's not so much that we're polarized, it's more that we're atomized. And sometimes football can transcend that atomization, especially during a World Cup.'

I also asked Kuper for a short answer to a very big question: does football improve lives? 'Supporting a world-class team gives people an enormous feeling of pride and of being connected to people around the world, even though most people never leave their own country. Football gives you release from the pressure and perhaps the misery of life. It allows you to dream.'

Again, my mind flickered back to the images of the kids kicking a ball around in Aleppo. Football allowed them – for a few minutes at least – to dream.

⚽ ⚽ ⚽

In early 2017, I asked the actor David Morrissey if he would help me to draw up a list of potential fans and footballers for the book and also tell me about the work he does for UNHCR, the UN Refugee Agency, as one of their Goodwill Ambassadors. He agreed and, in March that year, we travelled with UNCHR to Lebanon to meet various Syrian families, including two who had been identified as vulnerable and were due to be resettled in the UK.

On the first day we met families living in an abandoned shopping mall in central Beirut. The air inside the gloomy space was considerably colder than the mild spring air outside. There was one bathroom for nine families with a total of twenty-seven children. Washing was hanging at the end of the corridor and the place was spotlessly clean, but the smell of damp was pervasive; during a recent rainstorm, the entire place had flooded. The families lived in small, windowless shopping units. We sat on the sofa cushions that doubled as beds and drank tiny cups of the strongest coffee while children played with old plastic toys or stared at us, their blank faces impossible to read. The adults all said the same thing: they wanted to go home to Syria and, if that wasn't possible, they wanted their kids to have a decent education.

We drove across town to an abandoned block of flats to meet the first of the families due to be resettled. Water sloshed down the communal stairs and junk was strewn everywhere, but the couple had done everything they could to make the flat habitable for their young son. Their respective mothers had travelled from Syria on a bus to say goodbye, knowing they might never see their children or grandchild again. The daughter talked eagerly about learning English and her dream of studying to be an architect while her mother wiped away an endless stream of tears. I thought of those who want to close our borders, but I said nothing.

At a community centre in Beirut we spoke briefly to older Syrians who meet once a week to cook and chat and discuss various issues, their eyes dull with disappointment. We were introduced to Syrian kids who jumped from one foot to the other, excited at the opportunity to show off their English. And to teenagers who talked about family members drowning as they tried to get to Greece by boat. 'It's not fair that we are seen as terrorists or as dangerous people,' said one girl. 'We have done nothing wrong.' Her friends could only nod in agreement.

The next day, we drove to the Beqaa Valley, where UNHCR and UNICEF have built emergency shelters as a short-term solution to a long-term problem. Every family we spoke to echoed those in the abandoned shopping mall: when they left Syria, they assumed it would be for six months but they had now been here for six years; they desperately wanted their children to have an education. If some of the adults had given up on their own futures, they were determined to find a way to get their kids out of the refugee camp.

Driving closer to the Syrian border, we parked next to a jumble of shacks with corrugated roofs. Here, the second Syrian couple who were moving to England lived with their two daughters. The two-year-old kept kissing her father's cheek while the six-year-old bounced on his lap, vying for his attention like all kids that age do. The mother, cooking her family a lunch of rice and potatoes and apologizing that she didn't have enough to go round, explained that they hadn't wanted to leave their family in Syria but that they had to protect their daughters – from war and then, as they turned eleven or twelve, from being sold into sexual slavery.

I knew what the mother and father wanted for their daughters: an education and a future in a country free from war. It wasn't much to ask and yet they knew they were the lucky ones.

⚽ ⚽ ⚽

Shortly after the trip to Lebanon, David Morrissey and I met up with Gary Lineker. An outspoken supporter of refugees on Twitter, he agreed to write a foreword to *A Game of Two Halves* and to help us get some of his *Match of the Day* and BT Sport colleagues on board. We agreed that there should be no more than two players or managers, past or present, from each team. I wanted the list to be as geographically diverse as possible, but the pairings were logistically challenging and the book limited in its length, so apologies to Newcastle and Sunderland fans. And Wales fans. And all the other fans whose teams aren't represented in this book.

Between October 2017 and May 2019, twelve fans met twelve footballers. (I came off the bench to chat to the Arsenal and Netherlands star Vivianne Miedema after the brilliant poet Hollie McNish moved heaven and earth to meet Miedema at her home in St Alban's but was finally defeated by her never-ending touring commitments.) The twists and turns of the 2018–19 Premier League season will live long in the memory – Liverpool and Tottenham's respective routes to the Champions League final in Madrid, beating Barcelona and Ajax against all the odds, is the stuff of dreams; Manchester City winning the League by one point – and as such made it impossible to keep all the chapters up to date.

It was hard enough to get two busy people in a room once, let alone be afforded the opportunity to update their chapters. When Liverpool-born David Morrissey met Steven Gerrard, for example, Gerrard was still managing the Under-19s at Liverpool and had not yet taken on his job as manager of Rangers; when I met Miedema, she was already a superstar in her native Holland but had yet to become the all-time top scorer for the Netherlands women's team, as she did in the second game of the World Cup. Nevermind; each chapter captures a moment in time, a revealing and sometimes surprising glimpse of the real person behind the myth.

I sat in on and moderated all the interviews except Val McDermid and John McGlynn, which took place in Kirkcaldy, Fife, and clashed with another interview in the book. It was fascinating to watch the famous fans relate to the footballers or managers they admired and vice versa. When my iPhone wasn't recording, the shy and serious Steven Gerrard relaxed and started chatting to David

Morrissey about playing golf in Liverpool and the friends they had in common. Six months before the Women's World Cup kicked off in France and pushed the women's game onto centre stage, Clare Balding and Lucy Bronze had a heated discussion about how women's football needed proper, across-the-board support.

Omid Djalili arrived on his motorbike to chat to Frank Lampard at the private health club at Stamford Bridge and Lampard stayed for over two hours even though he had only promised one, while Rachel Riley cycled across London to meet Rio Ferdinand at his London Bridge offices to discuss the good old days at Manchester United. Gary Lineker – his flight from Munich delayed the morning after the Bayern v Liverpool second leg – dashed across London to meet former Syrian goalkeeper Fahd Saleh at UNHCR's offices and then listened to Saleh's painful story thoughtfully and solicitously.

Sometimes I felt as though I was intruding on a kind of blind-date-for-mates. The fashion-conscious Héctor Bellerín got so carried away when chatting to Romesh Ranganathan about veganism and social media that he didn't have time to go home and get changed out of his tracksuit before going to see Ricky Gervais live. Wretch 32 and Ian Wright finished each other's sentences and the latter then posted a photo of the two of them on Instagram above the caption, 'It will never feel normal chilling with this legend.'

Johnny Marr was genuinely thrilled – and thrown – when Pep Guardiola asked him to sign a vinyl copy of his most recent album. Guardiola's office at the heart of Manchester City's Etihad campus was dominated by a white board detailing upcoming opponents. Psychology books were piled up at one end of his desk. The yellow ribbon that Guardiola sometimes pins to his jumper in support of political leaders jailed following the Catalonia independence referendum in 2017 sat next to a photo of his wife and kids. Right in front of me on the desk was a document entitled 'Liverpool', written in Spanish. At the end of his chat with Johnny Marr, Guardiola led us out of his office, chatting away and making jokes about this and that. Someone mentioned the fact that I was seeing Jürgen Klopp the next day and that I support Liverpool, and Guardiola took me by the arm as we stood at the top of the stairs.

'So, tomorrow you see Jürgen! Give him a big hug from me. A big hug! Tell him to be calm. He's a really nice guy.'

I smiled. I tried not to be partisan while working on this book, but at times it was a real challenge. There I was at the Etihad, making small talk with the only manager who could stop my team from winning the Premier League for the first time since 1989–90.

'So,' the hugely likeable Guardiola continued, beaming, 'I was just the appetiser. The main dish is tomorrow with Jürgen. We are a humble team, a humble club. We built our club stone by stone, like a cathedral. Liverpool are looking at us, thinking that they've done it all, which of course they have.'

The next day, I passed on Guardiola's message to Klopp, who replied: 'OK, good. I'll give him a hug back when I see him next time.' Football remains an alpha sport, but this hugging business that Klopp excels at is heartening. (I later watched the six-minute video filmed after Liverpool won the Champions League, in which Klopp walks around the pitch hugging *everyone*, including bereft Tottenham players. It might have been a small act of humanity, but it somehow felt like a bigger gesture.)

While waiting for Klopp, John Bishop and I had a super-healthy lunch at Melwood, Liverpool's training ground, and watched the first-team players come and go. There was James Milner asking about a secret stash of chocolate while Alex Oxlade-Chamberlain chatted about navigating his long-term injury in the most positive way possible, and Andy Robertson and Trent Alexander-Arnold passed through, grinning at some private joke.

I was born in London but spent school holidays in Liverpool, where my grandfather – a surgeon who occasionally operated on elite athletes – once operated on Graeme Souness and brought home autographed photos of that magnificent early-1980s Liverpool team. I spent time around the club in the mid- to late 1990s, watching Robbie Fowler, Steve McManaman and then Steven Gerrard play great football but win very little. Alongside many Liverpool fans, I feel that Klopp has a special affinity with the club, like Shankly, Paisley and Dalglish did before him. A couple of Scots, an Englishman and a German. Sounds about right to me.

When Bishop interviewed Klopp – and it was an interview more than a chat, which is just the way some of these pairings turned out – Liverpool had yet to win the Champions League and lose the League. Klopp was less laid-back than Guardiola, despite both having just returned from an international break, but he was no less attentive. Klopp was in fact so fired up by racism and politics when we went into his office (with its map of the UK on the wall so that he could see the location of away games when he first arrived from Germany) that he talked about these subjects non-stop for a third of the interview. I, for one, was happy; after all, this is why I wanted to do the book. This is what I hoped the book would be, especially when racism reared its ugly head as the season wore on and Raheem Sterling spoke out for himself and other young black players who were being unfairly maligned by the right-wing press and abused by a small number of fans.

Right at the end of the season, after Man City had won the Premier League by a single point, I asked Sterling if, having found his voice, he might consider writing a foreword to sit alongside Lineker's. He immediately agreed and wrote it straight from the heart.

David Lammy and Eric Dier were the final pairing to meet for *A Game of Two Halves*. They were supposed to be one of the first, but as David Lammy and I were heading for Tottenham's training ground in December 2018, Eric Dier was forced to cancel; he was suffering acute abdominal pain that turned out to be appendicitis. Then, with his immune system compromised, Dier got flu and cancelled again. But he finally made it to Parliament towards the end of May 2019, when both he and Lammy were still full of hope that Tottenham could win their first ever Champions League trophy.

A footballer asking a politician, unprompted, about the minimum wage and the London riots was a fitting end to a book in which there was also much levity (see Marr asking Guardiola about his apparently endless supply of round-necked cashmere jumpers). There is no denying that football is, at times, political or that it can transcend atomization. Maybe I'm being ridiculously optimistic, but through the prism of football, we can perhaps see ourselves more as a global 'us' than an 'us v them'. We can stop the dehumanizing 'othering' encouraged by Brexit, when people who 'aren't like us' are classified as 'not being one of us'.

As twenty-four-year-old Raheem Sterling points out in his foreword, Britain is great because 'we are diverse, we are cultured, but most importantly we are one.' He has the first word in this book, but he should also have the last.

David Morrissey

&

Steven Gerrard

David: What was going through your head the first time you came onto the pitch as a first-team player?

Steven: When Phil Thompson shouted me down at the Kop end to come on for the last few minutes, it's the one time as a footballer where I've been close to needing a nappy.

BT Sport, London, October 2017

David Morrissey was born in Liverpool in 1964. He joined the Everyman Theatre at sixteen and, two years later, was cast in the television series *One Summer*. He attended the Royal Academy of Dramatic Art and spent time both at the RSC and the National Theatre. He found global stardom playing the Governor in *The Walking Dead*, but in Britain he is rarely off our TV screens, starring in *Red Riding, The 7.39, The Missing* and *Britannia*. His acclaimed theatre work includes *In A Dark Dark House, Hangman, Macbeth* and *Julius Caesar*. In 2007, he was awarded an Honorary Fellowship for contributions to the performing arts at Liverpool John Moores University. He volunteers for several charities, including The Felix Project and The Bike Project. He is a Goodwill Ambassador for UNHCR.

Steven Gerrard was born in Liverpool in 1980. When he was eight, following a recommendation from his local football team manager, he was fast-tracked into Liverpool's Centre of Excellence alongside players such as Michael Owen. At sixteen, Gerrard started a two-year training course at Melwood, Liverpool's training ground. He made his first-team debut on 29 November 1998 against Blackburn Rovers.

Although the Premier League title eluded him, he went on to win two League Cups, two FA Cups, a European Super Cup, UEFA Cup and a UEFA Champions League Cup with Liverpool. Gerrard captained both Liverpool and England, scoring twelve goals in fifty-seven appearances for his country. After playing for Liverpool between the ages of eight and thirty-five, he finished his career playing for LA Galaxy in the Major League Soccer. Gerrard completed his UEFA A Licence and took his first managerial role as Liverpool youth coach, before managing the Under-18s. In June 2018, Gerrard became manager of Rangers.

✪   ✪   ✪

David Morrissey: Let's start at the beginning: how old were you when you realized you were different from your mates?

Steven Gerrard: Probably around the age of thirteen; I knew then that I was going to be a professional footballer because I was offered a long contract by Liverpool. A two-year schoolboy contract, a two-year apprenticeship – called the YTS back in the day – and a three-year guaranteed contract after that. I didn't know I was going to play for Liverpool's first team back then, but it was the age I said to myself, 'I must be half decent...'

David: You must have known you were decent when you were knocking a ball around with your mates in the playground?

Steven: I knew I was a level above. A bit different. That sounds big-headed, but I don't know how else to put it. I just found it really easy. Sometimes I'd play with the ball on my own in the playground because playing with kids my own age wasn't enough of a challenge.

David: What are you earliest memories of watching football?

Steven: I lived in a street called Ironside Road on the Bluebell Estate and there were always street parties when Liverpool played Everton in a cup final. In May 1986, when I was six years of age, there was a crazy street party for the FA Cup Final. It was probably the first full game I watched.

David: I remember those parties! Are you saying that you got into football for the party?

Steven: Well, that party was certainly an eye-opener! What's this big occasion, why are we having a street party? I obviously knew my dad and my brother were Liverpool fans, but Everton scored in the first half. A Gary Lineker goal. At which point, I was thinking of being a blue. My mum's brother was a blue too. It was touch and go if I was going to be a blue or a red. My mum's side was more blues, my dad's side was strictly reds. And then obviously the game was turned around on its head in the second half and it ended up being 3-1 to Liverpool. Rushy [Ian Rush] scored a couple and Craig Johnston scored one. At the end of that day, worn out from watching the Cup Final and having enjoyed the street party, I officially became a red.

David: I had a very similar thing with my son, who grew up in north London. The first big game we watched together was Arsenal v Liverpool in 2001. I really talked up Liverpool, determined to make him a red. But when Freddie Ljunberg scored for Arsenal in the seventy-second minute, my son was really torn. He looked so guilty. And then, of course, with just ten minutes of the game left, Michael Owen scored two and Liverpool won. That was it, my son was a Liverpool fan.

Steven: It's mad how certain moments can decide who you support.

David: How would it have gone down at home if you'd have been a blue instead?

Steven: Not very well, because my older brother is a red as well.

David: I'm from a split family too. My older brother is a blue, as was my dad. My other brother and I are both reds. It's always tricky.

Steven: To be honest, from the age of six I've had a very nice time being a red because Liverpool dominated the city during that period. I think I made the right decision.

David: You absolutely did. What are your memories of being at Liverpool once you'd signed on to their YTS?

Steven: Well, for one thing, we all earned the same: £47.50 a week. I was sixteen, I'd left school and for the first time I had money in my pocket.

David: How did signing on for Liverpool go down with your mates? Did your relationship have to change?

Steven: Slightly, yes. I came from a council estate where gangs of lads used to get up to things that I couldn't get involved in. I suppose at times I was the boring one. I had to go home early. I was sent home on many occasions by my older brother if he saw me out after a certain time. Or if he saw me around, getting up to no good, I'd normally get a kick up the backside and get sent home. So I had the right people around, telling me what to do before I got involved in the wrong stuff.

David: I assume the club looked after you too, given that you were effectively an investment for them?

Steven: I wasn't aware of it at the time. But later I spoke to my dad and Steve Heighway [former Liverpool player who became director of Liverpool Academy] about it and Steve was regularly on the phone, asking where I was and what I was up to. He told my dad to keep me off the streets and out of trouble.

David: Were there dietary restrictions too?

Steven: It wasn't as strict as it is now. At fourteen, young players are now told exactly what to eat. And what not to eat. Whereas we were just told to keep an eye on the fast-food side of it.

David: I presume as a trainee you were expected to do some crappy jobs?

Steven: The jobs at Melwood – there was no Academy then – were organized via a monthly rota. For example, three or four lads were in charge of making sure all the floors were clean. Another three or four would be in charge of the medical department, making sure everything was tidy and the towels were clean. Others would be on laundry duty, cleaning first-team boots or sorting out balls, bibs and cones.

David: Was it pressurized or did you have a laugh?

Steven: There was pressure in the sense that you'd have Ronnie Moran, Sammy Lee and Phil Thompson barking down your ear, telling you that you're a lazy F-U-C-K. You had to make sure you were on it. We laughed on the job when we were sorting the balls, bibs and cones because they were kept next to the staff toilets. Most of the staff were quite regular of a morning so it used to stink in there. It could be a long month. Big Joe Corrigan always seemed to have been to the toilet ten minutes before we had to start work.

David: How much did you interact with the first team, some of whom were your heroes?

Steven: All my heroes were in the next dressing room. We used to go and watch them on a Saturday. Jamie Redknapp. Robbie Fowler. Before that, when I was a schoolboy, it was the likes of John Barnes and Ian Rush.

David: How were they with you?

Steven: Brilliant. Just great fellas.

David: Very early on in my acting career, I worked at the Everyman Theatre in Liverpool. In the company at that time were actors like Jim Broadbent and the late Pete Postlethwaite. I used to go up to them and ask about acting and they were always great. Rather than telling me to get lost or smacking me around the head, they really encouraged me. I made sure I thanked them when I was older and established.

Steven: Yeah, it's odd because I ended up sharing a dressing room with all these players. I went from cleaning their boots, putting their kit out for them and being intimidated around them to actually playing with them. It was a big learning curve, learning how you treat people younger than you, who are striving to make it.

David: When you are training with those players and watching them win, lose or draw at the weekend, how did it feel when you turned up at Melwood on a Monday morning?

Steven: There were these benches where all the young apprentices used to stand holding a couple of balls and a couple of shirts. Your responsibility as a trainee was to wait for every first-team player to walk past and make sure they signed the shirts and balls for local charities. If they'd lost at the weekend it was a long ten to fifteen minutes because you could just see by their faces…

David: Not just as a team, but individually?

Steven: Yeah, each of them was carrying the result from the weekend. Whereas, for the majority of us, as sixteen- or seventeen-year-olds, if you lost at the weekend you mostly got over it pretty quick. That's where football changes. It becomes less enjoyable the higher up you go simply because there's more at stake. It's only enjoyable when you win.

David: By the time Gérard Houllier brought you through to the first team, you must have been ready to make the transition. What was he like as a manager?

Steven: He was a father figure to me. He was always there for me. He basically changed the way I lived off the pitch. Growing up, I was quite relaxed. My diet, my social life, which nights I'd go out, where I'd go out and play with my friends. As soon as I met Gérard Houllier, my life changed off the pitch. For a start, I didn't get home till much later because after training he had me doing extra weights.

David: To build you up?

Steven: Yes, because I was a skinny, fragile player at the age of sixteen. Between the ages of sixteen and twenty, I had to do a lot of extra work so my days were longer. Gérard also had a meeting with my parents to make sure that after I came home from Melwood, I was in and resting for the rest of the day. We got all kinds of diet information, and the fridge had to change.

David: Do you think that was to do with Houllier being French?

Steven: He certainly changed the culture of the whole club.

David: Would it be too much to say his influence reached beyond Liverpool?

Steven: I don't think you can give him the credit for any other club, but the likes of him and Arsène Wenger – and the general influx of foreign managers at the time into the English game – changed everything. Prior to their arrival, there was a culture of drinking, overeating and eating the wrong stuff. And getting away with it. But then the foreign managers came in and changed the rules – and as a result their clubs improved and moved up the league and then everyone else tried to catch up.

David: Did you want to please Houllier by taking his advice? Did he ever bawl you out?

Steven: I had no choice but to take Gérard's advice. A couple of times he dragged me off the pitch and humiliated me in front of people. He always knew which button to press with me. He knew when to upset me, when to make me happy, when to care for me. He knew me inside out; he knew what I was feeling before I spoke or looked at him. He's a genius.

David: Tell me about the first time you came onto the pitch as a first-team player, in November 1998, against Blackburn. What was going through your head?

Steven: It was a flash. A couple of minutes. Like a dream. I've never really been petrified in my life, never been totally scared to the core, to the point where you feel like passing out. But when Phil Thompson shouted me down at the Kop end to come on for the last few minutes, it's the one time as a footballer where I've been close to needing a nappy.

David: I can only imagine! Did you have family and mates in the crowd?

Steven: Yes, they were sitting exactly where I was warming up. About eighteen rows up. I used to get four free tickets for a game and you'd get maybe eight to buy. I probably had about twelve people just in that area. You jog up to take your kit off and your heart is going a million miles an hour. You say to yourself, 'This is it. This is basically what I've been waiting for.'

David: And then it was over.

Steven: And all of a sudden, I'm in the car on my way home. I felt on top of the world.

David: And then it all started. The highs, the lows. When you scored that ninetieth-minute equalizing goal against West Ham in the 2006 FA Cup Final, I was doing a film in New Zealand. It was about four in the morning and it was one of the greatest moments in my life. What was it like for you? Did you know the moment the ball left your boot?

Steven: Yeah, with that one I did. It was one of those shots – you play golf yourself – where you hit it perfectly.

David: Well, I can't say it works for me…

Steven: I haven't hit many of those myself with a golf club. But the football hit a sweet spot. I was tired at the time. I was cramping up, I didn't have much left to give. Normally I'd probably have controlled the ball and tried to start an attack, but I knew the clock was running down. I heard the tannoy just before it. It was just a pot-luck shot really and it came off.

David: How aware are you of the crowd and of individual shouts when you're out on the pitch?

Steven: Very aware, me. Some players I've played with say they're not. I was always aware, always conscious. I used to take the fans very seriously. Especially at Anfield; I used to get a different feeling playing there to playing anywhere else. I used to play for the supporters really. They were the ones I always wanted to impress.

David: Was it a very different atmosphere when you played away in Europe?

Steven: Yeah, it was a different experience. It's a different type of game. Domestically against a lot of teams you can get results if you play averagely. For example, most teams in the bottom half of the Premiership will be similar. Most teams in the top half will be similar too. But going away in Europe was always unpredictable. There was a different type of pitch, a different type of noise, different weather conditions and different tactics.

If, for example, you were in Portugal or Spain, you'd know you'd get a really fast, technical game. In Russia you'd always know it was going to be cold. You'd maybe be playing on plastic pitches, which were common over there due to the cold weather. And the home fans could be really hostile.

David: Apart from during the match itself, was there any gamesmanship, anything going on to destabilize you?

Steven: The journey on the coach from the airport to the ground was always different. It was a lot more hostile. I remember hearing police sirens and getting a police escort everywhere. At a lot of grounds, home fans would be banging on the bus when you arrived at the stadium, especially as you progressed further into competitions. When we played in Dortmund in the UEFA Cup Final, we got stuck outside the ground because of the hordes of fans. The bus was shaking.

David: Going back to those early years with the big players, I wonder how much you learned from them. How did you interact with them on the pitch? Did you listen to some players more than others?

Steven: Early on was tough for me. When Gérard Houllier gave me my chance to play in the first team, I didn't feel ready. Looking back now, I probably wasn't ready for the first six months of it. So there were a lot of stray passes and maybe times when I underperformed. I was lucky to have a lot of local lads in the team to help me: Jamie

Carragher, Michael Owen. Jamie was older, but obviously I knew Michael well, having met him when we were both apprentices. They had my back if I gave away a loose pass. But the big leaders in the team, like Paul Ince, would let you know if you gave a pass away, so at times it was tough. You're in a sink-or-swim scenario.

David: If someone was having a go at you on the pitch, did you know it wasn't for the sake of it, it wasn't to knock you down?

Steven: At the time it felt as though they were being a bit harsh on me, but as you grow up and get more experience and mature a bit, you know they are doing it to help you. They are only doing it for the team. There have been many times when I've done it to people myself. It's not about singling a player out, it's to try and help the team.

David: Talking on the pitch must be one of the first things a player learns?

Steven: Communication is one of the most important elements of football. When I coached Liverpool Under-18s, I was on to them every day. I had a go at them if they weren't communicating, because that's where mistakes and mishaps happen.

David: Do you think there's sometimes a fear of talking on the pitch?

Steven: When you're young you let people get away with it, but as you get closer to the man's game, you realize pretty quickly that all you hear on that pitch is voices and shouting, communication and messages. You have to get used to it fast.

David: What about injury? I read in your autobiography that it's a complete myth for a player to be 100 per cent fit. How do you play through injury and who makes that decision for you?

Steven: Physios and doctors are guided by the information or feedback that you give them. There were times when I knew I was carrying a niggle, I had a swollen ankle or I'd been badly kicked... You know what you can play through. You can play through the majority of kicks and bruises. The ones you can't play through are muscle strains. They get worse and then you end up missing a load more games. At times you've just got to listen to your body.

David: Did you have to learn to do so?

Steven: I can't remember a game where I was perfect and my body felt like a million dollars.

David: Never?

Steven: No, not if you train properly from Monday to Friday, at 100 per cent high tempo, high speed. I used to train the way I played, so I'd probably have been making twenty to forty tackles a week. That's a guess. I'd be going up for ten, fifteen aerial duels. I'd be going to ground ten, fifteen times a day. How is the body going to be perfect coming up to Saturday? If you train right and you do it properly, your body shouldn't be absolutely perfect.

David: When you play with great players – you often talk about Luis Suárez and Fernando Torres – what do you think they give you on the pitch?

Steven: They gave me a buzz. I always felt with either of them in attack that we had a chance against anyone in the world. For me personally it was a joy – and that was the buzz, knowing that when I received the ball, I'd have their movement ahead of me. Playing with players like Suárez and Torres obviously gives the team a better chance. It gives the fans a chance of going home in a better mood. World-class players do world-class things.

David: Luis Suárez did things that you never saw other players doing on the pitch. He was suddenly in places that you didn't anticipate. Did he train like that as well?

Steven: He was exactly the same. He's a freak of a footballer.

David: He sort of arrived under the radar.

Steven: He did, yeah.

David: He was signed at the same time as Andy Carroll, in January 2011. Dalglish signed Carroll for a club record of £35 million and Suárez from Ajax for £22.7 million.

Steven: I was obviously aware of him when he was at Ajax. But having trained with him for a full week, it was one of those moments in my career where I was like, 'Oh yes, we've got an absolute gem.' The way he trained and the way he played – he was by far the best player I've played with.

David: And a very emotional player.

Steven: I love watching emotional players. Luis is one of those people who I'd pay any price to go and watch. You asked about injury: this is a player who never walked into a treatment room once during all the years I played with him. He never once had a bag of ice on his leg. He even played with a hamstring injury, which is unheard of. He was all about his family. And then all of a sudden people have this opinion of him because of his behaviour in certain games. But he was completely different as a person. An incredible footballer. Mentally strong.

David: And that filters around the other players.

Steven: It's infectious. We couldn't wait to get out on a pitch with him. We used to all go out behind him, knowing he could occupy a whole defence on his own.

David: At that point in your career, when you were Liverpool captain, did anyone at the club discuss its transfer intentions with you? Would they talk to you about who they were looking for?

Steven: I wouldn't be involved in any decision-making. Certain managers would tell me what they were thinking and who they were after. They might want me to speak to the player in question at some point. I suppose I was closer to the news than other first-team players, but never once did anyone say, 'Shall we?' or 'What is your opinion on this?' Never.

David: So you're playing for Liverpool – the greatest club in the world – and then you're called up for England. Were you ever at odds with Liverpool over commitments to England?

Steven: At times, if I was carrying a bit of an injury but still wanted to play for England, the club would be very cautious and advise me not to play. But they'd never stop you.

David: How did the two set-ups – club and country – compare?

Steven: England always felt very different to Liverpool. You always feel comfortable with the players you work with on a daily basis. At times, with England, it felt like we were all individuals. A lot of the time we played as individuals. I don't think we had a manager along the way who made everyone park their egos. Or who really fitted us into a system or a way of playing that suited the country. Did I have the right manager? Everything says not. I felt as though

I was surrounded by top players, top individuals. But when we went out to play, I felt as though we were a team of individuals.

David: What about the media side of being England captain? You always seemed very comfortable being Liverpool captain, but as England captain it always felt as though there was another agenda.

Steven: Being England captain was tough. There are agendas around the England set-up. You've got southern press. Northern press. Press that prefers southern or northern players. Certain journalists who have maybe asked for interviews over the years and, because you turned them down, they change their minds about you, even though they know what you can do and who you are. There were southern journalists who were close to players in my position who played for southern teams – Frank Lampard being the obvious one – so they ended up pushing those players instead of me. I got it. I understood. No problem. Because I had the northern press pushing for me. That's just the way it is and it's not going to change. It's something you need to accept and get on with as an England player.

David: When England smacked Germany 5-1 in 2001, the Germans changed the way in which they brought their young players through. The German FA and Bundesliga seem to work together.

Steven: Obviously that result hurt Germany and they had an overhaul of their system, but I'm not sure if it was specifically because of that result. I don't think they were in good form at the time anyway. Germany has certainly found a winning formula since then. I think it's this: when all these top German players come together, their egos are parked and they play as a team. Joachim Löw is a strong manager; if an individual wants to come in and do it his own way, he doesn't play.

David: And that filters into the Bundesliga too.

Steven: It filters everywhere. So everyone knows that, when they go and join up with Germany, they are playing for Germany and are sacrificing themselves for the team.

David: Which brings us back to bringing young players through in England. When you were Under-18 manager, how did you control young players' expectations, disappointments and egos?

Steven: Everyone has an ego. Trying to manage and control twenty-five egos is one of the most challenging aspects of the job. When I was youth coach at Liverpool, it was quite easy to always use the values of the club, which have been in place for a long time and will be in place for ever. That's what those kids had to understand: if they want to break through then they have to do it the Liverpool way. Which obviously means that your attitude has to be spot on; you have to work hard to improve on a daily basis.

David: I always noticed that if you were interviewed after a match alongside a younger player, and the interviewer excessively praised that player, you were keen to point out that it was a team game.

Steven: I was always protective of the younger players. I know how the media works. Going back to the England team for a moment, it's very easy for the media to build the young lads up. 'This is the golden generation' stuff and 'they're going to be World Cup winners.' The problem we've got in this country is that a player only has to have two or three good games and suddenly they're the next Bryan Robson, the next Paul Gascoigne. That's not the way. So, as England captain, if I ever felt a journalist was trying to go down that route, I'd always remind them to be constructive, be fair to the player. Yes, give him praise because he's played really well, but I need this player to have his feet on his ground because we've got another game in three days.

David: I have a similar thing with young actors sometimes. They'll come in and start snapping at people. I'll ask why and they'll say it's because they didn't get a job. But the reason you didn't get *that* job is because you're doing *this* job. That idea of envy and expectation can be really disruptive.

Steven: I can only speak for young players, but they have a lot of influences around them these days, especially compared to when I was starting out. They have agents much earlier – some have two or three. Parents can be very forceful. There's no patience any more. Everyone wants it yesterday. Whereas I was lucky: I had a family, I had good people around me who trusted the club, trusted the people at the club to make the right decisions for me and who believed in me. The best advice I ever got was from my dad: 'You'll get out of this job what you put in. If you commit to it and give it everything you've got, the rewards will come.'

David: Sports such as football and boxing are predominantly working-class games, and the promise of riches is often dangled in front of a young player early on. It must be tough telling players that wanting it all and wanting it fast is not the best idea, long term.

Steven: There are big risks. Big expectations. It's quite normal for families to want both success on the field and financial reward. At the same time, you've got to remind everyone to be patient. Give your kid the right advice and trust the people who know how to handle a young professional.

David: Is part of that also about looking after young players that don't make it?

Steven: To be fair to Liverpool, they do. The club isn't just interested in the two or three that might be about to break through to the first team. It helps every single kid with his education, with bettering his life, improving his CV, giving him something to fall back on. If it's not working out with Liverpool, they work their socks off to try and give them an opportunity to get signed by another club. I think a lot of academies do that now. I don't think it's right to set up a huge academy and just favour two or three players because they've got the best chance. Everyone is human, everyone deserves a chance. Liverpool are brilliant at it.

David: Do you think young players at LFC or Rangers listen to you because you were such a successful, high-profile player? When you were a player, did you have more time for a manager like Dalglish who'd been such an incredible player?

Steven: No. Managing and coaching are totally different to being a player. I don't think you have to have been a top player to be a top manager. Look at Klopp. Or Wenger or Mourinho. Those fellas are world-class managers, but they wouldn't mind me saying they were never world-class players. I wouldn't listen to Kenny any differently to Brendan Rodgers, just because Kenny was the best player ever to play for Liverpool and Brendan never really played much. I have huge respect for both. Plus I treat managers as they treat me. If they've got my best interests at heart, they get my respect back.

David: Can we talk about being a pundit?

Steven: We can talk about *trying* to be a pundit.

David: And now you are! But when you were a player, did you hate them?

Steven: I didn't mind them. I hated the ones that were personal. There is occasionally one who is trying to make a name for himself and who wants to stay in the job longer. If a pundit constructively criticized me after a poor performance, no problem. I'd shake their hand. I'd take it all day. Because I'm human and I'm not going to play well every single week. But if anyone was personal or it felt like they were going for me because they didn't like me or were jealous of me, I couldn't have that.

David: Do you have that in your head as a pundit?

Steven: I do have it in my head and I wouldn't have agreed to work for BT Sport if I was going to get personal with anyone, if I was going to dig them out for no reason. I get no personal gain by going for a player. I'm there to do a job and my job is to analyse a game. Teams, tactics, individuals. If and when I have an opinion and I say something, I'll only say it if I feel like I can back it up with constructive comments.

David: How do you find live broadcasting?

Steven: When I have time to do it, I enjoy it. It keeps my profile where I want it to be and it keeps me involved in the game. I'm learning all the time in terms of how managers choose a team, why they make changes. It gives me the chance to speak to managers too. I'm a big fan of the Premier League and the Champions League, so it's great.

David: You played for Liverpool for most of your career, turning down the opportunity to play for Chelsea on the way, but then you went to LA Galaxy. Did you enjoy the Californian lifestyle?

Steven: You probably know more about that than me! But yeah, I loved it. I had been in the pressure cooker of being Liverpool and England captain and that period of my life was coming to a close. I wasn't ready to call it a day as a player and I wanted to play at a decent level, but never for a team that could face Liverpool. The MLS was the perfect opportunity to do that for eighteen months. I also wanted to go to a city where I could relax and enjoy myself, where I wasn't getting stopped here, there and everywhere. Where I could go and do some of the things I hadn't been able to do for the previous fifteen years.

David: And the weather.

Steven: That always helps.

David: Did you travel around America?

Steven: Obviously with the team, to places like New York, Chicago and Philadelphia. I basically toured America.

David: Did the family go with you?

Steven: They came in and out because we didn't change the kids' schools. The schools gave us permission to extend every holiday by a week. It worked really well and it was a good experience for them. It was good to have a breather from Liverpool, freshen up and prepare to go back as a coach.

David: Has coaching thrown up things you weren't anticipating?

Steven: At the beginning it did. I was out of my comfort zone. I very quickly realized how different it was to playing. You go on the pitch on Monday morning and it's your responsibility to put on a training session for twenty-five players. As a player you have to worry about yourself and then try to help a few people around. As a manager I needed to do a couple of years of learning, making mistakes, collecting all types of different information from teams and players. Find out where I'm strong as a coach and a manager. Where I need help, guidance and support.

David: Why do you think there's a paucity of English managers? Why has the foreign manager become the go-to person?

Steven: I don't know. It's a difficult question to answer.

David: Is it just fashion?

Steven: At times it is. Because not every foreign manager gets it right and a lot of British managers are under-estimated. The leap for me was realizing that managing is a completely different job. The easiest thing for a player who had a career like me would be to cut corners and take job offers based on my reputation as a player.

Whereas I only wanted to consider job offers when I felt good enough to take them on. It gives me the best chance of succeeding. I think a lot of players come out of the game and automatically think they're going to be a great coach, and that's where a lot of people go wrong.

David: Is language a problem when you've got a dressing room full of players from all over the world?

Steven: It can be a problem when you've got players or managers who don't have an extensive English vocabulary. But 95 per cent of the time it's fine. Even players who can't speak English know the language of football.

David: And what's that, in a nutshell?

Steven: Receive the ball and keep possession!

Romesh Ranganathan

& Héctor Bellerín

Romesh: Just before I came up here to meet you, I was having a vape in the alleyway. This guy came up to me and said, 'Everyone is going to be so amazed I got a photo with you.' As we were posing he asked, without a hint of embarrassment, 'Sorry, what's your name?'

Héctor: That happens to me too! Sometimes people think I'm Nacho Monreal. 'Hey, Nacho, you were so consistent last season!' I'm thinking to myself, yes, *he* was.

Héctor Bellerín's management offices, central London, December 2018

Romesh Ranganathan was born in Crawley, West Sussex, in 1978 to Sri Lankan parents. He trained as a maths teacher and taught in Crawley and Surrey, spending every spare minute doing stand-up comedy. He did his first proper gig in Shoreditch at the age of thirty-one and four years later was nominated for Best Newcomer at the Edinburgh Comedy Awards. He has since appeared on myriad television shows, including *The Reluctant Landlord, Just Another*

Immigrant, The Misadventures of Romesh Ranganathan, A League of Their Own and, with Rob Beckett, *Rob & Romesh Vs...* In 2018 his autobiography, *Straight Outta Crawley: Memoirs of a Distinctly Average Human*, was published.

Héctor Bellerín was born in Barcelona in 1995. He played for Barcelona's youth team from 2003 to 2011 before moving to London and joining Arsenal's youth team. Since 2013, he has been playing for Arsenal's senior team, apart from a short loan period at Watford. He reached the semi-finals of the 2013 European Championship with Spain's Under-19 team and was picked for the senior team in 2016. He won the FA Cup with Arsenal in 2014–15 and 2016–17 and the FA Community Shield in both 2015 and 2017. He was young Catalan Player of the Year in 2015.

⚽　⚽　⚽

Héctor Bellerín: So sorry for the delay. Training finished late.

Romesh Ranganathan: No problem at all. By chance, we're going to the same gig tonight.

Héctor: You're going to Ricky Gervais too? I love him, man. I love English comedy, but sometimes I have to watch it a few times to really get it. In fact, I probably have to watch something three times before I fully understand it.

Romesh: Have you watched a comic's work-in-progress before?

Héctor: No, it'll be my first time. He'll be trying out new material, right?

Romesh: Yeah. I think it's the most exciting time to see a comedian. By the time a show like *Humanity* gets to Netflix, it's polished. Ricky's live show is pretty edgy anyway, but tonight he might say something for the first time to gauge the response.

Héctor: But the way he does it is smart. For me, the bit where he talks about Caitlyn Jenner in *Humanity* was so smart.

Romesh: That's the bit Ricky got the most shit for. I try to push the boundaries with my comedy, but it has become increasingly difficult because people get offended very easily.

When I do stand-up, I have thought very carefully about what I'm going to say. But if I see something on Twitter, I react to it very quickly, sometimes without thinking about what I'm writing. And then you get done for it. Everyone is on your back, telling you you're out of order.

Héctor: If I want to tweet something, I always ask Ehsen [Shah, his manager] what he thinks first. I let the idea brew for a bit and then write something. I want to be outspoken and I want people to know that I have opinions on things, but it's often not worth it. Not for me, at least. It's different for you; it goes with your job. Footballers generally don't have much to say publicly because they are afraid of the backlash. But I want to change that perception. I don't mind taking the backlash. But sometimes I'm not sure it's worth it; as you said, you can offend so many people so quickly.

Romesh: I often write a tweet and delete it immediately. And within the nanoseconds that the tweet existed, someone has probably taken a screen shot.

Anyway, I wanted to say that I'm a massive Arsenal fan and you are an absolute legend, mate. I don't want to fanboy too much, but the two things I would say about you are this: you are part of this generation of players that clearly have a personality and you're not scared to speak up on the Arsenal website or in interviews. You're also part of a generation of footballers who allow fans to see behind the curtains. Arsenal have had players with personalities in the past – you only have to read Tony Adams' autobiography to know that he got up to some shit – but he was the exception rather than the rule.

Héctor: Footballers are still told to stick to football and not to talk about anything else. For a lot of footballers it's easy to stay at home and post boring stuff after a game. I feel that we will never go forward if we keep doing that. There need to be people doing something a bit differently, slowly pushing the boundaries. Football is never going to change otherwise. Maybe if I do it, younger players will follow. 'Héctor's doing it, etc.' It makes me happy to influence other people in a positive way. At the end of the day, that's what social media is good for. It's bad for a lot of things, but we can also use it to show that we aren't machines that play every Saturday. We are ordinary people who have our passions and our problems just like everyone else.

Look at what happened when Raheem Sterling wrote about racism on Instagram. It seemed to come pretty much out of nowhere and it started a really important conversation. Racism exists. It's out there. Us footballers have the chance to change the world and we should be using that chance whenever we can. Because of his profile, Raheem making those comments is going to have a bigger effect than almost anyone else.

Romesh: It was a brilliant post. People don't expect a footballer to say those kinds of things. I used to do stand-up about footballers; they are easy targets because they are traditionally seen as stupid. That's the stereotype, anyway. A presenter read Raheem's Instagram post out on the radio verbatim, totally ignoring the fact that it was written in Raheem's colloquial language, while he was clearly really fucking upset. The presenter's vibe was slightly sneery.

Héctor: Like they were reporting the story but still having a laugh at him?

Romesh: Yeah and even though they agreed with the sentiment of what he was saying, they were mocking him. Without even knowing they were doing it. There was this prevailing attitude of, 'Who gives a shit what footballers have to say about anything?'

Héctor: It's always been the same in Spain.

Romesh: Even global superstar footballers aren't exempt. David Beckham is always seen as the thickest man on the planet. Too daft to even complete a jigsaw puzzle. But then you watch old footage of him playing – or of any world-class footballer – and every time he plays a ball across the field, he's intuitively working out the trajectory of the ball.

Héctor: Most footballers come from difficult backgrounds. If your mum or dad is a banker or a doctor then you're hardly likely to become a footballer; your parents will most likely put you through university and you'll have a career. My mum and dad raised me really well and I didn't have to hang around the streets all day, but I'm still from a lower-class family. When Alexis Sánchez was growing up in Chile, he used to clean cars in the local cemetery. It's why such a huge percentage of NBA players are black. It's so often about opportunity. Your family doesn't have the funds to support you through college so, if you're lucky, you play sport at a high level.

We are just as good at what we do as people who are college-educated. If Einstein was still alive, he probably wouldn't have a clue about the offside rule. We have a different kind of intelligence.

Romesh: There is definitely an element of elitism around sport, I think. In this country both footballers and football fans have been stereotyped – footballers as thick and fans as thuggish. It doesn't happen with cricket and rugby, both sports that are played in private schools. Cricket certainly wasn't played at the comprehensive school I went to.

Héctor: The people who play cricket and rugby at private school are privileged. Football is not a privileged sport at all. I've met so many footballers who haven't even been to school. The fact that they didn't have that opportunity doesn't mean they are stupid. They often have emotional intelligence, they are engaged, they are funny. They are street-smart. They might not know about some mathematical law, but then they don't need to know.

Romesh: Someone on social media tells me I'm stupid or shit at least once a day. In fact, I don't think a day has gone by when someone hasn't said, 'I hope you disappear.' The first time it happened, I was quite hurt. 'OMG, I'm just trying to be funny!' Sometimes you just have a shit day at work. Sometimes I've done *Mock the Week* and even though I've done the preparation, for whatever reason it's not felt right. I've just been shit. And every fucking time I get to hear about it on Twitter. But that's nothing compared to what high-profile sportspeople get on a daily basis.

Héctor: Yeah, it's really bad.

Romesh: You can post really innocuous stuff and still be thrown to the wolves. I swear to god, a footballer could post something as benign as, 'Enjoying an omelette before heading off to training,' and god knows how many people would start shouting in the comments. 'If you ate fewer eggs then maybe you wouldn't be so sluggish on the pitch, you fucking asshole!'

Héctor: It's exactly like that! It doesn't matter what you do, someone will always find something to complain about. And, of course, fans of other teams pick on you even more than your own fans. You probably like different comedians to, say, Ricky Gervais, but it doesn't mean you are actively *against* other comedians. Football is obviously very tribal. As an Arsenal player, you have Tottenham fans, Liverpool fans, City fans and all the rest chatting shit to you. And if you're not playing well, your own fans as well.

Romesh: Does it hurt more when it comes from Arsenal fans?

Héctor: I try not to care, man. When I started, no one knew much about me. No one expected anything from this kid, and I turned out really good.

Romesh: I remember when you came to Arsenal, you were one of a crop of young Arsenal players who nobody had really heard of. The fans were so excited. 'I don't even know where Bellerín has come from, man, but he's fucking good!'

Héctor: It was really good for me because when no one has any expectations of you, you play with a lot less pressure. And then you start to play well and the expectations start to grow. The pressure starts to build up. You feed off those positive vibes a lot, but then you do something wrong and suddenly the vibes are all negative. At a certain point, I looked for the positive vibes, but I couldn't find them. It used to frustrate me a lot. I used to get really upset by the comments people made. Then I'd play a very good game – it wouldn't just be me who thought so; the coach would tell me too – and still the comments would be negative. I realized I could do nothing to please those people. So now I am pretty chilled about it. It is what it is. Even when things are good, I don't look at the comments because at some point it'll be bad again and I'll be in the habit of looking. If the coach tells me that I've done well then that's all I need to hear.

Romesh: I come to watch Arsenal all the time. After the game, I can talk to a mate about the same player and we'll have a completely different opinion of how he played. Someone could watch you and say, 'Bellerín absolutely smashed it!' and someone else could be asking why you were even playing. It doesn't mean anything. It's the same with comedy. I'll do a show and think it's great – well, not great, I don't think anything I do is great; I'll think it's passable – and someone will say it's one of the worst things they've ever seen.

Héctor: It's a question of balance: you're never terrible and you're never amazing. The problem is that social media has given a voice to *everyone*. Before, fans would be happy just to read the match report in the paper. Now a kid anywhere in the world can post something after a match, saying something like, 'Héctor Bellerín is the shittest player I've ever seen.' You don't even know who this kid is, but it hurts you. I have talked to so many people in sport about this kind of thing and I have never met anyone who is fully immune to it. You just learn to deal with it.

Romesh: I think social media can be quite dangerous. I don't think people have figured out how to deal with it yet. You will know more about sports psychology than I do, but it's pretty obvious that a big part of it is to do with confidence. It's the same with comedy. If I'm feeling confident then I'm looser, stuff comes to me more quickly, I can improvise more easily. I just have to shut out that negative voice in head saying, 'That was shit, mate, I can't believe I just said that...'

Héctor: And move straight on to the next joke.

Romesh: Exactly. But it only takes a twelve-year-old kid – and I'm in no way disparaging twelve-year-olds, who are entitled to an opinion too – to say something shitty about you and it knocks your confidence. My agent tells me not to respond to anyone and generally I don't. But every now and again I can't help it.

Héctor: Isn't it good for you, as a comedian, to interact with people? So long as you do it in a funny way.

Romesh: Yeah. So, for example, I had a stand-up show that was broadcast on BBC2 over Christmas 2016. Somebody tweeted at me, 'I was forced to watch @romeshranga's stand-up show. Loads of swearing. Absolutely disgusting. Can't believe I was made to watch it.' I replied something to the effect of, 'I'm really sorry you've only got one channel on your shitty fucking TV.' Which loads of people then retweeted. I ended up feeling sorry for this guy who was irritated by me but who didn't deserve to be told to shut up by hundreds of my followers. 'Shut up, mate! Rom's absolutely rinsed you there!'

Héctor: There was a journalist who chatted shit about Mesut Özil. Then Mesut had a very good game, scored a goal and everyone from Arsenal started '@ing' the journalist, who then started complaining. But if you are willing to give it, you have to be willing to take it. Mate, us footballers deal with that shit every week, both on and off the pitch.

Romesh: How aware are you of what the fans are shouting during games? How much do you hear?

Héctor: I don't really hear anything on the pitch. Unless things are going really badly. You are so focused on the football that you block out everything else. Of course, I'm aware of the crowd if they chant my name. Or if they're having a go: 'Oh Bellerin, that ponytail!' You feel the crowd behind you when the team is winning or if they are frustrated when we are losing. If there's two minutes to go and we are 1-0 down and I pass the ball back to the goalkeeper, there might be a a low growl of 'Bellerin, send the bloody ball forward.' I would certainly hear that.

When I was sixteen, I only had to deal with newspapers and TV. And then, all of a sudden, I became professional and social media was a big thing and I didn't know how to deal with it. Every young player who is now coming up has to learn how to deal with it straight away.

Romesh: So much has changed since you moved to Arsenal in 2011. But even before that, there were significant changes. I'm thinking of Wenger becoming manager in 1996. No one knew what to make of him. He had a degree in economics and he had all these strange ideas about diet. This sounds ludicrous now, but the press questioned whether or not an English club should have a foreign manager. Even the liberal press was harsh. Arsenal were also one of the first teams to sign lots of foreign players. I remember a significant number of people saying that England weren't playing well because there were too many foreign players in the Premier League. People thought the north London derby wouldn't be as feisty because Arsenal and Tottenham's foreign players wouldn't understand the spirit of the game or the history of the rivalry. But then slowly players like Thierry Henry, who was at the club from 1999 to 2007, started to be seen as Arsenal through and through. You no longer had to be born in England to understand what the club was about.

Héctor: All that stuff about foreign players ruining the beautiful game is pure racism at the end of the day. It's an excuse to be racist. When you arrive at a new club, one of the rules is to find out about the club's main rivals. As soon as I got to Arsenal, I was told that I hated Tottenham. Ahead of a derby game you see how much that game means to everyone at the club; it doesn't matter where you're from. Even the travel manager, who plans all the trips, will make some comment like, 'I hardly ever say anything, boys, but we've got to win tomorrow.'

I know that some people play football for the money. They will play for Arsenal and hate Tottenham just because they are told to do so. But, for me, it's about my love of the club. Pure and simple. I used to love Thierry and I've always loved the kits because I used to play as Arsenal on the PlayStation. So, when I signed for them, I already had a connection with the club. I've been here for quite a long time now and it's been so good for me. I don't hate Tottenham because they told me to hate them. I hate them because I love Arsenal.

Romesh: I think – I hope – that the animosity towards foreign players has gone away now.

Héctor: If you're good enough, you'll play – it doesn't matter whether you are British or Spanish or whatever.

Romesh: The more recent change I was thinking about was footballers speaking out about issues that might previously have been taboo – like Danny Rose opening up about depression before the World Cup 2018.

Héctor: There has definitely been a change in the past few years but, as I said earlier, I don't think football has gone far enough in terms of footballers talking out. They still feel scared because football is still so associated with maleness. But you don't have to be an alpha male just because you're a footballer. It's not all about masculinity. Footballers are human. We go through so much shit. Aaron Lennon talked about his depression and someone asked how he could be depressed when he was earning so much money. But I don't see what one thing has got to do with the other. You can be incredibly isolated as a footballer – even if you spend the best part of the day with your teammates, if your family lives elsewhere then you are going home to an empty house. It can be really lonely.

Until recently, footballers had to pretend depression or loneliness weren't issues. You had to be man enough to get on with it. You couldn't cry as a footballer. And now I feel like things are slowly changing, not just in sport but also in film and music. Men are able to show more of who they are. I think it's important to show feelings because it helps other people who are going through stuff. Statistics show so many people are struggling with mental health but are still unprepared to speak up because of the stigma around it. I have so much respect for Rose and Lennon for talking about their issues.

Romesh: The contrast of being in the spotlight when you're very young and then suddenly not being in the spotlight at all can be really bad for your mental state. You see so many footballers struggle after they've finished playing, unless they become a manager or a pundit.

This is on a very different scale, but bear with me. I went on tour, did one of the biggest shows of the tour, the crowd were laughing and applauding, and forty-five minutes later I was sitting in a hotel room on my own, in my pants, eating a sandwich.

Héctor: That's so far from what people imagine! They probably think you're hanging around with twenty beautiful girls.

Romesh: And instead I'm in my pants, watching Netflix. If I'm close enough to go home and see my family, it's great. But mostly I'm stuck in a hotel room on my own. It's such a contrast.

Héctor: Yeah, it happens to me too. When I go home after a game, I'm on my own unless my family are over from Spain. I'm sure people think I'm living this glamorous life, but mostly I'm just home watching Netflix as well. It's weird. It goes back to the thing of people not thinking of us as being human. Sometimes you don't have a good training session or you're not in the mood to talk to fans but you know it'd be rude not to. It's the same for you, I'm sure: even if you're not in the mood, you still have to get on with it.

I have friends back home who ask if I'll go over to Spain to visit them. I can't during the season. I'm either training or playing. They can't believe I'm at the training ground from 9 a.m. till 2 p.m. every day. They can't believe that we sleep in a hotel before a home game to make sure we get the right amount of sleep and eat the right food. Then they ask when I'm on holiday. In June I might have a month off, if I'm not with Spain in the Euros or the World Cup. Maybe I'll only have two weeks off in June. It's not just about the expensive cars and the big houses. We actually do work hard! I'm guessing it's the same for you?

Romesh: You definitely have to work for it. But working hard has made me such a shit person at home. I get home from a gig – or, even worse, a tour – and I just don't want to talk to anyone. I want to eat and be depressed. My wife Leesa gets the worst of me. We'll go out and someone will want a photo of me and while they're taking it, they'll ask her, 'Is he funny at home?' She always pulls a face and says, 'You've got to be joking.'

I was a teacher before I did stand-up full-time and so I was teaching during the day and gigging at night. I had no social life. People couldn't understand why I was doing it because I wasn't making any money from it. I had to believe that, at some point, I was going to be able to do it as a full-time job. But not even my mates thought I could make it happen.

Héctor: Had you met your wife at that point?

Romesh: Yeah, I met her when we were both teachers. I told her straight away that I wanted to do stand-up. I started off doing gigs in pubs in front of six people and I was trying really hard to get better at it. And then my mother-in-law would come around and say, 'Oh, Romesh, off out again are you? Leesa will be at home on her own again, will she?' Now I can go off to a gig and it's my job and she can't say anything!

Héctor: It's hard to be 'on' when you're knackered. Sometimes my parents come over to visit and I'm too knackered to do anything. My mum probably thinks I'm depressed because I'm not really talking to her.

Romesh: My mum is the same. 'I see you on TV and you're chatty, chatty, chatty and then you come around here and all you can give me is one-word answers.'

Héctor: Don't do that to me, man! Don't start with the accents! Where are your parents from?

Romesh: Sri Lanka. That country with a great footballing history. Actually, the reason I'm a huge Arsenal fan is because when my dad moved over from Sri Lanka, he lived in north London and fell in love with Arsenal. Then he moved to East Grinstead and bought a pub, which he turned into an Arsenal pub. Dad was militant – nobody was ever allowed to criticize any Arsenal players. He would shout at anyone who was negative about the club. He would tear apart anyone who had anything bad to say about Wenger. One time we were sitting in the pub, watching Arsenal v Man United. The pub was absolutely rammed. We lost 4-2 and Dad was furious. He switched off the pub TV, turned to the punters and said, 'Everybody. Fuck off.' He was so pissed off that he closed the pub.

Héctor: Oh my days! That's so funny, man. Has he still got the pub?

Romesh: My dad passed away a few years ago. My brother and I tried to run it, but it turns out that we don't know how to run a pub.

Héctor: Sorry about your dad.

Romesh: Thanks, man.

✿   ✿   ✿

Romesh: We've talked about social-media trolls, but how do you feel about fans asking for a photo? The worst time for me is when I come to watch Arsenal, because of the sheer volume of the crowd. I can't imagine that you can go anywhere?

Héctor: Lately I've developed anxiety about crowded places. When I'm with my friends it's cool. I don't want to say no to anyone because I've been a football fan. But sometimes you've lost a game and you've relaxing with your friends or family and people ask for a photo as you're eating. Most people are respectful though.

I'm not a guy who goes around with security. I try to lead as normal a life as I can. I'll go for a coffee on the street by myself. Sometimes I get on the Tube and no one notices me. I feel like saying, 'Hey! I'm Héctor!' I'm joking, clearly, but it is weird how you can be invisible and then not. It all kicks off when one person asks for a photo and everyone else is trying to work out who you are and why someone would want your photo.

I asked Ehsen once about taking a girl out to dinner to this specific restaurant. I was worried that we might lose that day and people would ask why I was going out for dinner when Arsenal lost. People will make a story out of anything.

Romesh: Such as, 'Why the fuck is he eating?'

Héctor: Ehsen always says, 'Hec, you just have to politely say "no photos".' But I find it so hard. It's much easier if he's with me and he can say it.

Romesh: Can you imagine if Arsenal lost and you were seen at a *party…*

Héctor: I wouldn't go to a party! But I might have to go out for dinner with friends who have come over from Spain for that weekend. I always feel a bit guilty, as though I should stay home. Losing is the worst thing for me, but I have to be able to move on. I'm someone who will be in the dressing room, devastated, but then I get on the team bus and it's done. There will be another game in three or four days, let's make sure we play better.

Romesh: Arsenal lost and someone manages to get a photo of you smiling. Why is he eating *and* smiling?

Héctor: Haha, yes! Is it the same for you after a gig?

Romesh: To be honest, my instincts are completely the opposite to yours. If I have a shit gig, my instinct is to go out and get absolutely smashed and forget about it. What I should be doing is going home with a notebook and reflecting on what went wrong.

Héctor: But maybe getting smashed works better for you?

Romesh: I guess so. Going back to what you were saying about whether or not to refuse a fan's request for a photo. If somebody comes up to me and wants a photo, I will say yes 99 per cent of the time and it's all cool. But 1 per cent of the time it's really not fucking cool at all. My son is massively into Harry Potter. He loves you too, of course. If you were a wizard, my god… Anyway, I took him to see the Harry Potter play and we went for dinner afterwards. These two women came to the table, as were eating, and asked for a photo. It clearly wasn't appropriate. They then asked if my son could take the pic. My son said it was fine, but I was shocked.

If someone comes up to me and says they saw me in a show, can they please have a photo, that's great. But if they vaguely recognize me as someone off the TV who it might be quite good to have a photo with… I'm not so keen. Just before I came up here to meet you, I was having a vape in the alleyway. This guy came up to me and said, 'Everyone is going to be so amazed I got a photo with you.' As we were posing he asked, without a hint of embarrassment, 'Sorry, what's your name?'

Héctor: That happens to me too! Sometimes people think I'm Nacho Monreal. 'Hey, Nacho, you were so consistent last season!' I'm thinking to myself, yes, *he* was. For sure. They see someone take a photo, as you said, and think they must know you or they'll work it out later or whatever. I'm not going to correct them. I'm not that guy! Hopefully at some point they'll show a mate their great photo of Monreal and their mate will point out it's me.

Romesh: I did a show in America, where I've got absolutely zero profile. I was in the audience of a quiz show and the host recognized me and came over and introduced me as a British comedian and suggested everyone check out my work. I'd been sitting there anonymously all afternoon but after he pointed me out, I was swamped with requests for photos. I might be shit for all they knew!

Héctor: One time I was in Portugal with my ex-girlfriend, in a place where lots of Brits go on holiday. We went for a drink to the worst bar I've ever been to. This guy came up to me and said, 'Has anyone ever told you that you look like Héctor Bellerín?'

I was like, 'Who's that?'

He said, 'You don't know him? He's a footballer?'

I said, 'I'm a bit of a rugby boy.'

The guy went onto my Instagram account and was showing me pictures. 'You look *just* like Bellerín.'

We were about to leave the bar and my girlfriend said I should tell him. So I went up to him and said, 'I am actually Héctor Bellerín.' And he told me to get lost! He wouldn't believe it. I blew it.

Romesh: Are you ever tempted to just walk around with Bluetooth headphones on, like you do when you're getting off the team bus before a game? By the way, what are you listening to as you walk into the ground?

Héctor: Sometimes it's hip-hop, other times Spanish music. I don't have a playlist or a ritual. Some players have a pre-game playlist and they play something like Eminem's *8 Mile* soundtrack.

Romesh: Do people keep their headphones on in the changing room?

Héctor: No, but one of the players always chooses the music. At the moment it's Rob Holding. He has an incredible knowledge of music; he'll know a really small band from the 1960s as well as everything that has just come out. He's got great taste. If we lose he might play some sad songs, an R&B jam or something.

Romesh: When my dad passed away, his brother – my uncle – came over from Australia. He came up to my brother and me on the day of the funeral and said, 'Rom, I've got some songs that remind me of your dad. I was wondering if we could play them during the funeral.' My brother and I asked what the songs were. It quickly became clear that my uncle had listened to the chorus of all these sad R&B songs, but not the verses. The chorus had lyrics like, 'I really miss you.' OK, fine. But then it'd move on to, 'I really miss the touch of your body.' All these really sexual lyrics.

Héctor: Stop it!

Romesh: I didn't know how to tell him that they weren't remotely appropriate. He was standing there, waiting to be given the thumbs-up.

Héctor: That reminds of Ricky Gervais talking about his mother's funeral. It must be so hard to tell those stories on stage. Is there anything you wouldn't make a joke about?

Romesh: No, I don't think so. But the more difficult a subject, the better the joke has to be. Comedy works by injecting tension and then releasing that tension with a laugh. You see so many comics on the way up who create tension but then don't work hard enough on the pay-off and everyone in the room just feels really awkward. When stand-up really works, you sit there not quite believing what they're saying and then you laugh, almost despite yourself. It's an amazing feeling either for a comic or a punter.

Héctor: I guess most of your fans are probably used to your dark humour though?

Romesh: You'd think so. When I started out, I was performing in clubs to audiences who didn't know who I was. Apparently audiences make up their minds about comedians in the first thirty seconds. Hit them with a joke they like and they're on your side. When I started doing tours, I assumed everyone was there to see me because they liked my humour. But the reality is that one guy in a family or in a group of mates will see that I'm touring and will buy everyone else tickets. I can still back myself to have a good show, but it means that you can offend the people who aren't familiar with your material.

I sometimes talk about my three young kids and how they piss me off. I did one show and a woman in the front row had obviously never seen my stuff before. During the whole of the first half of the show she looked as though she was watching a murder. You always end up focusing on the one person who clearly isn't having a good time. I had zero chance with her.

Héctor: And you kept looking at her?

Romesh: Yes. And it gets worse. When I came back from the interval, she was gone. Clearly she hated the show. When I started doing the second half, I couldn't get her out of my mind. I had this internal monologue going on.

'Should I ask?'

'It won't be good.'

'But I have to know.'

Eventually I asked the guy sitting next to her empty seat where she was. He told me – and everyone else who was there – that she thought it was the worst thing she'd ever seen in her life.

Héctor: You already knew that! It was exactly what you wanted to hear!

Romesh: It's a form of self-harm! I'm a total fucking idiot. She left quietly and I had to make a thing out of it.

Héctor: As though you could do anything to convince that person to like you! She wasn't even in the room!

Romesh: What can I say? The highs and lows of comedy are extreme! Comedy is such a confidence game. Sometimes you don't even know why a gig is rocking. But that's when I'll start improvising lines. If the crowd is with you, it feels like you can say anything and it will go well.

Héctor: I usually watch comedy on TV, by which time the material is really polished. I've never seen a comedian die onstage on TV. And Ricky Gervais will be only my second live comedy gig – my first gig was Jack Whitehall. He's an Arsenal fan as well and he invited us to his Wembley show in 2017. I haven't been to more gigs because my spoken English is way better than my under-standing of it. I know it's an unusual way around, but it's always been that way.

When I landed at Heathrow as a teenager, this Arsenal guy picked me up. He was missing a tooth and had this broad north London accent. I was like, 'Hello, how are you?' – with my exaggerated Spanish 'h's – and when he started talking, I didn't understand anything! I realized I had to learn really fast.

Romesh: Your English is so fluent that I'd find it hard to believe that you had any issues understanding it.

Héctor: Thanks, but I guess it's a matter of confidence. I've been asked to do TV shows like *A League of Their Own* and I have turned them down because I'm scared I won't get the jokes. You have to react in the moment and it takes me a while. Or I might not understand the cultural reference because, although I've been here a long time, I didn't actually grow up here.

Lately I've been reading more rather than watching TV, but watching TV has really helped my idiomatic English. I don't watch the news or reality TV, which is crap – I only really watch Netflix. Dramas like *Narcos*. And I love watching stand-up. A friend of mine wanted me to go and watch comedy in a pub recently, but I didn't want to go because I didn't think it'd be any good. But I guess everyone has to start somewhere.

Romesh: Sometimes those pub gigs can be amazing. Or you catch someone early on. Sometimes I still drop into those pubs to do new material. See how dark I can go.

Héctor: I like the kind of dark humour that offends other people. I love Anthony Jeselnik. I watched comedy as a kid too, though obviously not the dark stuff. Paramount Spain had some great acts. In fact, I was really good at doing comedy at school.

Romesh: No way!

Héctor: Yes! This teacher asked everyone in the class to prepare a stand-up routine. There was a really good stand-up comedian in Spain called Toni Moog and I decided to write out his entire routine and spend two hours memorizing it – I've got a photographic memory. The next day, I stood up in class and recited the whole thing. Everyone was laughing. The teacher asked who wanted to go next and no one put their hands up because no one wanted to follow me! After that, my family asked me to do my stand-up every time there was a big family event. I don't think I could do it in English though. It's hard enough to understand English-speaking comedians.

Romesh: Especially if you watch it live and audience members are laughing really fucking loudly over the punchlines.

Héctor: Do you prefer doing live stand-up or TV?

Romesh: It depends. I do really enjoy doing TV, but nothing is as good as live stand-up. I did a sitcom in 2018 about my dad's pub called *The Reluctant Landlord,* which was my first time acting. It was great, but as soon as I started gigging again, I remembered that getting on stage was the most fun.

Héctor: It's the buzz. You can't get it wrong.

Romesh: It's so exhilarating. Whenever I think I'm getting good at stand-up, God hands me a gig to absolutely destroy my confidence. It's as though someone is saying, 'He's getting a bit cocky.' It's what I find so exciting: the thought that I could go out on stage and absolutely die on my arse.

Héctor: Do you remember your worst-received joke? When no one in the room laughed and you thought, 'What have I done?'

Romesh: Here's a story or two. If you want to stand on stage as a comic, you have to be able to perform for twenty minutes. It's a huge amount of material when you're starting out. I told this promoter who was looking for new acts that I didn't have twenty minutes of material and he said I should have a go anyway. I was brand new and really nervous. I went on stage in the foyer of this theatre and the first thing I said was, 'I was really excited to play this theatre, but I didn't realize we'd all be in the fucking foyer.' It turns out that everyone really loves that foyer. They are really proud of it. So the minute I opened my mouth, I offended everyone in the room. I performed to utter silence for twenty minutes. At the end, when I said 'I've been Romesh Ranganathan,' maybe one person in the entire room clapped.

Another time, I was hosting a gig in Leicester and, for some reason, they loved every other comedian apart from me. I was announcing acts, so I went on at the beginning. I was shit. I brought on an act who smashed it. I introduced another act. I was shit. That act smashed it. There was no way I could blame the audience; I was clearly doing something inherently wrong. Near the end, when I was again performing to no response at all, I said, 'Oh god, I fucking hate this.' And a member of the audience shouted out, 'Why don't you just fuck off then?' So I said, 'I think I will. Ladies and gentlemen, goodnight!'

Héctor: No! I feel so bad for you. You couldn't get it going and you had more chances than anyone else as well! At least if I have a bad game, I've got the whole team around me. I can always pass the ball to someone else. But you're there on your own, with everyone looking at you.

Romesh: Do you recognize when someone else is having a shit game?

Héctor: We all train together so we know what everyone is capable of. Everyone knows when they've had a crap game; they don't need the crowd or anyone else to remind them. I know how football works. I know when I haven't cleared enough balls. To be fair, football is way more positive these days and if you're having a bad time, you are given amazing support. I played for a team ages ago, when I was really young, and I passed the ball back a few times because I felt under so much pressure. The other side got the ball and the coach yelled, 'If you pass the ball back again, you're going on the bench.' I was young, we'd just started the game and I did it twice! It wasn't helpful for the coach to be shouting that. I just lost confidence. But that was the mentality back in the day. Now I'd be made to feel as though I could get it right, not that it was inevitable that I was going to get it wrong.

Romesh: It's that thing of football changing so much in the last five, ten years. I bet you couldn't have been a vegan footballer a decade ago. It's much easier being vegan now too.

Héctor: Are you vegan too?

Romesh: Yeah, since around 2012. It was hard back then, man.

Héctor: I started in 2016. It's much easier now.

Romesh: When I first started, I'd go to a service station or a hotel after a gig and I couldn't eat anything apart from chips. Now it's only when I go abroad that I struggle.

Héctor: When I became vegan, I don't think there were many footballers who didn't eat meat. I started doing a plant-based diet for a couple of months before I even told my mum.

Romesh: What made you do it?

Héctor: This sounds a bit arrogant, but I got a personal chef in 2014 when I was living with two mates and none of us were great at cooking. My body needs to be 100 per cent all the time, so it was worth paying someone to work out what I needed to eat to have a totally balanced diet. She's the best chef I've ever had. Not that I've had more than one! I'm not that bad. She's just brilliant. I tell her every day, 'You're my favourite.'

She used to make me chicken with all these vegetables, grains and pulses on the side. I started to love the stuff on the side more than the chicken. I asked a nutritionist about going vegan and he said, 'If you think about it, Héctor, cavemen killed animals to survive. They ate meat to survive.' Yeah, but we're not cavemen any more. I thought I'd leave it for a bit. Maybe become vegetarian first. But then I started watching all this stuff on Netflix about how animals are treated and the damage we are doing to the planet by eating so much meat. Kieran Gibbs said he was going to try and be vegetarian for a couple of weeks and then he was vegan for three weeks. He went back to eating meat, but he said it was worth trying a plant-based diet.

Because I already had that mindset and I'd been watching that stuff on Netflix, I was getting closer and closer to not being able to eat meat. Then we played Stoke away. We arrived at the hotel at around 4 p.m. the day before the game and had dinner around 6.30 p.m. I couldn't eat the meat. So my first vegan meal was the day before Stoke. I started doing proper research: was there a diet for athletes that didn't include meat or dairy? I told my chef and she went vegan herself. Ehsen went vegan too. It was great having so much support around me. But it was still quite hard to begin with and, as I said, I couldn't immediately tell my mum because the Spanish diet is all *jamon* and meat or seafood paella. I needed to be sure before I announced it to my mum. When I finally told her, she looked at me and said, 'What are you talking about? How will you have the energy to play? I've been watching you the last few games and you haven't been running the same.'

'But Mum, I've been doing it for two months! I'm feeling really good, don't worry!'

I'd had blood tests and the doctor said to me, 'Hector, I haven't seen a blood test this good in fifteen years.' He thought I must have been taking Omega 3, but I don't take any supplements. I don't need to.

In the summer of 2018, I took my chef with me to Spain because my sister was getting married and my mum wasn't free to cater for me being vegan. Since then, my parents only have meat once or twice a week. Before it was every day. They have seen the benefits and realized they have the time to sustain it. When they visit me, they eat vegan all weekend and they don't miss meat at all. It helps that my mum understands why I'm doing it.

Romesh: All of my mates are still pretty anti-vegan. They all make jokes when we go out. My wife tried it for a month and said it was the worst month of her life. She has since got into it a bit more, but not enough to actually be vegan.

Héctor: Why did you become vegan? To be healthier?

Romesh: I read a book about dairy production when I was twelve and came home and told my mum that I couldn't carry on consuming cow's milk, eggs and cheese. I just can't imagine ever going back now.

Héctor: Me neither. In the past two years I've been injured once, against Crystal Palace. I got a sprain that would normally take three weeks to recover from, but I was playing against Liverpool by the weekend. It took me six days to recover. I went to the training ground two days after the Palace game and the medics asked me how I was. I said I could barely feel any pain. They immediately put it down to the residue of the painkillers still working, but the next day I felt great. No one could believe it. However, I can't say such quick recovery is only related to veganism because I do so many other things like yoga and meditation.

Romesh: We might both be vegan, but I eat like shit.

Héctor: Vegan junk food is good!

Romesh: True. As you can see, I'm not an elite athlete, or any kind of athlete. But in fact being vegan stops me from eating even more junk. But I still piss my friends off.

Héctor: You don't want to be the guy who constantly orders off-menu. I try not to drag my mates to vegan restaurants all the time. Sometimes I'll eat before I go out and then just eat fries in a regular restaurant. It is getting easier all the time though. Have you tried the Beyond Burger?

Romesh: Mate. It is insane.

Héctor: It's so close to meat that some vegans think it's wrong to eat it. It bleeds. They sell it in Tesco now.

Romesh: Shit. I'm about to put on eight stone. The only thing that was stopping me eating it all the time is lack of access.

Héctor: I'm suddenly very hungry. Oh shit, Ricky Gervais is on soon. How is it so late? Have we been talking for two hours? I didn't bring a change of clothes. I'm going to have to go to the gig in this tracksuit that I wore for training. There's no dress code in the theatre, is there?

Romesh: Yes.

Héctor: Oh man…

Romesh: I'm joking.

Héctor: Of course you are! I really enjoyed chatting to you, by the way.

Romesh: You were great. This was great. Thank you!

Clare Balding & Lucy Bronze

Clare: What did you think about the eighteen-minute sequence on Sports Personality of the Year that celebrated the men's team reaching the semi-finals, when the women's team finished third in their World Cup, one place ahead of the men?

Lucy: My mum said, 'Does everyone realize they didn't win the World Cup?'

The Hive, north London, December 2018

Clare Balding was born in Hampshire in 1971. She read English at Cambridge University and was a leading amateur flat jockey in the late 1980s and early 1990s. She has worked on both radio and television, covering numerous sporting events including the European Women's Football Championships, Wimbledon, Olympic Games, Paralympic Games and Winter Olympic Games. She presented the Channel 4 documentary *When Football Banned Women* in 2017 and now presents Channel 4's weekly highlight show, *Women's Football World*. She has won both a BAFTA Special Award and an RTS Presenter of the Year Award.

Lucy Bronze was born in Berwick-upon-Tweed in 1991 to a Portuguese father and English mother. At the age of eleven, she was banned from her local boys' team because the FA didn't allow mixed teams beyond that age. She subsequently trained forty-five miles away from home, in Sunderland. She joined Sunderland's senior team when she was sixteen and then moved to North Carolina to study at UNC. Upon her return to the UK, she played for Everton, Liverpool and Manchester City, before leaving to play for Olympique Lyonnais.

Bronze won the FA Women's Premier League Northern Division with Sunderland and the FA WSL with Liverpool, then the FA WSL, FA WSL Cup and FA Women's Cup with Manchester City, and the UEFA Women's Champions League and the Division 1 Féminine with Olympique Lyonnais. As an England player, Bronze won the SheBelieves Cup in 2019. She won the PFA Women's Player of the Year in 2012 and 2017. In 2018, she was nominated for the inaugural Women's Ballon d'Or.

✪   ✪   ✪

Lucy Bronze: I loved watching Billie Jean King being honoured with a lifetime achievement award at the BBC's Sports Personality of the Year [SPOTY] the other night. As one of the presenters, did you have a chance to speak to her?

Clare Balding: I did, yes, but I also interviewed her in New York for the BBC's *Icons* series. I came away feeling that I was not doing or saying enough. It was as though I'd been plugged into a power socket for an hour. And she's seventy-five! She was outspoken even when she was playing. When you're contracted, it's so easy to feel limited in what you can say or how you should behave. I came back from the States thinking, 'Right, screw that. I don't care if I'm told that I shouldn't say this or that. I'm going to say it because I think it's important.'

Lucy: You've got to have the courage.

Clare: Exactly. I don't want to look back in ten years' time and wish I'd said or done this or that. I had constant discussions with my editor at the BBC about their netball coverage during the 2018 Commonwealth Games because I didn't think enough of the games were being previewed, shown or discussed in the highlights programme that went out every evening. Obviously I didn't know the team would go on to win gold, but I kept thinking that people should know their names. Ama Agbeze, the captain, is so ambitious and so smart.

Lucy: Oh my god, she's incredible.

Clare: They won the team of the year at SPOTY and I got the chance to interview them. I wanted to make sure that the diversity of the team was represented and celebrated so I made sure Ama was given a microphone and the opportunity to speak. I promised the editor that if Ama spoke, the audience would be blown away. And, of course, she was great. Going back to Billie Jean King's award at the SPOTY, there haven't actually been that many female lifetime achievement award winners, nor have there been many coaches of the year.

Lucy: Or, in fact, much recognition at all of women in sport, across the board.

Clare: I think lifetime achievement awards are really important because they are a marker of a whole career and if you make sure that it's evenly balanced, you are giving a real historical perspective. The late Rachael Heyhoe Flint should have won for inventing the Cricket World Cup before the men invented theirs. I know none of this is directly about you, Lucy, but it is about what you're going to achieve!

Lucy: Yes! Bring it on!

Clare: I'm fascinated to know what you see when you're in France with Olympique Lyonnais as opposed to what is going on here in the UK. How far have we got to go in terms of the Women's Super League set-up here in England?

Lucy: The French league is actually similar to the WSL in terms of a few clubs competing at the top of the table. It all comes down to investment and funding and sponsorship for the women's game, which still isn't where it needs to be. In France the women's game has more commercial partners and sponsorships overall and for each individual player. Hopefully as the profile increases, we will see those opportunities being taken up in England as there is a huge, virtually untapped market there for women's football.

Clare: What is Lyon doing that is different?

Lucy: Investing lots of money! Jean-Michel Aulas, the president, is a visionary. He doesn't think of himself as president of the men's team, but as president of both the men's and the women's teams. He flies to as many of our away games as he can. We played Montpellier away and beat them 5-0, which wasn't easy as they were third in the league at the time. After the game he came to see us and said, 'Right, I'm giving you all Christmas bonuses of £3,000 to spend on your families, to make sure you have a great break.' I've never heard of anything like that happening in England. Not even a bonus of £100. It's not about the money – it's the gesture. The acknowledgement.

Clare: It's about making you feel as though you are valued, and showing that you will be rewarded for performing above expectations. It must give you and your teammates a huge sense of self-confidence and self-respect.

Lucy: It also showed that Aulas understands that it was an important win for us. It wasn't a straightforward game and we had to play really well to win.

Clare: What are the crowds like?

Lucy: Lyon is a very strong team and we win a lot of games quite easily. For those easier games, we probably get similar attendance figures to the WSL. But when we play in the main stadium against teams like PSG or Man City and the game is advertised, we get as many as 15,000 to 20,000.

Clare: That's impressive. I went to Manchester City v Birmingham recently and I was shocked at how few people were there. They were second and third in the league, with players whose names are actually known. It wasn't a great game, but there are plenty of men's games that are rubbish and tens of thousands of fans turn up. I was surprised by the apparent lack of awareness that the game was even on. Why did nobody know about it?

Lucy: It doesn't help that there isn't a regular slot.

Clare: Building that live audience has to be the absolute priority. Ahead of TV contracts. Don't let television companies dictate what time you should be kicking off. I'm concerned about the push for 3 p.m. on a Saturday because I worry about the crowd and the other things people want to do on a Saturday afternoon. You can't compete with 150 other football matches. Because of the UEFA blocked-hour ruling, there's no live TV coverage on a Saturday afternoon. That rule exists to protect the live audience and keep crowd numbers up for men's football.

It might be a dead time for TV audiences, but you're not going to get anyone at the game and that would be disastrous. The main focus for WSL has to be pulling in a crowd. Netball pulls a crowd because they play in a much smaller arena. They have the atmosphere, but now they need regular TV coverage.

Lucy: Exactly. It's all about the atmosphere. If there aren't many fans cheering on the players, then it looks bad on TV. It looks dead so no one goes. And so the cycle continues.

Clare: Did you hear that in Mexico all the women's games are now being played on a Monday and it's getting an incredible response?

Lucy: Yeah, it's going crazy.

Clare: There are no men's games on a Monday. It's the women's night.

Lucy: That's what I mean: in England, you have to make an effort to find out which channel women's football is being broadcast on because it changes all the time.

Clare: And why are there only eleven teams in the WSL?

Lucy: There are only twelve women's teams in France, but the games are spread out over the season so we only play one game a week. They spread the games out because they want to make sure that the French teams make the finals of every competition. Whereas in England, all the games are crammed together because of certain schedules. I play the same amount of games as players in England and I'm never as tired as they are. We have ample recovery time.

Clare: I was reading about your Lyon teammate Ada Hegerberg being resolute in her decision not to play for Norway in the 2019 World Cup. Norway pay their men's and women's teams equally, but once again the money is not the point. It's the lack of respect for female players and the lack of professionalism within the national set-up. Did she become more aware of the gulf after joining Lyon?

Lucy: I think so. We go to away games in a private plane. We use the same training ground as the men. We eat the same food. We have the same chef. [Lyon men's player] Memphis Depay will come and have a chat and he knows all our names and whether we won or lost our last game.

Clare: Do you think that by training together and having the same access to the same facilities, you are busting the myth that you can't put the men's team alongside the women's because they will distract each other?

Lucy: That's such a ridiculous idea! I think it's good for the men's team to be around us. There was a new young Lyon player from the men's team who was by himself in the canteen because he's Dutch. I was sitting with one of the Dutch players in the women's team so he came and sat with us. We were joking about money and when we went to pay he offered to pay for us all because he was so aware of the disparity between our wages. He wasn't being rude or sexist, he just knew that we don't get paid as much as him. He only knows that because he's with us every day and he chats to us. He's still in his early twenties, but he has a healthy perspective on it.

Clare: Do you think some of the drive for change will come from the young male players?

Lucy: Yes. I always say that. We talk about inspiring girls and we are 100 per cent committed to doing so, but it's boys that I want to educate. When I was younger, it was boys who had a problem with girls playing football. It's boys – or their dads – who have the perception that girls can't play. Girls don't have the perception that they can't do something, but they often start to doubt themselves when the boys criticize or mock them. If we change young boys' perceptions, then they will grow up thinking women playing football – or any other sport traditionally associated with men – is normal.

Clare: The change happens when girls hit thirteen or fourteen. When I go into schools and talk to eleven- or twelve-year-old girls, they are game for anything. And then the boys start thinking they have to behave like men. Gender stereotyping kicks in and it's so damaging. You do, however, see some areas where things are changing dramatically. Sports broadcasting has, in my lifetime, changed completely. When I started out, there were only two high-profile female sports broadcasters on television. One was Sue Barker and the other Helen Rollason. Hazel Irvine is a few years older than me. Gabby Logan is a couple of years younger. We were the second wave.

Lucy: It's crazy that you can name everyone from your era.

Clare: But I can't name everyone who is coming up now. Thank god. There are so many more opportunities. Women are doing commentary now as well, which is great. I've been banging on about it for the last few years. There was a perception that women's voices didn't have the range, but it's bollocks. I was commentating at Wimbledon and Russell Fuller, who is a lovely man and a very good tennis correspondent, has a voice that is higher-pitched than mine. People's voices are different, but also you can train a voice. As a woman gets older, her voice tends to develop more bass notes. I kept telling my boss that he was looking in the wrong age group. Go for older women because their voice has a wider range. Equally, it's vital to target young girls and let them make their mistakes on local radio rather than pitching straight up on Radio 5 Live, making one mistake and—

Lucy: … everyone starts shouting about how terrible all women are at commentating!

Clare: We have to give women permission to fail. I still make mistakes. You just have to learn how to get over them. I think the hardest thing for anyone – and I don't think it's gender-specific – is learning resilience. God, I have had to learn it. I'm pretty good at parking it, but only because I'm very disciplined about social media. I won't look at comments when I know I'm vulnerable. I'll maybe look a month later, when I can laugh. I have to protect myself because it's just reams of abuse telling me I don't know anything and I'm shit at my job and so on. I've known athletes who read the abuse and then claim to use it to drive them on, but I don't think it's particularly effective.

Lucy: I can't imagine reading all that stuff would ever be a good thing. Why would you even pay attention to the opinion of someone you don't know and will probably never meet? What's the point? It's not helpful. Having said that, I do look. Touch wood, I haven't really done anything that would provoke that kind of abuse.

Clare: If it ever happens – and I hope it doesn't – it gives you an incredible sense of power *not* to look at social media. For all the major sporting events – for Wimbledon, the Winter Olympics, the Olympics – I don't look at mentions on Twitter. I might notice that Alice, my partner, has popped up on my timeline, having a go back at someone.

Lucy: It must be tough, but I think it's tough for everyone. Male footballers get abuse too. In fact, probably more because they are so high-profile.

Clare: And the racism in the men's game is staggering. I find it extraordinary and frightening.

Lucy: I don't understand it either. How do those people end up with those views?

Clare: I used to watch Chelsea in the 1990s and there was often a small pocket of racist fans hurling abuse at black players and fans. I went to see Chelsea v Man United back then and the Chelsea fans were baiting Man United about the Munich air crash while the Man United fans were doing helicopter arms in reference to Matthew Harding, the vice-chairman of Chelsea who died in a helicopter accident in 1996. I was speechless. That was the era in which the Chelsea player Graeme Le Saux was regularly branded 'queer' for reading the *Guardian*.

Lucy: It would be nice to think that times have moved forward since then, but...

Clare: ... but there's still not a single out gay footballer. Which is where women's football is, for want of a better phrase, incredibly gay-friendly. Plus, I've never heard a racist taunt while watching women's football. Before the final of Euro 2017 in the Netherlands, in which Holland played Denmark, I walked with TV cameras from the middle of Enschede to the stadium. All the fans were commingling. They were dancing, they were chatting to each other... it was so lovely. I didn't know football could be like that. I always feel slightly uneasy when I go to a big Premier League football match.

Lucy: You'd never get that edgy atmosphere at a women's game. The crowd is so different; it's not full of big men or yobs. There's more of a family atmosphere.

Clare: It simply doesn't have the same tribal element as men's football. Personally, I don't want women's football to ever aspire to be like men's football in terms of the way fans behave. Or the way players behave on the pitch as well. I'm not naive, I know a female player will dive for a penalty sometimes too, but there is a purity to the women's game. They will play and play and play to win. The crowd don't get angry in the same way as men's crowds. It's more like rugby league. It's a template that is worth analysing; I've covered a lot of rugby league games in my time and their crowds will have a go at the ref, but it's not tribal.

Lucy: Rugby isn't the same as men's football though. The way male footballers speak to the refs, the way the fans behave… it's crazy. Phil Neville [head coach of the England women's team] hates those things about men's football.

Clare: I think Gareth Southgate [manager of the England men's team] does too. Which is why what he did with the England team in the World Cup in Russia was so impressive. He virtually reinvented our relationship as fans with that team. Southgate has learned a lot from the Great Britain women's hockey team. After winning gold at the Olympics in 2016, the hockey team had a really strong sense of their place in history, the influence that they could have and their legacy. They didn't just want to win a gold medal, they wanted to change perceptions. It's a big thing to take on board, but they did it.

Lucy: We had that going into the 2015 World Cup in Canada. By coming third, we changed perceptions, but then what do you do next? It's so easy to get stuck unless you go on to actually win something.

Clare: As we know, the next three years are huge for the England women's team. The World Cup in France. The Olympics in Japan in 2020. The Euros in England in 2021.

Lucy: No pressure, then!

Clare: I'm not saying you have to go and win the World Cup! But you will be playing in the same time zone and it makes a huge difference. You're now a well-known, established player, as is Steph Houghton and about five other players. You've been through stuff together. You're solid. There are some exciting players like Man City's Nikita Parris, who's got real attitude. As a team you have already got a level of professionalism and a level of exposure that means you're not suddenly going to get over-excited. You're not going to go off the rails if you reach the final or if you win it. You're not going to suddenly turn up to every single soap award going. But you're right. What next? The FA needs to completely restructure the WSL. It needs to establish a regular slot for games. It needs commitment from the BBC or Channel 4 in conjunction with BT Sport.

Lucy: This is the first time there have been actual bids for the World Cup. Prior to that, the women's World Cup was pretty much an appendix to BT Sport, the BBC and so on. Phil has changed a lot of things in terms of media coverage – he was really surprised that we were giving so many interviews before huge games.

Clare: It's tiring to be answering questions all day. There is a tendency for the same question to be asked time and again, and often for that question to be about an athlete's weak points. Why aren't you a more successful penalty taker? Why do you make the same defensive errors time and again?

Lucy: That happens to the men's team too. Every time England play in a World Cup penalty shoot-out, they have lost before even kicking a ball, which is why everyone was so amazed when they won on penalties in Russia.

Clare: What did you think about the eighteen-minute sequence on SPOTY that celebrated the men's team reaching the semi-finals of the World Cup, when the women's team finished third in their World Cup, one place ahead of the men?

Lucy: My mum said, 'Does everyone realize they didn't win the World Cup?'

Clare: Which is why, as I said earlier, that I personally wouldn't want women's football to emulate men's football because it's such a bastardization of a sport. There are so many better models to follow. I said to Frank Skinner at the SPOTY that I hate men's football and he was shocked. He said, 'Imagine if I said that about women's football!' But they are not the same. I'm not making that statement based on gender, but rather on what men's football has become.

Lucy: It's the business that is problematic, not the game itself.

Clare: At the same time, there isn't enough professionalism in the women's game in terms of organization.

Lucy: The WSL is the first full-time professional league, but actually a lot of the players have to carry on working because they don't get paid enough to live. And I don't mean a lavish life, I mean just to pay the rent and eat.

Clare: So much of it is about profile. Think of Kelly Smith, arguably the most talented and incredible player England has had in a generation. An Arsenal legend. And hardly anyone knows her name. She's never had an award outside the world of football.

Lucy: The scale of profile is impossible to compare. Messi rarely gives an interview, but he's a household name because of the scale and reach of the men's game. In women's football, current players are working hard to promote themselves. Sometimes players get more recognition because, for example, they have the most Twitter followers.

Clare: I don't think that's true of you. I think you get promoted because you're bloody good.

Lucy: In women's football if you're pretty and/or you score goals, then you are automatically more likely to have a reasonable public profile. But that is more a reflection of society and the association with image and a focus on what is deemed attractive, and therefore more popular and apparently more commercially attractive. I am beginning to see a shift though, which is changing with the overall growth and awareness of the sport and in turn is becoming more reflective of players' actual ability on the field and women's football in general.

Clare: Marta, Brazil's number ten, won FIFA World Player of the Year for five consecutive years between 2006 and 2010. Her story is incredible – her meteoric rise out of the *favelas* – and her profile in Brazil is massive. She was used to promote the Olympics because obviously Brazil played both their men's and women's teams. I think that is based on her achievement and her play rather than her presence on social media.

Lucy: I agree, but I also think that she had a good team behind her who promoted her really well. She's obviously an incredible player, but what she did off the field was very carefully curated. I'm not being critical in any way, I'm just saying it's easier with a machine behind you.

⚽ ⚽ ⚽

Lucy: I read about your involvement, alongside Hope Powell, Tanni Grey-Thompson and Katherine Grainger, with the All-Party Parliamentary Group on Women's Sport. What was on the agenda?

Clare: I was talking about putting pressure on television – and particularly the BBC because it's licence-fee funded – to show more women's sports. And, to be fair, they have done, albeit with a reliance on the red button. I still get cross when 5 Live doesn't mention women's sport at all; I think they should be honest about it and say, 'Here's the men's sport.' If, for example, you were out injured before a big international game and England said it might take you a week to get back to full fitness, no one would hear about it. You would have to search for an update. And yet, in men's sport, you hear about Mourinho sneezing.

Lucy: It's so true! There are small signs of change though. I am starting to see slightly more coverage of women's football but, as we said earlier, it's not nearly enough.

Clare: We need fixtures, results and information. I write a column every week for the free magazine you get in Waitrose – which, I'll have you know, has a big readership – but I always try to mention a woman's sport fixture to follow. I have to tell you, it's difficult! They don't appear in general sporting calendars and you have to spend time trawling through information online.

Lucy: And it's not just about raising the profile of sport; it's also about the direct impact the profile of women's sport has on sexism in society.

Clare: Absolutely. It's so important. For example, Saudi Arabia having representation from female athletes at the Olympics or the World Cup really matters. When you are looking at countries in which women still don't have the right to drive a car, don't have the vote, don't have an education and aren't allowed out in public, that amazing visual image of women – either in a team or as individuals, being competitive and ambitious and getting sweaty and being allowed to be strong – it matters. It's even better if they have the eloquence to discuss that contrast when you put a microphone under their nose. But even if they don't, it's enough to share the joy of playing. They don't have to all be amazing orators. It's important that those women are simply seen.

Lucy: I don't think there will be significant enough changes during my lifetime. Much of the support at the moment still feels like box-ticking. It makes them look good.

Clare: I don't mind that. Tick as many boxes as you like. Just do it. Now, let's get back to you. Apart from playing for Man City, Liverpool, Everton and Sunderland in this country, you also played for the North Carolina Tar Heels when you were studying at the University of North Carolina. Were you impressed by that set-up?

Lucy: America was amazing. There is a written rule that dictates universities have to allocate a certain amount of money to women's sport. And it happens. It's not box-ticking. They certainly don't do it in a half-hearted way. I went there when I was seventeen, eighteen, and I got more kit and more training than I did in the England team eight years later. And it was only a college team.

Clare: Their national side has achieved great things and they haven't grown up with the tribal hatred that exists among the fans of male football here. I don't think that anger exists in America. Other sports might engender that, but it's not soccer.

Lucy: Not at all. It's totally different. The girls in America have never had to deal with the issue of men's football versus women's soccer because the women's game is respected.

Clare: What did [the American player] Heather O'Reilly think of the WSL when she came to Arsenal from FC Kansas City?

Lucy: Well, she went back to America after just one season. She was surprised by the set-up here. I played in America ten years ago and only now are we catching up. But then America went too fast with the women's game, invested too much money, effectively went bust and had to rebuild the game. They are rebuilding in the right way, because they know how to.

France is different again. At Lyon no one cares about Instagram or Twitter or self-promotion or the difference between women and men. They give the women loads of money. The only thing that is lacking is a comprehensive knowledge of sports science.

Clare: Sports science is really interesting. I recently found out that women are more prone to injury before or during their period. There is a lot of statistical evidence to suggest that during certain days of your cycle you are more vulnerable to fragile bones. Learning how to best protect yourself is key to getting through a season.

Lucy: I have to say that the set-up for the England women's team is amazing. We are treated pretty much the same as the men. It's a fairly recent thing, but now we have access to all the doctors and the most up-to-date sports science. It's always a welcome surprise when I turn up at the England camp. A personal chef travels with us. And a doctor. Four physios. Five coaches. Nutritionists. It's amazing. It makes us feel valued as players.

Clare: Are you being looked after in terms of mental health too? Do they do enough to protect you emotionally? I know Gareth Southgate is big on mental health.

Lucy: After the last World Cup, a psychologist started coming to every single camp and he stayed with us during the tournament. I personally don't feel I need someone to talk to, but it worked brilliantly for the team. Particularly for players who struggle with social media or have issues with their family. It made a big difference at the World Cup. When we ended up in third place, we were asked if anything made a particular difference and everyone mentioned the psychologist. As a result, the FA started to take mental health more seriously not just for us, but also for the men's team. Prior to that it was very easy for the male players to say that it wasn't important for them to talk about feelings and emotions. So, it's now been implemented in pretty much every team in England.

Gareth Southgate talks about how the England players doing team-bonding sessions made a huge difference – we saw all those photos of them messing around with blow-up unicorns in the pool during the World Cup in Russia. But it started with the women's team. Funnily enough, our former coach, Mark Sampson, took the idea from the All Blacks. He read about it in a book and started talking to sports psychologists about it and then mixed up all these ideas together. It helped us become a next-level team, going from twelfth to fourth in FIFA rankings in two years.

Clare: What did the psychologist do with you?

Lucy: He talked to us both separately and as a group. We did lots of activities. I admit that I was the last one to buy into it. I got on really well with him, but I always wanted to joke around. He'd ask me gently to talk, but I didn't think I had anything to talk about. I kept on saying I was fine. But I was impressed by an exercise where we each had to put on a white T-shirt and our teammates wrote on the back what was good about us both on and off the pitch. You then kept this T-shirt, with its motivational messages, for the rest of the World Cup. It worked because of course people don't always tell you what they think about you.

Clare: That's such a great idea. You hang the T-shirt in your room and it's always there if you're feeling a bit low.

Lucy: He also made us do speed-dating. We had to sit opposite each other and we had twenty seconds in which to tell the other player good things about them. Another time we worked out our personalities. Red, yellow, blue or green.

Clare: I've heard about that. I'm whichever colour type needs things to happen fast. Red, I think.

Lucy: I'm red too!

Clare: It means we're always thinking, 'Stop mucking about! Get on with it!'

Lucy: Lots of players are yellow, which means they wander around saying, 'Oh my god, the world is so amazing. I have so many feelings… I love this, I love that… I'm so bubbly.' And then there are three red players, including me, who are just like, 'Stop! Enough! Let's do it.' The psychologist said we had to understand each other in order to work together and it changed our outlook on pretty much everything and, in turn, changed the team.

Clare: Did you have to share your personal stories too?

Lucy: Yes, we all had to bring in two or three photos or objects that mean the most to us and then sit in a group of five and talk about them. I'm sure everyone will tut and dismiss this as being typical of girls, but we all cried. It was so important to understand that someone is a certain way because of what they had been through. It's not necessarily about treating them differently, but appreciating their back story.

Clare: It's so important in terms of building a team. The netball team came up with this concept called 'funetherness' – fun and togetherness – that Ama Agbeze talked about at the BT Sport Action Woman Awards. There will be tensions in any team, but that netball team know that both on the court and in training they are 100 per cent there for each other.

Lucy: The netball team came to see us a couple of months ago. Phil's sister Tracey Neville is obviously manager of the girls' team, although she's completely different to her brother. To us they are this amazing team because they have actually won something. We have access to sports scientists and a personal chef and we stay in St George's Park, the FA's national football centre, which is total luxury. The netball team don't have as much funding as we have and yet they are doing so well. They explained to us how they became a real team; being close and knowing each other so well made them play on a different level. It made us realize how much bonding work we had to do.

Clare: Sharing experiences across different sports is so vital. Because I work across different sports myself, I have talked to those teams. I spent time with the women's hockey team after they won their gold medal in Rio. I was furious when they didn't win team of the year at SPOTY. I've talked to female cricketers who have experienced their game becoming professional and how there's still so far to go – just because you're paying your players £23,000 does not mean that they have anywhere near parity with the men's game.

Lucy: And it's not as though you can play at a high level of sport until you are in your sixties, which presents another financial issue.

Clare: Did that make you think twice about playing football on a professional level? Did you think of doing anything else when you were younger?

Lucy: I was always sporty. I played tennis when I was very young, but I prefer playing in a team. I played this one game against another girl at the tennis club in Jesmond [a well-to-do suburb of Newcastle]. You don't use a referee when you're younger, and this girl – who was from a private school – was blatantly cheating. I was so shy and so honest. I was literally in tears. I told my mum that the posh girl was cheating and she urged me to call it, but the girl kept insisting the ball was out when it wasn't. I never played again after that day. Even though I was good – I could beat my brother, who is two years older than me. For ages after I gave up, Mum would still say, 'You could have been like Serena Williams!' She wanted me in little white dresses and frilly socks and I kept turning up in football boots and football kit. If not tennis or football, I'd have been an accountant.

Clare: Maths is a great thing to be good at. You could still be an accountant. I think we've got to allow ourselves different chapters in our lives. Apart from those who earn an absolute fortune, most sportspeople have to consider what they'll do once they stop playing. Footballers have to stop playing so young that they have to be positive about retirement.

Lucy: I don't want to ever retire! I want to play until my body gives up on me...

⚽ ⚽ ⚽

Clare: How did you feel when Ada Hegerberg was asked to twerk by the host, Martin Solveig, after she won the inaugural Women's Ballon d'Or in 2018?

Lucy: Everyone was talking about the twerking, which I completely get, but I was actually more annoyed about the fact that it had taken so long for women to even have their own Ballon d'Or. It's pathetic. But no one cares. All they care about is twerking. The show starts. Thirty men have been nominated and fifteen women. That's fine; we don't have as many great players because the game is not as big. There was a countdown for the men's prize in which minute-long video clips were shown of the top ten nominees. When it was time for the women's award, they stuck a photo of each of the top five players up on the screen and only showed Ada playing. It was a perfect opportunity to show women's football. And no one took that opportunity.

The twerking thing happened and I was like, 'I'm not really bothered right now!' There are all these male footballers sitting next to me and this is an opportunity to show them that WOMEN CAN PLAY. We've got these amazing players. And you stick a photo up! I was angry, but no one cared. It's normal. It's to be expected. Why take women's football seriously when you can stick a photo of them up? And not even the top ten, just the top five. What the hell is that about? I didn't make the top five, so it wasn't about my ego; I'd just love to have seen proper footage of some of my teammates. All the other girls I know felt the same as I did. But the media jumped on the twerking story. It was just a clickbait headline. It doesn't tell the real story of what happened at the ceremony.

Ada did this amazing speech in two different languages, neither of which is her first language. She's my teammate and it gave me goosebumps. Then she walked down the stairs and the DJ spoke to her. No one cared about her incredible speech because of the twerking comment.

By the way, the DJ also asked Mbappé to dance, but no one referred to that. Maybe because he was asked to dance and not twerk.

Clare: It's about finding the right time to say it and the right way of saying it. Keep saying it. Say it in this book. Say it again when the Ballon d'Or comes around again. By the way, were the photos of you in your playing kits?

Lucy: Yes! My god, can you imagine if they weren't? I'd have been even more furious. But I wanted to watch clips of the men *and* the women playing. It was the same when I won the PFA Women's Player of the Year in 2012. The men get these long, varied clips and mine was of me taking a throw-in. I won the award for the best player in the league and my video clip was of me *throwing* a ball. Not kicking it, but throwing it! Although, back in 2012, I do understand that it was more difficult to source the footage, which goes back to what we were saying about television exposure. When I won the award again in 2017, there was equal footage of the men's and women's game.

I feel like I'm having to chip away all the time. To stick my head above the parapet and say it's not acceptable.

Clare: Sometimes I feel as though we are shouting into a wind that is blowing right back into our faces. And then you'll win something and everyone will suddenly pay attention. But the support has to be there all the time. Otherwise you won't win. And it has to be sustainable. I try to speak out as much as I can and then I think, 'Well, you could sack me, and you will do one day but probably not just yet, so I'll keep saying what I've got to say.' I was really cautious in my thirties and I didn't want to stir up too much trouble. Now I don't think of it as stirring up trouble but of speaking the truth.

Lucy: I feel the same. Say what you want to say.

Clare: The bigger crime is not saying what you want to say. In speaking up, you are empowering other people to do the same.

Which takes us back to Billie Jean. She spoke up when she was playing. Her attitude was, 'Screw you for not letting women play in grand slams!'

Lucy: I watched *Battle of the Sexes*, the feature film about Billie Jean's televised 1973 match against Bobby Riggs. No one expected her to win, but she did. She was truly amazing.

Clare: And still now, in her mid-seventies, she is keeping the conversation going. Glory be to BJK. We love her!

Gary
Lineker

&

Fahd
Saleh

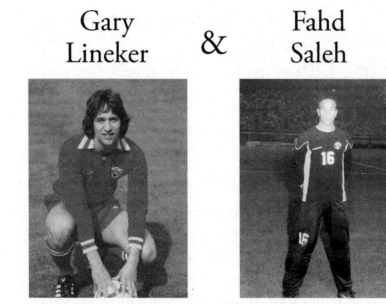

Fahd: I went to Jordan and tried to play but they said goalkeepers were not allowed because there are relatively few so they protect that job and only Jordanians can do it.

Gary: Now, I don't like goalkeepers, but that seems unfair.

UNHCR, London, March 2019

Gary Lineker OBE was born in Leicester in 1960. As a teenager, he captained the Leicestershire Schools cricket team and played football for Aylestone Park Youth. He joined the Leicester City youth academy in 1976 and the senior team in 1978, scoring ninety-five goals in 194 appearances. He played at Everton (1985–86), Barcelona (1986–89), Tottenham Hotspur (1989–92) and Nagoya Grampus Eight (1992–94). Lineker scored forty-eight goals in eighty appearances for England, winning the Golden Boot in Mexico '86. He is the anchor of the BBC's flagship football TV programme *Match of the Day* and also presents BT Sport's Champions League coverage. In 2019, Lineker and his BBC *Match of the Day* team won a BAFTA for coverage of the England v Sweden World Cup 2018 quarter-final.

Fahd Saleh was born in Homs, Syria in 1985. He was goalkeeper for al-Karamah in Homs and for the Syrian Under-21 team until war broke out in 2011. He left Syria for the United Arab Emirates and from there went to Jordan to join his family, who had also escaped from Syria. Fahd and his young family were recognized by UNHCR, the UN Refugee Agency, as being in need of resettlement and were flown to the UK (unlike many refugees, he didn't arrive here as an asylum seeker after making a dangerous journey from Syria). He was welcomed in Mansfield by Barbara Nestor, a former councillor and retired librarian who felt that the town should take some responsibility for the refugee crisis. She founded Maun Refuge in 2015 and the council supported her motion to welcome four Syrian families in December that year, including Fahd and his wife Tahrir. Since his arrival in Mansfield, Fahd Saleh has worked in local schools and completed a coaching course. Determined to perfect his English, he spoke to Gary Lineker without a translator.

✪　✪　✪

Gary Lineker: It's great to meet you, Fahd. I must ask which team you support here in the UK?

Fahd Saleh: At the moment, Liverpool.

Gary: Why on earth are you a Liverpool fan? Is it because of Mo Salah?

Fahd: Yes, it's Mo. Most of the Arabs in the Middle East support Mo Salah, which means they support Liverpool.

Gary: That makes sense. How are things? Have you settled into this crazy country?

Fahd: I'm very good, thanks. My family feel safe here and my sons can get a proper education.

Gary: You've got an interesting story to tell, and obviously a very emotional story. When did you start playing football?

Fahd: A long time ago, when I was six years old. I was always a goalkeeper, first for my school and then I started to play for a team called al-Karamah in my hometown of Homs. It was one of the best teams in Syria.

Gary: When you started playing as a young boy, Syria was obviously a very different place.

Fahd: Yes. There was no war, it was a great place to live and very cheap too. When I wanted to become a goalkeeper, my family supported me, especially my father and mother. My father passed away last year.

Gary: I'm so sorry. I know how tough that is; my father died recently too. What changed for you and your family when the war started?

Fahd: I was still playing football with al-Karamah in 2011, during the first year of the war. But then it started to be really difficult to get to training because of all the army checkpoints. The army spent so long looking at papers that it made it impossible to get anywhere on time. And then the army moved in around my home and it made life even harder.

Gary: You must have felt scared.

Fahd: Yes, of course. It was really scary, especially because my family were in Homs too. If I was there on my own then I could possibly have found a way to escape, but with my parents and my siblings, it was much harder. Around that time a group of locals started shooting at the army in my area. It made a bad situation even worse, so I moved into my father's place. After six months I decided to go back to my house to pick up some stuff. Because it was so dangerous there, I couldn't book a taxi and it took a long time to find anyone who was willing to give me a lift. Finally someone offered to take me and when I opened my front door, I discovered that there had been a fire in the house. Everything was destroyed. All my photos, all my medals. It was really hard.

Gary: Bloody hell. You lost all your football memorabilia. Did you have a young family at that time?

Fahd: No. I saved all my money to build the house and it was supposed to be a family house once I met my wife and had children.

But, in the end, I only lived in it for seven months before I was forced to leave. I lost everything.

Gary: It must have been a very difficult decision to leave your home.

Fahd: Yeah, of course. I didn't have a choice. It wasn't safe to stay, so I left. After living with my parents for six months, I went to the United Arab Emirates.

Gary: And during this period did you still try to play football?

Fahd: Yes, because it was my job. I was playing for a team called Ministry of Higher Education in the UAE, but it was becoming impossible. I was talking to my parents all the time about how they could leave Syria without talking to the smugglers and paying them huge amounts of money. They finally managed to fly to Jordan legally, with some money in their pockets. My wife, who I had met in Syria before going to the UAE, travelled to Jordan with our first son two days before my parents and I flew to Jordan three months later.

Gary: Before you moved to Jordan, was football an escape, a time during which you could forget all your problems?

Fahd: Yes, I was able to forget about everything and just play football. But then as soon as I stepped off the pitch, I thought,

'Oh gosh, my family. Are they OK? Did something happen when I was playing?'

Gary: And once you were in Jordan did you manage to carry on playing?

Fahd: I went to Jordan and tried to play but they said goalkeepers were not allowed because of the way the Jordan Football Federation works. They can bring in outfield players, but because there are relatively few goalkeepers they protect that job and only Jordanians can do it.

Gary: Now, I don't like goalkeepers, but that seems unfair. So what did you do then?

Fahd: I went to the Football Association of Jordan and said I'd like to do some coaching. They were happy for me to do a qualification, but first I would have to show them a document that I'd left back in Syria.

Gary: And it would have been too dangerous to go back.

Fahd: Yes, far too dangerous. But I was a little bit lucky. My friend was the first goalkeeper in Syria's national team and they were playing a game against Palestine in Jordan. I asked him to bring me the document and he did. So I did Level 1 coaching for goalkeepers in Jordan.

Gary: So you changed your career from goalkeeper to goalkeeping coach. How old were you by this point?

Fahd: I was about twenty-eight.

Gary: You were still young enough to play, but coaching was the next best thing.

Fahd: Yes, but I didn't start coaching straight away. It takes time to get the qualification and I had run out of money. So I found a job in retail, which I did for a year. After three months, the owner said he'd like me to open and close the shop and he gave me a key. It was a big responsibility.

Gary: And a display of trust. So you were the key-per. I'm allowed one bad pun!

Fahd: I understand your joke: the keeper of the football and the keeper of the shop! Very good.

Gary: After working in the shop for a year, were you able to start coaching?

Fahd: A friend told me about a team who were looking for a goalkeeping coach. He asked if I would like to work with them, and of course I said yes straight away! I met with the chairman of the club and he wanted me to work with them, but he couldn't offer much money, only around 150 Yemini Rials [around £46] a month. I was still working at the shop, but I needed to put my foot in the door so I coached the team for about two years and they gradually increased the money.

Gary: Did you miss playing?

Fahd: Yeah, of course, because I had been a goalkeeper since the age of six. I was still fit and healthy, but there was no chance of playing. It was frustrating, but at least by working with goalkeepers I had a chance to show them how to dive, how to catch and kick the ball. It was good.

Gary: So at this stage you were doing your coaching badges and your goalkeeping practice and working in the shop. Were you happy in Jordan? Did you intend to stay there for a long time?

Fahd: I was honestly just thinking of staying in Jordan and getting my badges because there are lots of courses there. For example, at the moment I have Level 1 coaching and Level 1 coaching for goalkeepers from the FA, but if I'd stayed in Jordan by now I would already have a UEFA A or B licence.

Gary: Can you get your A or B licence here?

Fahd: That's my aim. At the moment I'm doing my Level 2 coaching.

Gary: Where are you doing that?

Fahd: In Nottingham with the FA. I want to get as many qualifications as I can so that I can work here.

Gary: You said you were happy in Jordan; how did you end up coming here?

Fahd: I was coaching a local team and everything was fine. I was earning enough money and my wife and I had had our first child. Everything was perfect. But then life became harder when our son was ready for school because education is so expensive in Jordan. And education is everything. I want my children to have the best chances in life to do well and work hard. So I registered with UNHCR and after about two years they called me and asked if we'd like to move to America. I accepted. But then they called back and said there was another choice – the UK. I immediately thought of Manchester City! Liverpool! Chelsea!

Gary: Your first thought was the football! I would be the same.

Fahd: Gosh, I thought that if I moved to the UK, I could be working with Manchester United or Liverpool. With any of the Premier League teams.

Gary: Maybe in time!

Fahd: When we moved to the UK in December 2015, I was thirty and still young enough to be a goalkeeper.

Gary: Do you play now? There are so many teams in England, so much amateur football across the country.

Fahd: As soon as I got here, I got in touch with as many teams as I could. But unfortunately they didn't respond. I also asked my local club, Mansfield Town, if I could join in with training or watch them train. Anything!

Gary: Yes, teams are very difficult like that. Did you manage to get any coaching work?

Fahd: I'm working as a volunteer football coach in a local primary school and I've also started work as a volunteer with AFC Mansfield, a non-league team, as a goalkeeper coach. I am still studying English. When I first arrived here, I didn't have any English words at all, but I want to improve.

Gary: Have you only been learning English since you moved here? You've done really well. And does your family speak English now?

Fahd: Yes, especially my children. Their English is better than mine. And they've got the accent.

Gary: They've got an East Midlands accent! That's good. I've got an East Midlands accent, that's where I'm from. You know Leicester? They were champions a few years ago.

Fahd: Yes, in 2016. I remember!

✪ ✪ ✪

Gary: What was it like to arrive in a country you don't know, where you don't speak the language and where some people have a bit of a problem with refugees? Were you welcomed?

Fahd: We were very lucky. Barbara Nestor set up her charity in August 2015 and by December that year we had moved to Mansfield. She did so much work to help us settle down; if she hadn't, we probably would have moved to Nottingham, where there are a lot of Syrian families. Because Barbara worked to help us integrate, we are very happy in Mansfield.

Gary: How many Syrian families are there now in Mansfield? Do you stick together?

Fahd: We know each other and we studied English in the same class, but at the moment I prefer not to spend time with Syrian or Arabic speakers because I want to learn English fluently.

Gary: I did exactly the same when I went to play for Barcelona. I chose not to hang out with the expats because I wanted to learn Spanish. It makes life so much easier and so much better; it means you can communicate with your teammates and with the coaching staff.

Part of what I loved about playing in Barcelona was the incredible climate, but you moved from Jordan to the East Midlands!

Fahd: That was so hard for us. When we left Jordan in December, we were used to spending a lot of time outside. In Mansfield, it was dark just after 3 p.m. and everybody was locked up inside their houses. I went to the shop on the first day and there was no one else around. It was foggy, all the houses looked the same and I was scared. But I got used to it. I walked or jogged everywhere until everything was familiar.

Gary: And Barbara Nestor was instrumental in that. It just goes to show that there are good people everywhere.

Fahd: And not just Barbara, but the sixteen people who work with her. All of them worked really hard with us. For example, when we first arrived and didn't speak English, they helped book an appointment at the hospital for the children. They explained how certain things worked. They did a really, really good job for us and made a difficult situation much easier.

Gary: Now that you've been in this country for a while, how do you feel about being a refugee?

Fahd: It's a really hard question. Of course, I never wanted to be a refugee. Nor did my wife. But we had no choice. It hasn't been easy and it's still not easy.

Gary: Do you feel bad about being a refugee, even if the circumstances are completely out of your control?

Fahd: This is the situation and I have to accept it. But I have to move forward as well. Yes, I'm in the UK; yes, the government helped me; yes, the job centre is giving me some money for my family at the moment. But I have something to offer. I don't want to speak highly of myself, but I have the skills to give something back. I did a coaching course at Vision West Nottinghamshire College, and I worked for a year at Queen Elizabeth's Academy helping children from Syria who didn't speak English to do their homework and communicate with their teachers. I am thankful for every opportunity, but now I want to do full-time work that is paid.

Gary: You clearly want to be a good citizen.

Fahd: Of course!

Gary: But your dream is to be a full-time goalkeeping coach.

Fahd: When I first came to the UK, my English teacher asked what I'd like to be doing in five years' time. I said I would be a goalkeeping coach with a really important team. That is still my dream. Actually it's more of an ambition than a dream; it's not something that goes away when I wake up in the morning. I think about it all the time. Hopefully an opportunity will come my way.

Gary: Would you eventually like to go back to Syria? If the war ever ends and the cities are rebuilt.

Fahd: I'm very happy in the UK just now.

Gary: You've got used to the fog.

Fahd: Not yet! But I have made some friends. More English ones than Arabic ones, as I said.

Gary: Have you experienced any racism since coming to the UK? Have there been any kind of bad feelings about you being from Syria or being a refugee?

Fahd: During the first year or two a few people swore at us, but no one hit us. Perhaps because my wife wears a hijab and they didn't understand why. But we didn't respond. We just ignored them.

Gary: It must have been hurtful though?

Fahd: Yeah, it is difficult. People say 'go back to your country'. But you don't know what happened in my country, you don't know the reason I came to the UK.

Gary: It is quite hard to believe that people don't have any empathy towards those who have been forced to flee their own countries, leaving behind their homes, their friends and often their families.

Fahd: Especially, as you say, when you leave your country without choice. When leaving is mandatory. One of my friends, who also played for al-Karamah, was shot dead in the first year of the war.

I lost other friends too. And I told you I was forced to leave my home. I designed it, I built it and I lived in it for just seven months. I even built two apartments for my future children to live in, but everything has been destroyed.

Gary: It's impossible for me to imagine how hard it's been for you.

Fahd: Thank you.

Gary: Have you got a nice house in Mansfield?

Fahd: Yes, a house with two bedrooms and one living room. It's great!

Gary: I know you said you want to keep looking forward, but I'm aware that it'll be eight years tomorrow since the war started, and I wondered if you still read or watch news about Syria?

Fahd: I stopped watching the news three or four years ago. Every time I watch it, my heart breaks.

Gary: What do you tell your children about Syria?

Fahd: It's really important for me to talk with my children about Syria. Most of the time just simple things: it's a beautiful country that we had to leave because of the war, but that one day we will be able to visit it. And maybe live there again. But first of all

– education. My children ask me why we came to the UK and I explain first about the war and secondly about education. We came here to give our children a chance. I want them to have the choice, to be a policeman or a doctor or whatever they want to be.

Gary: How old are they?

Fahd: I have three children, aged seven, five and a half, and 26 days. All boys.

Gary: I've got four boys. Between us that's nearly a team!

Fahd: I'll be in goal. You will have to try and score.

Gary: My scoring days are gone. I'm finished. Too old!

Fahd: Never too old! Can we have a photo together?

Gary: Well… I don't normally do that with goalkeepers. But I'll make an exception for you, Fahd. It's been a pleasure to meet you. I hope everything works out for you.

Fahd: Thank you. It's been a pleasure to meet you too.

Johnny Marr & Pep Guardiola

Pep: By the way, how many guitars do you own? Millions?

Johnny: Funnily enough, I was going to ask you how many grey cashmere jumpers you own!

Pep Guardiola's office, Etihad Campus, Manchester, March 2019

Johnny Marr was born in Manchester in 1963. At the age of thirteen he formed his first band and at the age of nineteen he formed The Smiths with Morrissey. They became one of the most important and talked-about bands of the 1980s, but by 1987 they had gone their separate ways. Since The Smiths' demise, Marr formed Electronic with New Order's Bernard Sumner and later joined Modest Mouse, The Cribs, The The and, briefly, The Pretenders. He has also worked with the Pet Shop Boys, Billy Bragg, Talking Heads and Beck. He is now a successful solo artist. In 2012, he received an honorary doctorate from the University of Salford for 'changing the face of British guitar music'. In 2013, *NME* honoured Marr with a Godlike Genius award.

Josep 'Pep' Guardiola was born in Santpedor, Spain, in 1971. He joined La Masia, Barcelona's youth academy, at thirteen and rose through the club's C- and B-team ranks until he joined the first team as a defensive midfielder in 1990. He was part of Johan Cruyff's so-called 'Dream Team' that won Barcelona's first European Cup in 1992, as well as four Spanish league titles. He left Barcelona in 2001 and played for Brescia, Roma, Al-Ahli and Dorados. He also played for Catalonia's national team and Spain.

In 2008, after a year managing Barcelona's B team, Guardiola took over the first team; by the end of his first season they had won La Liga, the Copa del Rey and the UEFA Champions League. In four years he won fourteen honours, a club record that – even with Messi in the team – is so impressive that it has to be broken down: three Liga titles; two Champions League; two Copas del Rey; three Spanish Super Cups; two European Super Cups and two World Cup Championships.

Between 2013 and 2016, Guardiola managed Bayern Munich, winning four trophies in his first season. He won the Bundesliga four times in a row; in all, he won seven trophies at the German club. He became manager of Manchester City in 2016 and won the Premier League title in his second season, breaking domestic records in the process as City became the first team to attain 100 league points. In the 2018–19 season, Manchester City won the Premier League, the FA Cup and the EFL Cup.

⚽ ⚽ ⚽

Johnny Marr: You look very well. I'm guessing you went away during the international break because you would never get a tan like that in Manchester. I'm used to the weather here, but I always worry about the players not getting enough sun.

Pep Guardiola: It's OK when you're winning, but if you lose a game and it's wet and grey, it can be pretty awful! I'm feeling good just now because I'm just back from a holiday in the Dominican Republic with my wife.

Johnny: Do you enjoy taking time out during the break or does it mess with the team's momentum?

Pep: I always have doubts about it because of the issue of losing momentum. When you're winning back-to-back games, you have a kind of rhythm that can easily be disrupted by the international break. There are more international breaks to come this autumn. It's tough; it means that the schedule is never-ending. At least it's a change of environment for the players and that tends to do them good. As soon as they come back, they have to get right back into the swing of things at City.

Johnny: I saw the Germany v Serbia game in which Leroy Sané was viciously fouled. He somehow escaped serious injury, but it must be hard to know your players could come back injured.

Pep: I didn't watch the game because I was away with my wife, but my son sent me a frantic message asking what had happened. And then, thankfully, Leroy sent a message telling me he was OK. But you're right, it could have been terrible.

Johnny: I wondered if I was over-reacting as a City fan, but Serbia were clearly all over him for the entire game.

Pep: I know. It makes no sense. But the game has become so physical that there is always going to be a risk.

Johnny: How is Fernandinho, if you don't mind me asking?

Pep: He's doing well. He might need more time because he's thirty-four, you know. It's easy to pick up an injury when you've been playing for so long.

Johnny: Fabian Delph lives a couple of doors down from me. He was out late last night...

Pep: Dancing, raving.

Johnny: Obviously I'm joking!

Pep: I know. But I want the team to be happy. If they have the occasional drink, it's not a problem. I judge what happens on the pitch. What happens off the pitch is your business, but if you're not able to be professional because you haven't had enough sleep, then you'll be rubbish and you won't play. And next season you'll be at another club.

131

Johnny: It's the same in my profession. You know the musicians who want to be really great and who therefore take care of themselves.

Pep: I'm not a policeman. The players' private lives are private. But when the money first starts to arrive, their heads are always turned a bit. It can become a problem. But then they realize they have to compete with each other for a place in the team so they can't afford to take their eye off the ball even for a minute.

Johnny: I have some questions for you, if that's OK?

Pep: Of course, no problem at all.

Johnny: Where were you born and what did your parents do?

Pep: I was born and raised in Santpedor, a village seventy kilometres from Barcelona. My mum was a housewife; she stayed at home with the kids. My dad was a builder who ran a small company with eight or nine employees. He fixed kitchens and so on. We were a normal working-class family. I have two older sisters and a younger brother. It was a happy childhood.

Johnny: Do you still see a lot of them?

Pep: We are all in touch, yes. More so with my brother because he lives in London. My sisters live in Barcelona and in Tarragona in Catalonia so I don't see them as much, but we know we are there for each other.

Johnny: This is a basic question, but how did you get into football?

Pep: My dad was a Barcelona fan. I played in the street all the time; there were no traffic lights and hardly any cars, so we could play and play. Mum had to call me in: 'Come and have lunch, Pep!' Then, later: 'Come and have dinner!' I was only ever at home to get my homework done, to eat and sleep. Otherwise I was playing football.

Johnny: It's a very working-class thing, to be out on the street playing all the time. It's the same all over the world.

Pep: Yeah, of course. I was in Central America last summer and whenever we went to the poor areas, all the kids were playing football on the street. My kids have never played on the street. Partly because they grew up in Barcelona, which is a big, busy city.

Johnny: Has Santpedor changed much since you were a kid?

Pep: A little bit. There are traffic lights now! Unfortunately…

Johnny: Some of the things I wanted to talk to you about relate to the things I'm often asked about. For example, when people talk about you, they nearly always mention you being a perfectionist. Is that too simplistic?

Pep: Yeah, it is too simplistic. I always believe I can do better. That I can do more. But I have a family to think about; I probably wanted more during my first years as a manager than I do right now. Before I might have spent twelve hours before a game analysing the opposition. Now I am more selective about my time, and my assistants are incredibly well prepared, which takes some of the pressure off me. But I love my job. Because I enjoy it, it rarely feels like a job. I can watch footage of the next team we are going to play, have a coffee, watch more footage. I love watching the way a team defends and working out how we could break it down. At the same time, as much as I love sitting in this beautiful office with its beautiful view, I love going home and having a nice glass of wine with the family.

Johnny: Is that partly because you know yourself better as you get older and therefore you know how to protect your energy?

Pep: Yes. Before, I used to be exhausted by the time I had to face my players before the game. Now, one of my targets is to be in the moment and approach the game more freely. Sometimes I even prefer to arrive in front of the players without having *every* bit of information about the opposition. I can be more relaxed instead of arriving at the ground puffing and panting. As you say, that comes with age. You learn over time what is important.

Johnny: Especially when you've had huge success, because it's only natural to want to keep repeating what you've done before.

Pep: In the end you learn that nothing changes too much when you do all that extra work. Instead you could talk with a player for two minutes and make him feel wow! Make him feel really good about himself. It can be more productive than spending hours focusing on something like strategy. One of my weak points is that I'm not in touch with everything, but every season I am a little more in touch. At the same time, it's good for me as manager to be there when the players *really* need me.

Johnny: Do you feel as though you've always got your foot on the gas?

Pep: Definitely – although maybe less so compared to the start of my career.

Johnny: In the sense that you are always in cruise control but at times you want to be aggressive and really put your foot down hard on the gas?

Pep: I certainly don't want to be aggressive all the time, but sometimes they have to feel that I am angry, I am sad, I am disappointed. Sometimes they have to feel my emotion so that they give their best performances.

Johnny: You have to be real.

Pep: Exactly. When I am happy, they see me happy. When I am sad, they see me sad. I am not fake. If I am disappointed in the way we played, how can I be happy? The next day I will be here working, but I don't want to see the players at breakfast. I don't like them because we lost. But to return to your expression of 'putting your foot down on the gas', I don't really want to do that all the time when I might retire in several years' time.

Johnny: As I've got older, I've developed a similar attitude. I don't want to put my foot on the gas in a manic way, but if you take your foot right off the gas, you lose your edge.

Pep: You have to learn to be more selective. To spend your time more efficiently. Or you will not survive in this world. You have to adapt to the times; for example, as players have knowledge about football, so they demand more of me.

Johnny: I've been in a lot of bands over the years and I'm always very exacting. I get pissed off when we do a bad show and someone hasn't given it their everything, no doubt because I've always been a grafter. I'm the same when I'm asked to produce a young band: I like to be the first one in the studio in the morning and the last one out at night. I put a lot of my energy into the process and I really enjoy working in a team. For me, being a leader in that situation isn't related to ego – I actually enjoy the psychology of it. Like noticing that the guitarist's head was down after he'd talked to his girlfriend on the phone. You want to be nice, but you have to get the song done. So you go over and put your arm around him and say something reassuring. Of course, you've got a whole squad to consider: do you enjoy the man-management side of your job?

Pep: Like musicians, footballers are still people! Sometimes they are sad because they are getting divorced or their kids have health issues. You don't always know what is going on in their lives, of course. There are sixty, sixty-five people working here altogether and of course I can't solve everyone's problems. But they know we are always there for them, twenty-four hours a day. Hopefully, if I see a footballer I used to manage a few years after we worked together, we can hug each other and talk about good memories.

It's about trying to do our best given the circumstances we find ourselves in. There's no sense in trying to lift trophies and titles if you have a ridiculous relationship with each other, if you shout at each other for no good reason. If you are in a team, you celebrate the good moments together and support each other during the bad times. People think that because I'm a manager, I have to solve all the problems, but who solves *my* problems? I need someone to say, 'C'mon, Pep, everything is fine. We'll get there in the end.'

Johnny: So you need support as well?

Pep: Of course! Journalists turn up to press conferences thinking I am some kind of magician and I know all the secrets of the game. I have doubts, I have fears. Bad moments, bad days. Bad periods. As well as the good moments and the good days.

Johnny: Is the British media any easier to deal with than the German and Spanish media?

Pep: In general, it's the same: if you win, you are top; if you lose, you are a disaster. When we lose it's as though we have killed someone. All of us. Not just the managers, but the players too. It can be ridiculous. But they expect you to give the media much, much more time in Spain than here or in Germany. It's far more stressful than it is here. In Spain journalists try to watch training when they are not allowed to do so; here we see the journalists at press conferences and that's pretty much it. It's therefore much more comfortable working here in England. But in every single country around the world, if you win the pundits say you're a great manager and if you lose you have to be replaced.

Johnny: It's crazy.

Pep: Yes, but there's another way of looking at it. A friend of mine who is a writer says to me: 'I would rather my book was criticized, analysed or in fact discussed in any way rather than be ignored.' It makes sense; I wouldn't like to do this job with no one paying any attention to what I'm doing. If the media is always talking about the club I manage, the stadium will always be full! You can't have it all ways. I don't want to be like a painter who has created an impressive piece of work that no one ever sees. I'm sure you wouldn't like writing great songs that nobody ever hears. We have to remember how privileged we are when we feel as though we're going to crash into a wall. It's never that bad. It's just football! Perspective is essential.

Johnny: I know what you mean about people having access to your work, but it can go too far! People can get really obsessed. When I first started playing music professionally, at the age of eighteen, my first proper band got big really quickly. In the end, I had to leave that band because it got too crazy.

Pep: You mean The Smiths?

Johnny: Yeah… it's a long story. I left The Smiths thirty years ago and I've been in loads of bands since, but I'm still asked the same question all the time: when are The Smiths going to reform? I've tried to be gracious, I've tried every single answer. I've never got too pissed off, but I do end up saying, 'Look, just google it, man.'

Pep: 'Just google it!' I like that.

Johnny: I don't know what else to say! Of course, I don't want to be ignored but, then again, I don't want to have to deflect questions about a band I was in thirty bloody years ago when the work I'm doing now is pretty good. In the end, I always come back to the same thing: it's good to be working. And even better to be doing a job that you love. Everyone knows how much you love football.

Pep: It's true. I do really love it.

        ✪   ✪   ✪

Johnny: Even before I knew we were going to meet for this book, there's something I wanted to ask you about that relates to my own work. Sometimes, for example, I write music for movies and I will work really hard on the track, making it as perfect as it can be, in the full knowledge that actors will be talking over it. When I've been at a game and City are winning 3-1 or even 3-0, I've noticed that you are sometimes still frustrated and I wonder if you always want the game to be as perfect as it can be? It is perhaps because the game doesn't have the rhythm you want – I've noticed you use the word 'rhythm' quite a lot about football, which is unusual. I suppose my question is: even when we're winning, do you get frustrated if we're not playing right?

Pep: Sometimes when we are winning 4-1 or 4-2, I am still scared of losing the game. I want the players to be paying attention regardless of the score. I want them to feel that we always have a job to do. I'm not asking for big actions or big performances; I become really angry when they don't do the simple, simple things. I hate it when, instead of making a simple pass of two metres, they give the ball away.

It goes without saying that – like you when you are in the studio – we have to try to do our best. It's our job to do so. The fans have made a lot of effort to get to the game. Many, many good and bad things can be said about all the teams I've worked for, but there's one thing I don't want anyone to ever be able to say: my players don't run; my players don't fight. Look at Agüero. He fights and fights and fights. I think it's the best way. If I didn't think that, I would retire.

Johnny: It's not only about winning with a clean sheet, but you also want to see the game played well and with conviction.

Pep: Of course. We have a plan. When it works, there's no better feeling and it's why we are managers. When it doesn't work, we know the reason why and we have to change the plan. You can't wait till tomorrow, that'd be too late. Sometimes you have to change the plan during the game or at half-time. There's no timeout like there is in basketball, so the pressure can be very intense.

Johnny: I was reading a book about you a while ago in which you refer to this moment of inspiration. And it is just a moment. As far as I'm concerned, that moment of pure inspiration is the best part of being a musician. It's pure gold. Better even than the shows. It's what I live for. An older musician I know always used to say 'be inspired' instead of saying goodbye. It's the best thing to say because *everything* comes from that. I can work really hard, but I can't always be inspired. You have to open yourself to it. It's the bit you can't predict.

Pep: I don't know how you compose or how your process works, but the creativity is always there for you. I tell my kids to look for a job that they like, where they can be creative. You and I are really fortunate in that sense. When I watch how creative my players are out on the pitch, I'm blown away.

Johnny: Do you know that quote by Picasso? 'Inspiration exists, but it has to—'

Pep: '... find you working.' It's true.

Johnny: There are all these stories about how classic rock-and-roll songs were written. The musician will say they were in the super-market or in the car and they heard this song, perfectly formed. It's bullshit.

Pep: Totally.

Johnny: Like you have to watch endless videos of games, I have to be in the studio day in, day out for that moment of inspiration to come. Sometimes I get stuck with my process, but I just persevere – out of stubbornness or pride or fear – and sometimes the music has still not been right. But I'd feel worse if I gave up.

Pep: Of course. You cannot give up.

Johnny: I'd feel like I'd failed. I'd feel lazy. I always want to push myself. I reached a certain age and gave up pretty much everything – alcohol, cigarettes, meat – and started running. Because I'm so obsessive and suggestible, I started buying running magazines and of course I wanted all the gear. But I wouldn't let myself buy the gear unless I became a proper runner. I very quickly became Forrest Gump.

Pep: That's so funny!

Johnny: I played with Modest Mouse when they opened for REM in America in June 2008. I decided to run for fifteen miles before the show even though I'd never done it before. By the time we were on the fourth song, I was almost on the floor, exhausted. It comes back to what we were talking about earlier: knowing yourself and being more efficient.

Pep: Everyone who excels at their job is a machine. They work every day. It doesn't matter what their job is – a musician or an Apple guy – the talented, brilliant men and women out there all have a crazy work ethic. It's impossible to achieve at that high level without it. Inspiration isn't enough. Then you have to work doing something you like. Without that… it's a big failure.

Johnny: We've talked about perfection and inspiration and work ethic, but I'd love to know if you are superstitious.

Pep: A little bit. I used to be really superstitious. The last phone calls before a game were always to my wife and my daughter. Or I had to wear a suit. But not any more.

Johnny: Were you more superstitious as a player than a manager?

Pep: About the same. I'm not really, really obsessed. Superstition won't win me a game. I have to work and it depends on the players, not because I've worn a certain jacket. Routines and rituals are more important to me. Having said that, it would be impossible to find a manager who's not a little bit superstitious.

Johnny: Do you feel like you are still learning?

Pep: Of course; it's why I moved on from Barcelona to Germany and now here. Basically, it's a test for myself. Between 2008 and 2012, I was managing my home town, with Messi and Neymar in the same team, so why would I leave? I had everything there. I won two Champions Leagues in 2008–09 and 2010–11. It was the best ever.

Johnny: What was it like working with Messi?

Pep: He was top, top. I learned so much about how to be a competitor. The desire to win, again and again. The simple training sessions. He is an incredible competitor. The best ever.

Johnny: He's super-driven.

Pep: It's part of his personality.

Johnny: When you left Barcelona in 2013, you had a year off in New York. What did you do while you were there?

Pep: If I had a year off in Barcelona, it would have been crazy. I had to disappear. I thought the best place to go and not get bored would be New York. My kids were at an age where they could move schools and, at that point, they didn't speak one word of English. We had an incredible time. After one or two months, I signed a contract for Bayern Munich and I started German-language lessons for three hours in the morning with a teacher and then did homework in the afternoon. The restaurants, the theatres, Madison Square Garden… And my wife loves museums.

Johnny: Did the time go really quickly?

Pep: So quickly! In the summer of 2018, my assistant coach Domènec Torrent left City to become manager of our sister club, New York City FC. My wife asked why I didn't want to go to New York too! So maybe, when it's time for me to leave City, I will try to convince our chairman to send me there. I don't think I could live there for a long time because it's such a stressy city, but I love so much about it.

Johnny: Didn't you meet director Woody Allen when you were living out there?

Pep: A friend of mine was producing his movies around that time, so we met and talked about how much we love the New York Knicks.

Johnny: Do you like Sergio Leone and films like *Once Upon a Time in America*? That's one my favourite films.

Pep: Of course. I love movies so much; I like the whole thing of going to the cinema with a Coke and sitting there in the dark with other people. We met lots of different people in New York, not only Woody Allen but also [the chess grandmaster] Garry Kasparov and Knicks players. I went to a few of the Knicks training sessions too.

We did many things that we probably wouldn't have been able to do in Europe because football is everywhere and you can never be remotely anonymous. I got to be myself in New York. Not Pep Guardiola, football manager. Maybe in a restaurant some South Americans recognized me, but most of the people didn't care.

Johnny: I remember taking my daughter to New York for the first time, when she was twelve, thirteen. She was so excited.

Pep: Yeah, my family love going to New York, even if it's just for four days.

Johnny: You mentioned Kasparov. How did you meet him?

Pep: We have a friend in common. Or, rather, a friend of a friend of a friend! It was fascinating. You realize those chess masters are above. They are another level. We were having dinner and I asked him if he could beat one of the best young chess players. He was eating a salad. He wasn't looking at me. He didn't answer me immediately. And then he simply said, 'No way.'

I asked why. I pointed out that he has more experience, maybe more skill. He shook his head. 'No way.' Why? 'Because I can no longer focus on one thing for four hours. After half an hour, I'll start thinking about something else, like the political situation in Russia. It's not the young man who will beat me, but time.'

For him it is all about time and how your relationship with it changes as you get older. People ask why I left Barcelona. It wasn't because I'd won everything or because I was provoked by a specific event. It was a question of time. I started managing them when I was thirty-seven, and I was forty-one when I left. I wasn't the same person.

Johnny: Does Kasparov still play?

Pep: Not professionally, no way. Maybe exhibition games or on a more casual basis. He realized how much quicker the younger guys are. There is no avoiding it! But his brain is still incredible. You're in a busy restaurant with him and he very quickly knows what everyone is talking about. There's no doubt he has a gift.

Johnny: It must be hard for him to be in semi-retirement, or whatever he might call it. People ask me about retiring but I can't imagine it.

Pep: You won't retire. You will die playing guitar. For sure. Why would you retire when you love it so much? I will never properly retire either.

Johnny: It's different in your profession because it's so physical. Do you stay fit by going to the gym?

Pep: I should, but I don't. I have a lot of interviews with Smiths guitarist legends.

Johnny: Hey, this is the real work! Sitting around, chatting to me!

Pep: I love it! I'm very relaxed today, very open. I'm just back from holiday and we don't have a game for a few days. To be here talking to you helps me a lot.

Johnny: That's very kind of you, but—

Pep: Believe me, it's true. It helps me to learn. I should be watching games on my Mac, but it's perfect for me to stop and have a break.

Johnny: Well, if you ever need me to stop you from working, I'm always around.

⚽ ⚽ ⚽

Johnny: You were talking earlier about your relationship with your players. Did Raheem Sterling ask for advice when he started being racially abused by other fans and targeted by the right-wing press?

Pep: No, he didn't. He's an adult. The point is that we are never safe from these kinds of attitudes. Never. The media has a lot of power. Alongside politicians, they can manipulate what people think. Whether you are talking about racism or what is happening to refugees in the Mediterranean Sea. People have to be so active. All the time. People forget so easily. Every time something happens, we have to react. Every time. Like a machine. React, react, again, again.

Raheem has the power to make a difference because he's a public person and he's playing football at a big club as well as for his country. It's important for the new generation to be reminded that we are never safe. There is always racism. It's like constantly pulling at the levers on a pinball machine. We have to keep the pressure on. These kind of humanitarian issues won't go away.

Johnny: Did you see the *New York Times* article about Raheem?

Pep: I know about it but I haven't read it yet.

Johnny: A friend of mine who lives in New York told me about it. He couldn't believe what he was reading about a young black athlete enduring all this racist abuse.

Pep: People think that we have sorted these issues out. We haven't. Have you seen a German movie called *The Wave*? You must watch it. It's an amazing movie that explains exactly why we are not safe from what happened in the past [*editor's note*: the feature film is based on an infamous experiment in California in 1967, in which a high school teacher attempted to help his pupils understand fascism by re-enacting the conditions in which the Nazis came to power, with chilling results]. The pupils respond really quickly and start pointing out who is different and who is the same.

The Wave touched me because it's so easy to think fascism will never happen in Germany again. Or Spain. But look at what is happening now in Europe. In Italy, in Britain. Populist politics are on the rise pretty much everywhere.

Look at what happened in my country, in Catalonia. It's why I wear a yellow ribbon. Our elected politicians are in exile or in prison just for asking people to vote in a referendum in 2017. They went against the constitution, but the people wanted a chance to vote. To be heard.

I have a really good friend, Òscar Camps, who works for Proactiva Open Arms [a Spanish NGO engaged with search and rescue of refugees at sea]. My daughter is always helping them and I try to be a little bit involved when I can. They explained to me what happened: Italy won't allow any refugee boats to come ashore and so people are dying. These people don't leave their homes because they want to. It isn't a choice. They leave because they have *no choice*. Their country is at war or they can't find food to feed their kids. They have nothing to lose.

I realize it's a huge issue. The problem in Syria or Jordan or wherever has to be solved. Everyone in Africa clearly can't come to Europe. That's not the solution. We have to make a better Africa.

But coming back to what Raheem has done… He did well to speak up, but he has no choice. I will say it again: we cannot let these things just happen. Racism at football grounds. Racism in the newspapers. Racism on social media. And, more widely, we cannot accept the rise of populist politics. We can't.

Johnny: If we're talking specifically about Raheem, the British media has got so much to answer for. The way the narrative around him has built and built is shocking. Even when he was at Liverpool, I knew it wasn't right. A player being booed everywhere he went? Just awful. The positive thing is his response. A handful of Chelsea fans were verbally abusive and he responded brilliantly.

Until recently, no one really knew if Raheem was a quiet guy; in the *All or Nothing* documentary series on Man City, he seemed to be a quiet guy. Unlike Vincent Kompany, who I know a bit and who is the opposite! I'd go as far as saying the Chelsea incident was a watershed moment for modern football. Raheem has been so dignified about the racism he's facing.

A few years ago, I would never foreseen that loads of people – irrespective of their club allegiance and whether or not they are into football – would be giving Raheem a pat on the back. I'm so happy for him. He's become an empowered guy and, best of all, he's scoring loads of goals to shut everyone up.

Pep: Every single time it happens, it has to be condemned.

Johnny: Is racism worse here than in Germany or Spain?

Pep: Quite similar. It's partly why I travel and move on – to experience new cultures and meet different people from diverse backgrounds. It's a pleasure to be in England, to learn about your reality. When I leave the UK at some point, I know I have friends here who I can come and visit.

Johnny: I've travelled so much in bands and I keep discovering new places. Like Hamburg. My god, what a city!

Pep: I lived in Munich. You cannot imagine how beautiful it is.

Johnny: And Manchester?

Pep: Oh well, yes, Manchester too!

Johnny: Did you know before you came here that Man City had all the cool musicians?

Pep: I knew there had been a boom in music here, but not much else. Now I know everything! Talking of cool musicians, will you sign my Johnny Marr vinyl? I'll have to buy a record player now.

Johnny: It'd be my pleasure. But if that turns up on eBay, Pep, I'll know it was you. I also wanted to give you one of my plectrums.

Pep: Maybe I'll put it in my pocket and it'll bring me luck for the rest of the season. By the way, how many guitars do you own? Millions?

Johnny: Funnily enough, I was going to ask you how many grey cashmere jumpers you own!

Pep: I have many. Very many! But the jerseys are easier to find than the guitars.

Johnny: I do have a lot of guitars, it's true. When Noel Gallagher started out, I gave him a couple of my guitars because he was a fan of mine. Obviously I had no idea that Oasis were going to be so big.

Pep: I don't think anyone did!

Johnny: Before I go, I want to thank you for what you're doing here. I've been a City fan since 1972. I've said this to Vinnie and some of the other players, but I'm not fixated on winning everything; I just want to see players in good shape, who really love the club. There were some good guys in the 1990s, but lots of them were out of shape and just not properly committed. I just love seeing you guys try. And really work. So thank you. I won't ask about the quadruple.

Pep: I have an answer for you: google it! I'm here any time. Maybe we can go for dinner and you can explain your period of music to me. You can tell me what it was like being in The Smiths.

Johnny: Or we could talk about great footballers. Did you know about George Best before you came to City?

Pep: No, but Mike Summerbee always starts to cry when he mentions George Best. It's nice; a legend from City, a legend from United.

Johnny: Those two owned a shop together. For a kid like me growing up in the 1970s, you know who was really cool? Brian Kidd. He was a street kid. A perfect number eight. He scored a lot.

Pep: He's great to work with now [as co-assistant coach] because of his history with the club.

[a knock at the door]

Pep: I'm coming!

Johnny: If the sun's out and you ever want to go for a run, just call me. I'll go slowly.

Pep: I might prefer dinner. What a pleasure this has been. Thank you.

Johnny: Thank *you.*

John
Bishop

&

Jürgen
Klopp

John: Can you ever imagine just sitting and watching a game?

Jürgen: Yeah, I think it would be possible in the future. Because I'm already much calmer than I was. I know it's difficult to believe!

Jürgen Klopp's office, Melwood training ground, March 2019

John Bishop was born in Liverpool in 1966. He played non-league football for Hyde and Southport and worked as a medical sales representative. When his marriage broke down in 2000, he started to perform stand-up as a distraction (he reconciled with his wife eighteen months later). In 2006, just before he turned forty, Bishop became a full-time comedian. Three years later, he was selling out arenas and, in 2010, won the British Male Comedy Breakthrough Artist award at the British Comedy Awards. In 2014, two years after raising over £4 million for Sport Relief, he was awarded an honorary fellowship at Liverpool John Moores University in recognition of his contribution to the arts and charity. He is a regular on television panel shows and presents his own shows, including *John Bishop: In Conversation With...*

Jürgen Klopp was born in Stuttgart, Germany in 1967. He played for his local clubs and hoped to be a doctor, but didn't get the right grades. He studied sports science at the Goethe University Frankfurt and played for Rot-Weiss Frankfurt. In the summer of 1990 he was signed by the second-tier team Mainz 05 and, eleven years later, became their manager. With a small stadium and an even smaller budget, Mainz were promoted to the Bundesliga in 2003–04. Klopp left to manage Borussia Dortmund in 2008, winning the Bundesliga twice, the DFL-Supercup twice and the DFB-Pokal cup once. Dortmund were runners-up in the UEFA Champions League in 2012–13. In 2015, he became manager of Liverpool. Liverpool were runners-up of the League Cup and the UEFA Europa League in 2015–16 and of the Champions League in 2017–18. After taking teams to six finals, Klopp finally won the Champions League with Liverpool at the end of the 2018–19 season.

✧ ✧ ✧

John Bishop: Thanks for doing this. Do you know what it's for?

Jürgen Klopp: Charity? I read the word 'charity' and your name and said OK!

John: It's to raise money for refugee kids because football is the most universal game in the world. And it also, to some degree, reflects what is happening in a country. For example, we have this dire situation with Brexit and at the same time racism has become a really big issue in football again.

Jürgen: One hundred per cent. A French magazine journalist was talking to me about racism the other day. He told me that George Weah and a few other very famous former footballers felt under-appreciated when it came to awards such as the Ballon d'Or. They were pretty sure that it was racism. Wow. I couldn't understand it. It's not how I see the world. As far as I'm concerned, the dressing room is about whether or not you can play football, regardless of colour, religion or race. You can either play football or you can't. That's all that matters. The other stuff, nobody thinks about.

We have a prayer room here for Mo Salah and Sadio Mané. There are other Islamic procedures that we respect, including washing before a game, which we include in the pre-match preparations. Everybody here accepts that we are all different, but we are 100 per cent on the same page.

John: I think it's a relatively new thing, particularly for British football. I remember the abuse John Barnes had when he first became a Liverpool player in 1987. When Howard Gayle became our first black player ten years before that, people said, 'Liverpool don't sign black players.' I'm not saying there was a policy; it's just that those players stood out because they were the first ones. Football is now so international, which is brilliant. A decade ago, I would never have thought there would be a Muslim player in the Premier League. It was such a white, working-class game.

Jürgen: It's absolutely true. When I was a player at Mainz, Yugoslavia collapsed and there were a series of wars in the Balkans. There were Croatian and Serbian players in the team, alongside those from other former Yugoslavia countries. They were completely fine with each other. The only thing they didn't talk about was the war. They were actually playing for Mainz *because* of the war; they managed to escape it because they could play football, which meant they had a chance to make a new life in another country. They probably watched the news at home, but whatever the Serbians thought about the Croatians and vice versa never became a problem in the dressing room.

I'm not saying there are no problems out there. Of course there are. We are all human beings and we have our strengths and our weaknesses. But it's not about pointing the finger at the weaknesses and saying, 'That's why you are different.'

I really thought racist abuse had gone from the game. When I heard what happened in Montenegro, with Callum Hudson-Odoi and Danny Rose being subjected to racist chanting, I was shocked. I watch football without the sound because I'm not interested in what the pundits are saying, and so I didn't really get what Raheem [Sterling] was doing when he pulled at his ears in front of the Montenegro fans after scoring England's fifth goal. I was thinking, 'What are you doing?' And then I read about what had happened. I can really imagine how harsh it is for these boys. I cannot *feel* it exactly because it has never happened to me, but it's so crazy that it has started again. We are making other people responsible for our failure. Brexit is a good example of that. Why have we got Brexit? Because we want to have a border. Why do we want a border? So that certain people don't come into the country. Oh sorry, you don't tick the right boxes, you have to go away.

That's what I don't understand about racism in football.

Football throws everyone together to play the same game from all over the world. It works out brilliantly even if you all speak a different language. Of course, you have to learn the language of the country you are in; a player like Naby Keïta isn't playing all the time because he only understands about 30 per cent of the things we're talking about. Everyone likes him, but he doesn't understand enough yet.

John: You mentioned playing alongside Serbians and Croatians when you were a player at Mainz. Was that the first time you realized politics could affect a player's performance?

Jürgen: I never thought about football like that. For me they were only teammates, not people from another country. It's like going on holiday and trying the local food. If you don't like it, don't eat it. But if you do like it, it's wonderful. It opens your mind. There were African guys playing for Mainz while I was there, both from famous footballing nations like Ghana and from smaller countries. If you listen to people from different places, it makes you smarter. You can learn something about those countries without even going there. Your world-view should always be getting wider not narrower. It's not about thinking that other people look strange. The more you know about the world, the better you feel about yourself.

In football there are never problems with smart players. Of course, you could bring in a right fullback from Africa and another right fullback who is a local lad and they might not be best friends because they are always going to be fighting for the same place.

Only a silly person would say, 'You're not playing because you're from Africa.' I have never had that kind of discussion at Mainz, Borussia Dortmund or here at Liverpool. In football it's clear: the best player plays.

It's the same outside football. If you didn't bother listening at school and you don't have any education or skills, you can't expect to get a good job. And when someone turns up from another country who has worked hard and has studied economics or whatever, they don't get the job because they are black or foreign. They get the job because they are the better candidate. And they're not taking *your* job, by the way. If you have no future, that's your problem and no one else's. You have to create your own potential – if you have the chance to do so, if you live in Western Europe. Sometimes people have one, two, three chances and they waste them all. And then they blame people who have absolutely nothing to do with their own failure to take those chances. They blame outsiders, foreigners, refugees. Anyone but themselves.

That is the best way I can think of explaining the fear that some people have about open borders. I have friends from all over the world and I like that, it's cool. But we are in a difficult moment where some people think we have to go backwards. We have regressed to a time where we are always pointing fingers at strangers and making them responsible for our problems.

John: You've come into Liverpool—

Jürgen: As a German!

John: You've come to Liverpool to manage a team and, all of a sudden, you've found yourself in a country that's in political turmoil. So you're a European—

Jürgen: One hundred per cent.

John: … living in Britain—

Jürgen: Cool.

John: … with a high-profile job that has a high level of—

Jürgen: Attention!

John: … attention and also responsibility that's beyond almost any other job.

Jürgen: Yeah.

John: Has that placed you in a more difficult position in terms of being able to look at the future?

Jürgen: First of all – and I've said this a couple of times already – I'm really happy that I'm here while Brexit happens. Because otherwise, from the outside, you would've said, 'Are they all mad in England?'

John: You can say it from the inside too!

Jürgen: I know, I know! It's a sign of the moment. Communities everywhere in the world are a bit like that just now.

John: That's very true.

Jürgen: Angela Merkel has the most difficult situation to deal with in terms of how many refugees try to come to Germany. Because of our awful history, we have to be good people. We are still paying for our past. We have to care. England is in a different position because it has a different history and it's an island and not part of mainland Europe. It's harder to get to. And yet people are still worried about having open borders. England is a relatively wealthy country, but of course not everybody is well off; there are cities in industrial crisis and the focus is very much on London, Manchester, maybe Birmingham, I'm not so sure. Liverpool benefited from the EU years ago when it was Capital of Culture.

John: Yeah, in 2008.

Jürgen: Liverpool is a nice city. It has the Albert Dock, the Museum of Liverpool. But, as I was saying, there are other cities in crisis. I remember going to Dortmund in 2008 and it was still in transition from being a city whose mining and steel industries had collapsed to a city that is recognized as the most sustainable and digital city in Germany. It doesn't help the miners, but it gives the city another chance. The world changes, and you have to find a way to move on.

John: Did you always think, at the back of your mind, that you would one day leave Germany for England?

Jürgen: I came here when I was eighteen and I loved it. Loved the people, loved the bed and breakfasts. It was brilliant. So yes, I always wanted to work here. And I am here now and it's still a wonderful country with wonderful people. But what I don't understand – and I cannot really discuss it because I don't know enough – is that there must be a reason why half the population thought Brexit was a good idea. I think it's a bad idea, but they think it's a good idea. Why? Why do they think it makes real sense? Theresa May is still fighting for it and I don't understand why. Maybe I'm not smart enough or *they* are not smart enough, I don't know. How can democracy be working when such a huge issue is decided by just 2 per cent?

John: I don't think people fully understood what they were voting for – or against.

Jürgen: And now Theresa May is still saying, 'We have to do it because people voted for it.' No, they didn't! Just over 70 per cent of the population voted and lots of them were over the age of seventy.

John: Since the referendum in 2016, the electoral demographic has changed. The older Brexiters are dying off while many Remainers are turning eighteen and are now eligible to vote. If we wait long enough and vote again, we'd probably vote to remain.

Jürgen: I really hope so. It's not up to me to make decisions that will affect my grandchildren. My childhood was brilliant, but the childhood of my grandchildren will be completely different. They might not be so happy to just climb trees or kick a football around.

John: I'm very interested in what you said about Angela Merkel's position and the guilt Germany has had placed upon it. You're the first generation who has grown up without the direct guilt of recent history.

Jürgen: Yes, it's called *vergangenheitsbewältigung* – there is no direct translation, but it basically means coming to terms with the past.

John: Does it mean that you were brought up with the idea that it's better to be unified as opposed to being divided or pushing people away?

Jürgen: Look, I love my country. I love living there. I really love it. But I don't love it *more* than other countries, to be honest – but I know more people there and I'm German, so that's cool. I know this wonderful country was able to make one of the biggest mistakes in world history. Following an asshole in the wrong direction. Of course, he didn't do it alone, but people were ready to follow him. The generation before me always said, 'Yeah, but we didn't know exactly what was going on.' But not being informed doesn't make you free of responsibility. It's not the same situation here – it's nowhere near as extreme – but you can't pretend you don't know what's going on.

My generation are the last generation to feel the responsibility of what Germany did in World War II. We were directly related to the men who fought in the war. My sons have a different relationship with Germany. But we can't forget what happened. We have a responsibility for the past. But not everyone cares. If not all your lights are switched on, perhaps it's easier to ignore the past. If you have proper morals, if you're a Christian or whatever, you cannot ignore it.

John: Germany has been reflective on its past while we have this awful Little England mentality that relates back to our colonial past. Some people still have this idea that England is somehow better than other countries and doesn't need any help or support from Europe.

Jürgen: As a generation we have all benefited from Europe. When I was eighteen I travelled through Europe on Interrail for 400 German marks – less than £200. I visited England, Greece, Italy, France. There was this fantastic freedom of movement. Of course, the EU is not perfect, but it's the best idea we've had so far. We saved Greece together. We look after each other. That's how the world should be.

England can't go it alone again, pretending they are still an empire. They were an empire when ships were the best way to travel across the world. Not any more! Our generation has grown up without a world war. We learned from previous generations that war doesn't work. Now we have to use that knowledge. We have to be unified.

John: I think pretty much everything we've been talking about will resonate with Liverpool fans because Liverpool is, for want of a better phrase, a socialist city. I think you've bonded with the people of Liverpool in a way that is really, really special. But I wanted to ask you about your reaction when you were offered the chance to manage Liverpool. Why did you feel it was the right job for you?

Jürgen: I knew a little bit about the city because I was here a couple of years ago for a commercial and I saw the Albert Dock. People told me about the ongoing regeneration of the city. But I didn't know much more. As a football fan, I knew that the club wasn't in a good moment and hadn't been for the previous four or five years, with the exception of very nearly becoming champions. Of course, I knew that Liverpool had this incredible history of winning trophies both in Europe and at home.

To be honest with you, I really wanted to bring that glory back to the club. It was clear to me that the heart of the club was brilliant; it was like a garden that needed a bit of work to bring all the flowers back again. I knew that it wasn't the best team Liverpool had ever had, but I liked a lot of the players. I really wanted the job. I can't explain exactly why, but it just felt *right*. I knew that if they came for me, I'd really want to do it. I only hoped it would be at the right time for me, because I needed a holiday after managing Mainz and Dortmund. In the end, I only had four months off!

John: Sitting here, talking to you, you're so full of energy that I can't imagine you not working. But you've talked in the past about taking time off after leaving each club.

Jürgen: Yes, and unfortunately it hasn't happened! From Mainz I jumped immediately to Dortmund.

John: And when you left Mainz and then Dortmund, you had that unique thing of a manager leaving with the supporters' applause ringing in your ears. You left with their goodwill.

Jürgen: Yeah, absolutely. For me it's the only way to do things. It's the only way to live your life. If you are together, enjoy the time together; if you leave, leave as friends.

John: But that very rarely happens with football managers.

Jürgen: OK, that's true. And of course I never expect it. But I give each club I manage everything I've got. I became really good friends with the CEO and Sporting Director of Dortmund and now I'm really close with Mike Gordon [a director at LFC and president at the club's ownership group, FSG]. Mike is the guy who will tell me at some point, 'We enjoyed working with you, Jürgen, but…' When that time comes, it shouldn't mean anything about the time we've had together. It's like our attitude to death: we die one day and we can wait every day for that day or we can enjoy the time we have. I choose to enjoy the time I have. I have the only job in the world I'm good at. I'm not skilled in a lot of things, so it means I'm a lucky guy.

John: What I was trying to say just now is that you are so committed to your job and seem to enjoy it so much, that it must be hard to take time off.

Jürgen: You wouldn't believe how skilled I am at doing nothing. Honestly, you wouldn't believe it! I'm *unbelievably* good at doing absolutely nothing. When I took those four months off, I didn't watch football for two months and Ulla, my missus, couldn't believe it. She was really worried about me. But I enjoyed it so much. The plan was to do nothing but relax for three out of the four months. I had a tennis lesson every morning from 8 a.m. to 10 a.m., which was brilliant. The first day I turned up and the coach said we'd do fifteen minutes' warm-up first. The next day I arrived at 7.45 a.m. and when he turned up at 8 a.m., I said to him, 'I'm warm.' I was ready to play.

I wanted a few months of thinking only about me and my missus and what we wanted to do. And if we wanted to go out, we had to think about where we could go because people recognize me. I can't, for example, go out in Liverpool. I'm not a party guy, but if I was a bit more interested in having a social life, it would be difficult. It's getting more and more difficult to find a country where not everybody knows my face. I don't want my private life to be discussed in any newspaper or seen on any website.

John: No one wants that! After your break, there was talk of a number of jobs you might take, but you came to Liverpool. I remember watching your first press conference and being struck by your command of English.

Jürgen: It's easy for you English guys because you don't have to speak another language! If my first language had been English, I wouldn't have learned a second one because you don't need it. English is the first foreign language taught in German schools, but I was never very good at it. The next generation is really good – my sons are fluent without ever having lived here, probably because of the English-language music they listen to.

My English is still not too good, but it's good enough obviously to send out my message. And I'm really interested in language because I like to communicate. Before I came here, I listened to TalkSport! They talk unbelievable bullshit, but I picked up English football terms and heard different dialects – Scottish for sure, probably Irish. I carried on listening when I got here; just half an hour on the way to work and half an hour on the way back improved my language a lot and gave me a range of words.

John: So now that you're surrounded by English every day, do you think in German or English?

Jürgen: English. I just spent a week with my family, so I've gone back to thinking in German, but I'm now at the point where I'll be speaking German and I'll be searching for the German word for something and all I can remember is the English word. It's really embarrassing!

John: Funnily enough, I spoke to [former Liverpool player] Didi Hamann when he was a pundit on Sky Sport in Germany and he told me that he kept struggling to remember certain German words.

Jürgen: He's still in Manchester, right?

John: Yeah, I think so. So you arrived at Liverpool and, as you said, it was like a garden that needed to be replanted. And, four years on, the club's in a much better position. You are obviously a successful leader, but how important are the people around you?

Jürgen: This is my understanding: to be a really good leader, you need to have enough confidence to have strong people around you. Weak leaders always struggle with that concept because they can't work with people who might be better than them at a specific thing. I can easily accept that. When I started my managing career at Mainz, I had to learn everything about the job because we didn't have a scouting department, we didn't have analysts, nobody helped me with training, whatever. I did *everything* by myself. Which means that I can really appreciate and respect the work everyone does at Liverpool.

I want to have the very best around me. Everyone who works here is better at their jobs than I would be. I think I'm the only one at the moment who can bring them all together, which is why I'm still important. We brought Pep Lijnders back to the club to be assistant manager. We brought Mona Nemmer over from Bayern Munich to be head of nutrition. We brought a physiotherapist from Germany because I'm still yet to fully understand how English physiotherapists work. It's a completely different job to mine; they are more like doctors than like masseurs.

That's all that I had to do to build the team. We then created such a positive atmosphere here at Melwood by inviting all the staff to go to Tenerife with the players. And to bring their missus, their husband, their kids, whatever. We've done it three times now; last time I think there were ninety adults and fifty kids. LFC pays for a decent hotel and they have a phenomenal holiday with brilliant weather. It creates an atmosphere and brings everyone together. Football clubs often talk about the team behind the team, but it's not just words here. Everyone who works for the club knows they are important. Of course, they can't score a goal or keep a clean sheet, but they are unbelievably important to the day-to-day running of the club. Hopefully you felt that a bit when you were having lunch earlier today in the restaurant here. They're nice people and they are close to each other.

John: I did feel it, yeah. The players seemed very relaxed and close to the staff. There wasn't any sense of the players being more important. I first came to Melwood when Kenny Dalglish was manager and it's obviously changed so much. I think, back then, food was just food. No one would have had the idea of bringing someone from another country to be head of nutrition. I know that diet has become a big thing in football, but are you particularly interested in that side of things because you studied sports science?

Jürgen: I finished studying sports science in 1995, when I was playing for Mainz, and absolutely everything I learned about it has changed since then. One of my strengths is understanding that I have to adapt to changes by working with people who are informed and completely up-to-date in their field of work. They bring the information to me and it makes me smarter.

John: Is it true you did your sports science dissertation on walking?

Jürgen: It's true. I was a very busy twenty-seven-year-old. I was a father, I was playing for Mainz in the second division and I had another job because playing football didn't pay proper money. I wanted to take the easy route, to write about back problems or an issue that had already been widely researched. My tutor insisted I do something new. I said, 'Oh my god, I don't have time for all that!' And then he told me about Gary Yanker's walking workouts, which were a new thing at the time. And wow, I had to do real work! I think it was the first dissertation in Germany about walking. People ask if they can see it, but I have no clue where it is and hope that nobody will find it, ever. It was poor work, but I did at least finish it.

John: I'm interested in what you were saying about having confidence as a leader, and I wondered if that relates to being comfortable with having legendary former players around the club. Kenny Dalglish is a non-executive director and you don't appear threatened by his presence. You brought Steven Gerrard in as Liverpool Under-18 manager. There are some managers in your position who would say, 'I'd rather make sure former players are out of the way,' but you've actually embraced them.

Jürgen: First, Kenny and Stevie have both been a really big support from day one. Second, my position as a manager has nothing to do with the people around me. If Liverpool were to sack me tomorrow, maybe Kenny would be first choice to replace me, but they would probably bring Stevie down from Glasgow. If you ask who should follow me, I'd say Stevie. He was here earlier on today, just for ten minutes. I help him whenever I can. If someone gets your job, it's not about them, it's about you not being good enough.

I am old enough to know that I give this job everything. I am not a genius, I am not perfect, but I give the club 100 per cent. If that's enough, great. If it's not, then it's just the problem of the situation. I'm not jealous, I'm not sceptical. I'm completely open. If you want my help, you'll get it. My family often thinks I'm too quick to open up, but I think being any other way is a waste of time. I love life, I love my job, I like most people, that's how it is.

John: Have you always been like that as a person or have you adopted that position since becoming successful?

Jürgen: Well… I always wanted to be a manager, but you cannot say, 'Oh, by the way, I have an idea, I could manage that team.' It doesn't work like that. You have to wait for it to happen. One Sunday I was taken off by the coach after fifty-seven minutes, not because of injury but due to a bad performance for Mainz. On Monday, I became manager. The transformation was from an old player to a young manager. I was like a kid! I couldn't use experience to do the job because I didn't have it, but I felt comfortable in the sense that I was happy to give the job a go.

You have to build confidence as a manager. It's not always easy. For example, I've lost the last six finals my teams have been in. But, in a way, I don't feel like I lost six finals – I took my teams to six finals. But the world out there doesn't appreciate you being in the final unless you win it. I'm never happy about losing, but I can easily accept it. My life is as perfect as it can be. My family is healthy. I am healthy. I am doing what I want to do. I am confident that we will win finals in the future. Not everything, but some. Having lost six finals isn't the biggest problem in the world!

John: Is your Christian faith part of the bedrock that gives you that confidence?

Jürgen: I never think about it like that. In a press conference two weeks ago, I talked about being judged by God one day and that is how I understand it. I am prepared for that. I don't do bad things. I don't harm or hurt anyone. With my players it's sometimes different. Maybe they're not in the squad or I have to sell them. It's the hardest part of my job. But if we lose a game, judge me, no problem.

So yes, being a Christian means for me, in very simple terms, making the place you work in a little bit better. Don't think only about yourself. We are all selfish, but don't be *too* selfish. If I come into a room and the mood is average, but it drops the moment I step through the door, something is obviously wrong. That shouldn't happen if you are open to talking to other people. Don't do what you *want* all the time, do what you *have* to do most of the time. It's really not that difficult.

I'm not a priest. I don't go out and tell people what they have to do and how they have to live. Christianity, as I understand it, is a very good thing.

John: Your summary of Christianity is to behave in the way any reasonable person would surely want to behave: do no harm and do your best.

Jürgen: Yeah, I think a lot of people are like that, actually. But they aren't asked why they're like that. In my position I get asked about it and so I share my view and that's it.

John: Purely from a supporters' point of view—

Jürgen: Will we win the league?

John: By the time this book comes out, we will hopefully have won the league. There are three other things I've got to ask you. Number one: why do you stand on the halfway line watching the other team warm up?

Jürgen: I see my team all week long, so I don't need to watch them warming up. Before the game, you get the opposition's line-up, but you don't know the formation they will play. Sometimes, when they are warming up, they will play in that formation. You can find out if they are going to play with four at the back. Sometimes they play with three or five at the back, but if the last line is made up of four players during the warm-up, that is probably how they will play.

I stand there to get as much information as I can, but also to get a feeling for the other team. That's the truth; I want to get a feeling. When we played against Dortmund in the Champions League, I knew it would be awkward for my former players if I did it. It didn't stop me! As I watched them, they could look and see that I was really there. That was the first small victory of the night.

John: It's like the manager's version of boxers at the weigh-in – it's that stare-out, isn't it? And it's a real sort of statement of intent.

Jürgen: When the players come really close to me, it's kind of awkward, but I'm used to it. I know they're thinking, 'What's he looking at?' I can hear the opposition's assistant managers shouting at their players to turn away from me. I'm not trying to be intimidating; I'm just interested in what the other team's players are doing.

John: Number two: you've been pulled up for being so passionate on the side of the pitch. As a supporter, you want to see the players play how you would play and the manager manage how you would manage. And you manage how I would manage.

Jürgen: [raucous laughter]

John: Can you ever imagine just sitting and watching?

Jürgen: Yeah, I think it would be possible in the future. Because I'm already much calmer than I was. I know it's difficult to believe, but really, I'm already completely different. The thing is, I talk to the players all week long. We prepare things. We give advice. We give out information. In a game, it's difficult to give out many instructions because it's too loud, play is too fast. So you can only talk during half-time.

So I think my job is being like the reserve tank for the boys. If their energy level drops, I have enough to share. I've said to players a couple of times, 'I will give you all my power, I don't need it. So really go for it. I will kick your ass when you need it. I will shout at you when you start to feel weak.' It's better for them to be aggressive and angry with me than to not respond to a situation and end up thinking, 'Oh, I missed the chance.' It's better they think, 'Boss, you're a wanker!' and then go off and prove what they can do.

I never thought about how I might behave on the sideline. It just happened. It's just me. I'm not interested in what people say about me, but I do know that people think I'm not a tactician because I'm too lively to be a tactician. I'm the emotion guy.

John: Whereas they see Pep Guardiola as the tactician.

Jürgen: Pep is lively as well, but not *that* lively. He looks better when he's shouting. Pep always looks perfect – body, clothes, everything is perfect. When I shout, I look like a serial killer. It's my face, I bite my teeth in a certain way. I look at babies with exactly the same face. Like, 'Oh, you're so cute.' And very often the babies start howling.

John: There's no doubt that your passion is what binds you with supporters at every club you've managed. I think it's one of the things that resonates with everybody about you.

Jürgen: Pure coincidence.

John: You say it's coincidence; I think it's also part of the reason you're here.

Jürgen: What I mean is that it's pure coincidence it fits because if that passion didn't please the fans then I couldn't change it. If people expected me to stand there and passively hold up three fingers to the players to mean X or Y, then I couldn't. I'm not that person. The truth is that for those ninety minutes I'm on a different planet.

John: And that brings me to my third question. How do you build up to the intensity of those ninety minutes? Do you have a routine? How quickly are you able to process a game, regardless of whether we've won or lost? Can you put it away and deal with it on Monday?

Jürgen: I've never been able to switch on or off, but I'm much better at it than I used to be. I give around twelve, thirteen interviews after a game so I don't really get a chance to think about myself.

John: Just say that again – how many interviews?

Jürgen: Around a dozen. Perhaps six of those are for television, I think, then radio, radio, radio, then the club TV channel.

John: Are they all contractual commitments?

Jürgen: Yes. The post-match interviews for the Champions League games are even more demanding.

John: Does that mean you've already had time to decompress because you've said everything to the press?

Jürgen: I'm not sure! After the game, you go straight to the dressing room for a minute and then you go out and [LFC head of press] Matt McCann is waiting for me and off I go. How can I explain it? It's like being a piece of meat that is not cooked. I sometimes feel a bit raw, but I have to go out there and sometimes I'm immediately presented with a silly question like, 'Why did you play that player?'

You have to learn to bite your tongue sometimes. I have a problem with losing, I'm not a good loser, but I accepted long ago that sometimes you lose. So far, so good. But if somebody isn't sensitive or isn't really interested in what I've got to say, they're just after a quote or a headline or they ask, 'How could you let this or that happen?' then it's really hard to be composed. From time to time, I do go for them with words.

I'm famous in Germany for giving really weird interviews. When, live on television, I went for the interviewer: 'Which game did you see? Blah, blah, blah.'

John: I haven't seen you do that here.

Jürgen: I'm not that person any more. I'm calmer.

John: Age brings that.

Jürgen: Absolutely. After I've done all the interviews and seen the players, I don't think about the game. Both my boys, who are now thirty and thirty-three, are completely football-mad. So when they come to Liverpool, they talk to me constantly about football. Or text me from Germany. After a game, I have to say, 'Please, shut the fuck up.' I saw the game. I was there. I don't want to talk about it now. I have a meeting about it tomorrow morning.

John: I anticipated a similar answer. I can see you put so much into it that you need space to be away from it. I remember the first time I saw you here at Melwood, you turned up in an Opel, not the flashiest of cars—

Jürgen: I still drive an Opel.

John: … and that's great, but it's not the image of most of the people involved within the football world. I don't feel as though you've bought into the flashy side of football. You have your world away from football. What do you do when you're not working?

Jürgen: Wife, dog, friends, family. My two sons are my best friends, so that's really cool. They both work in Germany. As I said, they are both football maniacs, so they come over as often as they can, especially for the big games. They text me constantly, giving me tips for players to watch. I'm just back from six days in Dubai with my wife, my sons, their girlfriends. I couldn't be happier.

To be honest, I started enjoying my job as a manager the moment I didn't need to worry about money. That happened to me pretty early because I don't need money really. It's crazy what we earn in football, but there is always the chance of losing your job and your name being killed. If they – the press, the fans – decide to go for you, you won't work again. It's happened a lot in Germany. So for me, when it worked out at Mainz, I was completely free because I knew I could do the job. I could be national coach of the Fiji Islands. I would still enjoy that like hell and I'd be good at it. Until then, the pressure is intense because you have to deliver. I'm not as good at anything else as I am at football. Which means if I'm not doing this, what else can I do? I'm sure it's the same for you: if you're not being a comedian, what would your second big skill be? We are both lucky we are doing the things we are good at and enjoy. You're probably in the same situation: the moment the money is sorted, you can really start enjoying it.

John: It's funny with me because I went into stand-up comedy late in life and all of a sudden I realized, 'Oh, OK, I can be a comedian in a massive arena or I can be a comedian in a pub, but I can always be a comedian.' The money bit doesn't matter, nothing else matters – just knowing that you can do it matters.

Jürgen: For me it was important that people realized I could do the job. Then I thought, 'OK, now I can do it as long as I want,' and that's exactly what I do at the moment.

John: And you're here till 2022, is that right?

Jürgen: My contract is until 2022.

John: So is this home? Or is the Black Forest home perhaps?

Jürgen: I left the Black Forest at nineteen. Mainz is home. We go back to Mainz when we can. We are building a house there. One of our boys lives there, the other one is in Berlin.

John: This is bad, but I don't know where Mainz is.

Jürgen: Oh, it's directly next to Frankfurt in the south-west of Germany. There are 180,000 people living there, mainly students. It's built on the Rhine river. It's a famous wine area. It's really nice, I have to say. The weather is much better than here or in Dortmund.

[a knock at the door]

Jürgen: I'm sorry, but I have to go! Thank you for coming.

[runs out of office]

Val
McDermid

&

John
McGlynn

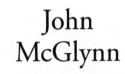

Val: I remember meeting you for the first time in the dressing room, where you were folding the freshly laundered kit. You'd already replumbed the shower area and retiled the dressing room.

John: Yeah, I cleaned the place up and painted it.

Val: The way you got stuck in was extraordinary. I tell people this story and they say, 'That's your manager?' I say, 'Yeah, he's part of the team.'

Stark's Park, Raith Rovers FC, March 2019

Val McDermid was born in Kirkcaldy, Fife, Scotland, in 1955. She was accepted to read English at St Hilda's College, Oxford, at the age of seventeen, becoming the first undergraduate from a Scottish state school. McDermid worked as a journalist on national newspapers in Glasgow and Manchester before turning her hand to novels. Her first attempt, written when she was twenty-one, was turned down by every publishing house in London; her second, *Report for Murder*, was published by The Women's Press in 1987. Since then, McDermid has become a best-selling crime writer, shifting in excess of 16 million books worldwide. In 2011 she was awarded an honorary doctorate from the University of Sunderland, and in 2017 she was elected a Fellow of the Royal Society of Edinburgh as well as a Fellow of the Royal Society of Literature. A lifelong Raith Rovers fan, she has sponsored the players' shirts and was on the board of directors at the club until 2017. The north stand at Stark's Park was renamed the McDermid Stand in memory of her late father, who was a scout for the club.

John McGlynn was born in Musselburgh, Scotland, in 1961. He played for Bolton Wanderers' youth team from 1979 to 1980 and then for Berwick Rangers, Musselburgh Athletic and Whitehill Welfare between 1980 and 1997. He went on to manage Easthouses Lily, Musselburgh Athletic, Heart of Midlothian, Raith Rovers and Livingston. He was a first-team scout for Celtic from 2015 to 2018. He returned to Raith Rovers as manager in September 2018. As a manager he won the Scottish League Second Division with Rovers in 2009 and the Fife Cup in 2012.

⚽ ⚽ ⚽

Val McDermid: So here we are at Raith Rovers Football Club, where John McGlynn is the manager for the second time in his life. A man who is clearly no stranger to masochism.

John McGlynn: I'm delighted to be here.

Val: You were born in Musselburgh in 1961. What was your upbringing like?

John: My parents came to Musselburgh from the west of Scotland. I was born there and raised in Wallyford. My father was a miner. As soon as I was tall enough to kick a ball, I started playing football. I played for the school team and then, when I was eleven, for Haddington United boys. It was a half-hour bus journey from where I lived, so I spent a lot of time going back and forth on the bus with two or three other lads. Nowadays parents take their kids to games, wait on them and bring them back. We had to fend for ourselves back then!

Val: Did you have siblings?

John: Aye, I had an older brother, Charles, named after my father. Unfortunately, my mother died of cancer when I was eight, so I was brought up by my dad and my older brother.

Val: That must have been tough.

John: It wasn't easy. It wouldn't have been easy for my dad either. I got annoyed at school because everyone else had a mother and it wasn't fair.

Val: I suppose that, after your mum died, football gave you a place that you belonged?

John: Yeah, definitely. Football has been my life, all the way through. Jim Jefferies was a local boy who was friends with my brother. Jim was playing for Wallyford Colts when he was really young, just seventeen. Along with some other people, he set up a boy's club team for Under-14s in Wallyford. He was coaching our team when I was thirteen; it was good to have someone to respect, someone who had knowledge of the game and was a professional footballer.

Val: Is that when your love affair with Hearts began?

John: I was basically a Celtic supporter as a boy coming up. I suppose it was a natural thing because my folks were from the west coast and I went to a Catholic school. I never actually went to a Celtic game when I was young because it was too hard to get there.

Val: Without taking a *lot* of buses.

John: Exactly.

Val: What's your first football memory?

John: Playing football at school with my friends. And then, after school, there were loads of wee games going on all over Wallyford.

We could just play in the back garden and it could be the greatest game on earth.

Val: Wee girls played football on the streets and in back gardens too. It was only when we got to school that we were told 'girls don't do that'.

John: Exactly. There were some skipping ropes…

Val: Do you remember the first game that you went to?

John: I remember going to watch Hibs and Dundee, way, way back. I'm sure that Bobby Ford and Eric Sinclair were playing for Dundee at the time. And John Blackley was playing for the Hibs. All good players. It didn't matter to me then who was playing; I was just happy to go to a football match. Another time, my brother took me to see Celtic v Dundee United in a Scottish Cup final.

Val: My dad used to take me to Stark's Park when I was wee, I think mostly to get me from under my mother's feet.

John: Were you from Kirkcaldy?

Val: Aye. I can vividly remember being sat up on those U-shaped metal barriers on the terraces and how cold they were on my bum. The best bit was a Pillans pie at half-time; I remember I'd bite into it and the juice would run up my sleeve. A moment of warmth away from the wind and cold on the terraces. It was those physical sensations that stay with me most acutely. That and the thrill of the game, obviously! But you were playing more than watching.

John: Yeah. After Wallyford Colts, I joined Salvesen Boys Club in Edinburgh. When I was fourteen, I signed an S-form – 'S' for schoolboy – with Dundee United. Jim McLean was manager and they were just starting to be extremely good.

Val: Jim McLean was quite a character.

John: Quite extreme, yeah. He was way ahead of the game, tactically and training-wise. A few of us from around Wallyford would get driven up to Dundee in the school holidays. We stayed there for a week, training and everything. It was great. Then, when I turned sixteen, the club let me go.

Val: That must have knocked the wind out of your sails a wee bit.

John: Not for long! By this time, I was playing for Musselburgh Windsor Under-18s and I got spotted by a Raith Rovers scout. I came here to Stark's Park on a Tuesday evening to play against a Fife select team and scored two goals. It was supposed to be a behind-closed-doors game, but it turned out that there was a Bolton scout watching the game. He called Musselburgh Windsor's coach and asked if I'd go down to Bolton for a trial. Of course, I would!

Shortly afterwards, I went down and played very well for Bolton's youth team and then again for the reserve team against Coventry at Highfield Road. Ian Wallace was playing for Coventry at the time. I don't know if you remember him, but he was one of the first million-pound players. A small, ginger-haired lad who used to play with Dumbarton. Believe it or not, Sam Allardyce was just coming back from injury so he was the centre back in Bolton's reserve team that night. Bolton liked what they saw in me and so I signed for them at the age of seventeen.

Val: Did you sign a professional contract?

John: Yes, but I was at the lower end of the pay scale. I'd been working as a plumber for a year at this point, and I went to college one day a week in Bolton so that I could qualify as a plumber. Moving to Bolton was brilliant. I was there for eighteen months, in both the A team and the reserve team – I never really broke into the first team. Then I signed for Berwick Rangers in 1980. Berwick were bottom of League One and were, sadly, relegated. But I had three great years there.

Val: When you moved back to Scotland, to what extent were you aware of the sectarian divide between Catholics and Protestants that afflicts certain elements of the Scottish game? Mostly it's concentrated on the Old Firm, Rangers and Celtic, but its ugliness does spill over elsewhere.

John: Living in Edinburgh or on the east coast of Scotland, we don't know the half of it. I worked as a first team scout for Celtic for nearly four years from January 2015 till I moved back to manage Raith in September 2018. I didn't move house to live in Glasgow;

I just travelled through when I needed to. But I still got a real sense of the tension.

Val: We should probably keep the story chronological! After your stint at Berwick, you went back to play for Musselburgh Athletic?

John: Yep. It just made sense because I came from that area. I knew of lot of people associated with the club, like Peter Ramsay. That was the thing that motivated you back then – mates, not money. We got about £100 as a signing-on fee and that was it, you went off and played your football. I wasn't bothered about the money because I earned a living from plumbing.

Val: You went from Musselburgh to Whitehill Welfare, a team based in Rosewell, Midlothian, and had a good run there.

John: I was at Whitehall Welfare for three years. We won the Scottish qualifying cup and beat Albion Rovers in the actual Scottish Cup, but we were beaten by St Johnstone in the next round. Around that time, I started helping out with Musselburgh Windsor, the team my young nephew was playing for. When my brother and some of his mates started a new team called Lothian United, he volunteered me to coach the team. So I was plumbing, playing and coaching! But it led to me coaching different age groups and working my way up the coaching ladder.

Val: After coaching Musselburgh Athletic, you were caretaker manager at Hearts for a short spell, followed by six years at the

Rovers from 2006 to 2012 and another year at Hearts from 2012 to 2013. What was your first spell at the Rovers like? It must have been a tremendous relief after what you'd been through at Hearts, with the constant changing of managers and so on?

John: The chopping and changing at Hearts was a nightmare. Not only managers coming and going, but eleven players were signed on the last day of the transfer window! I didn't know how safe my job was from day to day. It was a relief to come to Rovers. With the greatest respect to the club, I came here to cut my teeth as a manager without any of the distractions that were going on at Hearts.

Val: The Rovers were really happy to get you, but you didn't find us in a great situation. You had to be up for a challenge.

John: Rovers were second-bottom. I know lots of other people were interviewed for the job, and I had two or three interviews myself. I was *really* up for the job. I wanted the challenge. I needed the experience. I needed to get involved and put my ideas across and get things going. I felt that this club had a fan base, it was a sleeping giant that could be rekindled, it just needed a kick up the backside! Thankfully we did get fairly quick results albeit not the dream of promotion. But at least we went from second-bottom to the play-offs.

Val: You had to adjust to the Rovers – a club with very little money – after working at Hearts, where there was money for bouncy castles and fireworks.

John: That's true, but I had worked at Boys Club level and at junior level and I've always been the type of guy who rolls up his sleeves and mucks in. Whatever it takes, basically.

Val: I remember meeting you for the first time in the dressing room, where you were folding the freshly laundered kit. You'd already replumbed the shower area and retiled the dressing room.

John: Yeah, I cleaned the place up and painted it.

Val: The way you got stuck in was extraordinary. I tell people this story and they say, 'That's your manager?' I say, 'Yeah, he's part of the team.'

John: I wanted people to respect the place and the only way they would do that was if it was clean and tidy. I didn't think it would ever look like the Ritz, but I didn't want it to be a pig sty. Once you start letting go, everything starts falling apart. I thought if I replumbed the showers and retiled the dressing rooms, people might start to respect the club a bit more and feel pride in playing for it. Simple housekeeping can make such a difference. I also felt that if I showed my commitment to the club at every level, the players would respond and be motivated on the pitch.

Val: It's such an obvious but brilliant approach because people take pride in their surroundings.

John: That's what I tried to achieve. It wasn't about throwing money at this or throwing money at that. It was a matter of rolling the sleeves up and working extremely hard to raise standards on and off the pitch. I wasn't soft, I knew we'd have to lose a few players to get one player who'd make a big difference, but I wanted everything about the club to show its ambition. And we did it that first season, going from second-bottom when I took over in November to third-top by May. It was a great achievement.

Val: You could probably have had a free pint in any pub in Kirkcaldy at that point.

John: Aye, you're probably right.

Val: The following season, you built on that success and we got the Second Division championship.

John: We had battles with Ayr United all the way through my time at the Rovers. They played us towards the end of the season and left thinking they'd won the League, but we won eight games in a row and won the title with a game to spare. It was an amazing feeling – everything you come into football to achieve. We then did well in the Championship, got to the Scottish Cup semi-final and I was awarded Manager of the Year.

Val: How did that feel?

John: Amazing actually because I didn't really expect it. It was enough to be one of four nominees; to win was incredible. I was so proud. You see the names of some of the people who have that award and it's frightening. But it wasn't just me who won the award; it was all the staff at the club. Paul and Pud the physios, Gunter the kit man and Wayne the goalkeeping coach. We were so tight, so close. We all had each other's backs and the players recognized that spirit and reacted to it on the pitch. Spirit is everything at a football club.

⚽ ⚽ ⚽

Val: How would you describe your coaching style? What's important to you when you're working with the team?

John: I like to see attractive football. To pass the ball. There's a simple catchphrase that I always have in mind: the ball is round to go around. It's meant to be passed around. Barcelona is the obvious example, because they pass the ball to death. People try to copy that style of play, but there is only one Barcelona. I like to see good goals scored from good passing movements but, at the end of the day, it's about winning. You've got to try to put tactics in place to win a football match. Which is not as simple as it sounds. I think over the years I've got better tactically, partly because I've learned from absolutely everyone I've worked with. I came back to the Rovers for a second time as manager after my spell at Celtic, and I have to say that Brendan Rodgers is the best I've ever worked with. I've worked with a number of great people along the way: Craig Levein and George Burley went on to manage Scotland, while John Robertson, Jim Jeffries and Billy Brown were all magnificent in what they did. But Brendan Rodgers is head and shoulders above the whole lot of them. He's good at everything. It's all very well for a manager to be effective in the training ground, but can he see what needs to be done during a game? Can he change it? Can he see a player he admires, bring him to the club and settle him down? Brendan ticks ten out of ten in all the boxes. Just fantastic.

Val: You don't get many of those. Sir Alex Ferguson is another.

John: I like to be hands-on when I coach, to be involved in everything. But attractive football is the aim. If you just roll the ball along, it might end up in goal, but it's not a good spectacle for the fans.

Val: I find it so frustrating when the players forget themselves and just start lobbing the ball up the park, hoping somebody will be on the end of it. To whom are they passing it? One day in the directors' box I got the piss taken out of me something terrible because I shouted out 'To whom? To whom?' I sounded like a bloody owl. But, to be fair, I think we sometimes forget how young some of the players are.

John: Aye, very young and inexperienced. You've got to remember we're in League One, unfortunately, and the players are here for a reason – generally because they're not good enough to play in the top flight. They might well be on their way up, but they're not yet the finished article.

Val: When you bring a player in, are you always looking at him in terms of what can be fixed?

John: I'm looking for a player who can score a certain number of goals. Or keep a number of clean sheets. Someone who will improve. At the moment, for example, we don't have enough winners. Players who are real aggressive winners. A mentality of, 'Thou shall not pass, I will clear this ball.' We have very nice tactical football players who can pass the ball very, very well. But not many who are willing to fight till the end. Real winners.

Val: Sparky [Mark Campbell] was great for that. He wasn't the most technical on the park, but he was absolutely a rock. He was committed. An amazing player. Watching him play brought a smile to your face because you knew he was there to win the game and that's what mattered to him.

John: Mark was exactly the kind of winner I'm talking about.

Val: You've got to have that desire, that burning sensation.

John: You've got to have a fire in your belly.

Val: But you've always seen the value of youth, you've always had a really strong commitment to youth players?

John: Absolutely. I don't think there's a lot of difference between a young player and an experienced player if they've both got ability. It's also about the right mentality and the right physical strengths, but I am always up for giving young players the chance to prove themselves. They can only learn by playing. That is, of course, assuming they are enthusiastic, motivated, full of desire and hunger.

Val: You were with the Rovers till 2012 and then you went to Heart of Midlothian for a season and Livingston for a season, before returning to the Rovers in 2018. All clubs with very little money.

John: I wanted to come to Raith Rovers, make a name for myself and go back to Hearts. But it was the wrong time to go back. Hearts knew that they were going down the tubes, but I wasn't aware of the full extent of it. I was told it would be tough but that I'd get support. They weren't happy when the club started to slide down the league, even though I took Hearts to a League Cup final. I was sacked three weeks before the Cup final. A lot of bad things were going on at the club – players weren't getting paid, there was a transfer embargo. But I don't regret it. We almost took Brendan Rodgers' Liverpool to extra-time at Anfield in the 2012 Europa League play-off. We were beaten 1-0 at home and then, when we went to Anfield, David Templeton scored in the 85th minute. Luis Suárez got a goal three minutes later so we didn't get the opportunity to go to extra-time. It was frustrating, but I've got great memories of Liverpool coming to Tynecastle Park and then going down to Anfield, where the atmosphere was amazing. In the end, however, it wasn't enough and I left in 2013.

Val: The fans never have the opportunity to understand what's happening behind the scenes. They see what's in front of their faces but have no understanding of the kind of juggling that goes on in board rooms and management meetings, trying to square the circle, trying to make the impossible possible.

John: The Hearts fans obviously realized things weren't hunky-dory because the players weren't always getting paid. The Hearts fans were great, raising money and all sorts of things.

Val: And then Ann Budge came in with the white horse, putting together a consortium to buy Hearts in 2014. I've got a lot of respect for her.

John: So have I.

Val: It's great that Edinburgh clubs are being run by women, with Ann Budge at Hearts and Leeann Dempster at Hibs.

John: Aye, that's true.

Val: Livingston were another club struggling for money.

John: Which meant we had to sell players to other clubs. I was trying to bring young players on, but it was too hard. Once again, I got a team to the semi-final of the Champions Cup and was asked to leave. I've got Hearts and Livingston to cup finals and yet have never taken a team out.

Val: It's a scunner. You were doing great things with clubs that were really struggling. But your ability to spot young players and bring them through is what drew Celtic to you.

John: That's the difference between football people and, with the greatest respect, the normal kind of fan. Football people will recognize that Hearts were in a terrible situation and it's doubtful anyone could have done any better. Same thing with Livingston. I spent a lot of time firefighting. There was so much blood, sweat and tears at both clubs. It was a real grind to raise standards and be successful.

Val: Which is why Celtic wanted you as a scout. My dad was a scout for Raith Rovers – he loved football and he passed that passion on to me, just as his father did with him. It was a part-time job that he did on his days off. He discovered the great Jim Baxter, but he was very modest when he talked about signing him for the Rovers. He just said, 'A blind man could have scouted Jim Baxter.' He also signed Ian Porterfield, who went on to score the winning goal in the 1973 Cup Final. I had these endless afternoons standing on cinder pitches, watching miners and shipyard workers kicking seven bells out of each other. My partner Jo and I were at Stark's

Park one freezing cold January afternoon, the rain in our faces, and she turned to me and said, 'How could your dad not have scouted for Barcelona?' I went to so many games with my dad that I learned a little bit about the trials and tribulations of scouting. You have to watch a lot of games before you see a player that sparks your imagination.

John: That's the thing about scouting: you put so many hours in, with very little to show for it. Celtic have got the infrastructure set up and they've obviously put money behind developing the squad, so I was watching games all over Europe. And it becomes competitive; the others scouts might say that they discovered a player like Virgil van Dijk [who was at Celtic from 2013 to 2015]. For me, it wasn't about personal ambition, it was just about what is best for the club.

Val: It was a lot easier in my dad's day. He saw a player, suggested he'd be a good buy and, if the other club was willing to let that player go, the Rovers would sign him.

John: These days the initial part of scouting is done on a computer. There's a website called Wyscout that is for agents, scouts, players, journalists and referees. By Monday morning, every game is on the website. When I was at Celtic, on a Saturday I'd be on a 5 a.m. flight to Belgium, where I'd pick up another plane and maybe even take a third flight, to watch a game in the back of beyond. It was normal to get back to your hotel room at midnight and be on another flight by 7 a.m. the next day.

Val: Did you enjoy the travel, the strange, distant lands, the weird football grounds?

John: I got used to the travel, and going to unusual grounds was exciting! But I never got to see the cities I was visiting.

Val: It's like book tours. People think my life is so glamorous, but you barely have time to register where you are. I could be in Paris and all I'll do is book signings, back-to back interviews and sitting on trains. I'll be in the gastronomic capital of France and I'll be lucky if I get a decent meal. There's no glamour in it at all.

John: That's a real shame. I loved doing match reports because Celtic were in the Champions League, so I got to go and see Man City or Borussia Mönchengladbach in Barcelona. Or PSG v Bayern Munich. That was amazing. To go to those stadiums and watch those games was top drawer.

Val: How lucky you were! I have to say one small thing here about the glamour of book tours, though. A couple of years back, I was doing the Cologne Literary Festival. I arrived in the city on a Saturday morning and my event wasn't till the evening. I looked up who Cologne were playing that day. Turns out it was Bayern Munich. I asked my publicist if I had time to go. My publicist thought it'd be too late to get a ticket. It turns out that the main sponsors of the Cologne Lit Fest are also the main sponsors of FC Köln. So, not only did I get to go to the football, but I also went as a VIP and got the full treatment.

John: And they know how to look after you in Germany, by the way.

Val: Absolutely! The director of the book festival was over the moon because it gave him an excuse to go to the football. We did actually for once have a glamorous afternoon, but that's not usually how it goes. And for some reason, the Köln fans sing a song to the tune of 'The Bonnie Banks o' Loch Lomond', though obviously they've changed the words. It was quite weird sitting in the VIP area in Cologne, listening to the strains of an old Scottish folk song.

✿　✿　✿

Val: What was the irresistible magnet that drew you back to Stark's? Because it clearly wasn't the money.

John: I always wanted to come back, to be fair. I missed the football side of it, I missed the daily involvement with players. And I never lost touch with the Rovers. When you're in Scotland, you're never far away from the Rovers. Although I like Celtic, the Rovers feels like my club. The place I could always come back and make an impact. Roll my sleeves up and muck in. It's a small club so everyone has to multi-task.

Val: There's genuinely a lot of love for you here. People were excited and delighted that you were coming back. But it's been a difficult season, with a new pitch and a lot of injuries to crucial players.

John: The injuries are crucial. Absolutely crucial. We've had hardly any use from Lewis Vaughan and we've really missed him. He got three goals against Dunfermline Athletic—

Val: What a game that was!

John: Aye, brilliant. That was the game of the season. Lewis scored three goals, he's on cloud nine, he's flying, and then a week later he picks up a serious knee injury. We've been creating opportunities that Lewis could stick in the back of the net. We'd have more points... I'm not making excuses, it's a fact. We've currently got four key players out. More than any other team in this league.

Val: It's hard because with clubs like ours, you don't have a bottomless well of people to put in their place.

John: There are some younger players who we can put in the team; we've had sixteen-year-old boys on the bench this season. But you can't replace the quality of someone like Lewis.

Val: And you've got a new board, as well, who don't all necessarily understand the ins and outs of football. I'll say no more than that. But you've also got a very vocal fan base. It's an intimate ground, this. There's nowhere for you to hide from the fans.

John: You've got to take the rough with the smooth, haven't you? But it has been a difficult season, much more difficult than anticipated. I came here to win the league, but we've had injuries *and* the opposition have been better than I expected. Not an awful lot of credit has been given to some of the other teams – there are actually decent teams. And, unfortunately for me, a lot of players have got their heads screwed on and are leaving full-time football for part-time football and getting a job so they can earn a decent living. Even last season a few former Rovers players went part-time and they'll be earning much more money now than when they were at Rovers. And they're good, good players.

Val: When you're having a tough season, what does it feel like when the fans have a go at you? Do you feel secure in yourself and think, 'I'm doing the best I can do' or does it make you question yourself?

John: The buck stops with the manager. That never, ever changes. Which means that I question myself all the time. As you said before, there's nowhere to hide. I'm a human being and it's never nice to be criticized, but it's part of the job. You've got to be strong enough to accept it when the team has lost and try to win the following week. You have to hope that some players will come back from injury and others will hit form. Being a manager is a lonely place. You have to dig deep inside yourself every day. And never look at any social media.

Val: That's probably sensible in your position.

John: I've never looked at fan forums online. There's no point in looking when you're playing well and it will only bring you down if you're playing badly.

Val: That's what Laurence Olivier said: you can't read the reviews, because if you believe the good reviews, you have to believe the bad reviews as well.

John: Exactly. In the early days of Sir Alex Ferguson's tenure at Man United, he was getting slaughtered by the press. He went to Sir Matt Busby and said, 'Matt, I'm getting absolutely slaughtered in the papers.' Sir Matt's reply? 'That's simple, don't buy them. Don't read them.' I took that advice. My job is preparing the team for their next game. To be more prepared than any other team in the league.

Val: We've talked about your commitment to youth players. One of the hidden issues of football, which is finally being talked about more openly, is depression. Some of the players you are working with might not have much support outside football. Do you find yourself counselling them as young men as well as footballers?

John: Depression is not an issue I have to deal with every week or even every season, but I have come across it. It's very, very difficult. I don't know if I'm particularly good at dealing with it. Some young guys have come to see me and right out told me their issues. Some really nitty-gritty stuff. I've been shocked and stunned by it, to be fair. It's not easy. In the end, I phoned the PFA and got them involved because they've got experts who know how to deal with these situations.

Val: They're young lads in a highly pressurized environment. There's a certain glamour to what they do and people expect them to present in a certain way. If that's not their natural predisposition, you can see where difficulties come from. It's not just depression that's an issue. Racism is another one. A shocking one.

John: Racism raises its ugly head every now and again. More so recently, which is very sad.

Val: And homophobia. I can't believe there's not a single football player in this country who's gay.

John: Not a single player has come out. Which betrays the rule of averages, eh?

Val: And women are quite open about their sexuality in the women's game. There are out lesbians playing football for Scotland and nobody has an issue with that. But in the men's game, it seems to be the last taboo.

John: It will be like everything else, though; it will just take one high-profile player to come out. And that's just one of the huge social issues in football. In this day and age, we're still talking about racism and sectarianism.

Val: That's one thing I've been quite proud of at Raith Rovers. We've had a succession of black players and I don't recall there being that kind of racist abuse either about players or between players.

John: Certainly not in the dressing room, not when I've been here.

Val: The South Stand took Harry Panayiotou as their mascot, even though he couldn't score a goal unless it hit him on the bum by accident. Do you think that football has a social responsibility? Do you think the game as a whole has a responsibility, in the wider community?

John: I think it does because people relate so much to a football club. The work that a lot of clubs do in the community will directly affect the community, so it definitely has a social meaning. There's a number of community projects going on at the Rovers, including bringing people into the stadium for Christmas dinner. I came in to chat to them and they loved the fact that the club was looking out for them.

Val: It's hard to talk about social responsibility when the lower-league teams are impoverished and the Premiership is overflowing with money. You've got experience of both sides of this: at Celtic where there's money and at a club like ours, where there's no money to spare at all. Do you think big business is corrupting the game at the top end?

John: I think the money they've got is absolutely frightening. Sky is putting those fortunes in the game and we're all buying into it. We like watching our football, obviously, and so we pay the subscription fees and the money goes into the top flight and the top players get paid an absolute fortune. In England, they can create jobs just to spend their money. Meanwhile, there are many clubs – more, in fact – that are putting every bit as much effort into the game and who are scrimping and scraping just to get by. Not every club spends its money well, but the money at the top and the wages being paid is distasteful to say the least.

Val: Do you think the money ever trickles down?

John: Sadly not. It would help the greater game if it did. Put money into the youth, put money into smaller clubs. But it doesn't happen. Not to any noticeable degree. It's not right. Everyone is so greedy and they are just going to get greedier and greedier. And they are obsessed with finding the new Mbappé and signing them for a world-record fee.

Val: It's changed the demographic of fandom as well; if your local club is a Premier League club and you're on a minimum wage, there's no way you can afford to go and see your club.

John: No way at all.

Val: You have to go to the pub and watch it on Sky. We recently hosted a hospitality day here at the Rovers for twenty friends. It was a fantastic day out that ended with us all eating fish and chips in the street in Edinburgh at midnight. You couldn't do that at

Chelsea. Or Man United. Which means the demographic of the game changes, as does how people watch it. People who can afford to watch Man City or Liverpool go because they can afford to, not because they care passionately about those teams.

John: It's not like it was when we all lived in mining villages. My dad went to school with Jock Stein. And then there's Matt Busby, Alex Ferguson, Walter Smith – all men with a mining-village mentality.

Val: And they came up through football because that was all there was. Football or boxing.

John: Anyone could play football and everyone *did* play it. Nowadays, there aren't enough people playing street football.

Val: One of the big positives of recent years has been the development of the women's game. Your daughter coaches, does she not?

John: Aye, she doesn't now, but she did for a while and she enjoyed it.

Val: We're going to Paris to see Scotland play Argentina in the Women's World Cup.

John: Hopefully we'll do all right.

Val: I'm really excited about it. There has been investment in the women's game in recent years and here we are in the World Cup finals, which will in turn bring money back into the game. I would have loved to play football when I was growing up, but I had to play hockey because back then girls didn't get to play football.

John: Did you dad ever play?

Val: He wanted to play professionally, but he got TB in the bone in his legs and he could never play after that. But he was always part of the game. It's in the blood, isn't it? You can't escape it.

John: Exactly. You find a way to be involved.

Val: You've had an extraordinary career. You've made a life out of football. What's left? What are your remaining hopes and dreams?

John: Well, I suppose a goal in the short term is to get this team into the Championship. That is the immediate goal, and that's still a possibility, but it needs to be done as soon as possible. If by any chance it doesn't happen this year then it needs to be next year. It would be brilliant to take this team into the Championship and then into the Premier League. That would be everything to me.

Val: It would be brilliant!

John: It's definitely not beyond us, especially when you can see what we did against Dunfermline that day, with those three goals coming from Lewis. I don't want the players to entertain the idea of going part-time. Negative energy just drains every last bit of optimism and hope right out of you.

Val: Great. Go for it!

John: So yes, that's my dream: getting the Rovers into the top league. There'd be so much money coming in and I could be director of football and orchestrate things from above.

Val: You could get a private jet…

John: The Premier League would do me!

Val: I think that's a good thought to end on. That's been great. Thank you so much for giving me so much time.

John: I'm delighted to do it.

Omid
Djalili
& Frank
Lampard

Omid: How upset were you when your goal against Germany was disallowed at the 2010 World Cup?

Frank: At least it forced FIFA to introduce goal-line technology!

Chelsea Health Club, March 2019

Omid Djalili was born in London in 1965 to Iranian parents of the Bahá'í faith. He studied English and theatre studies at the University of Ulster before taking a series of successful shows to the Edinburgh Festival. He made two series of *The Omid Djalili Show* for the BBC, co-starred in the American NBC sitcom *Whoopi*, alongside Whoopi Goldberg, played Fagin in the stage version of *Oliver!* and voiced a character in *Grand Theft Auto*. He has appeared in various films, including the Oscar-winning *Gladiator*, *Sex and The City 2*, *The Infidel*, *Mamma Mia! Here We Go Again* and *Spy Game*. He has won several awards including Best Actor for *The Infidel* at the Turin Film Festival, the Time Out Comedy award for Best Stand Up, the One World Media Award for his Channel 4 documentary *Bloody Foreigners* and has been nominated for the Perrier Comedy Award at the Edinburgh Festival.

Frank Lampard OBE was born in Romford, east London, in 1978. He played as a midfielder for West Ham's youth team from 1994–95 and then for the senior team from 1995–2001. His father, Frank Lampard Sr, was assistant manager and his uncle Harry Redknapp the manager. He played for Chelsea from 2001 to 2014, scoring 147 goals in 429 appearances and is still the club's all-time leading goalscorer. While at Chelsea, Lampard won three league titles, four FA Cups, two League Cups, the Champions League and the Europa League. In 2014, he left Chelsea and played one season apiece at Manchester City and New York City FC. He won 106 England caps, scoring 29 goals. He published 20 children's novels between 2013 and 2018. Since retiring as a player, Lampard has been a pundit for BT Sport and *Match of the Day*. He managed Derby County during the 2018-19 season. In July 2019, he became head coach of Chelsea.

✪ ✪ ✪

Omid Djalili: I put a tweet out yesterday, asking if anyone had a question for you for this book. Of the 250 people who immediately responded, I'd say at least half were asking when you're going to be coming home to Chelsea as manager.

Frank Lampard: You know I can't answer that! I'm very happy at Derby. It would be the dream to manage Chelsea at some point in the future, of course, but I would have to be good enough and the club would actually have to want to employ me.

Omid: I suppose I wanted to start by saying how much us Chelsea fans still love you! But let's move on. How is your first season at Derby?

Frank: When I took on the job the owner, Mel Morris, made it clear that there was no pressure to reach the play-offs in my first season. He wanted me to focus instead on bringing in younger players and encouraging a better style of football. Mel's a massive Derby fan and he's put a lot of his money into the club, but he has done so with his heart. He's very open to ideas and very communicative.

Omid: That sounds great. So much better when the channels of communication are open at all levels in a club. One good season at Derby and we'll have you back... Anyway, I have a long list of questions for you, but there's one in particular that I'm burning to ask. I'm talking about the West Ham fans' forum in 1996, when you were just breaking into Harry Redknapp's side.

I hope you don't mind if I refresh readers' memories. Harry is obviously your uncle so there were inevitably accusations of nepotism flying around and some fans didn't think you were up to being in the first team at just seventeen. If you rewatch the video of the event online, one fan in particular has a go at Harry, insisting that you aren't 'quite good enough yet'. He adds, 'I also think that in the last couple of years, you've let some good midfielders go for peanuts, like Scott Canham.'

And then Harry jumps in with: 'He definitely wasn't good enough. [Frank] *is* good enough and he definitely will be good enough. Scott Canham has gone to Brentford but he can't get in Brentford's team. I let him go 'cos young Frank is seventeen, eighteen, and he's miles in front of him. I will tell you now that there's no comparison with what Frank Lampard will achieve in football and what Scotty Canham will achieve in football. There is no favouritism. I didn't want to say this in front of [Frank], but I'll tell you now, he'll go right to the very top. There ain't no doubt about that in my opinion. He's got everything that's needed to become a top-class midfield player: his attitude is first-class; he's got strength; he can play; he can pass and he can score goals.'

Do you remember what you were feeling as you were sitting there?

Frank: I was hugely embarrassed – I was literally crying inside. I was a shy kid and I'd been quietly sitting on the end of the table because no one had asked me a question. As you said, I got a lot of stick when I signed for West Ham because Harry was manager and my dad was Harry's assistant, but I never really knew what Harry thought of me as a player. I don't think Harry planned to say any of those things, but he felt moved to defend me.

That moment meant so much to me. It was a real boost. When I look back now, I've got lots of love for Harry for what he had to put up with for having me in his team, and that forum wasn't the only time someone had a go at him for playing me. I was still a chubby kid, a decent player but nothing more.

Omid: But you had a strong work ethic?

Frank: Yeah, I was always pushing myself to improve. But it wasn't that simple. I had a fear of playing for West Ham because of the stick I was getting.

Omid: From your own fans?

Frank: Yes. Luckily my dad, who's a pretty tough character, kept telling me not to listen. He was always my idol. He's much tougher than me and he dragged me through some emotionally difficult moments by telling me to keep working, to keep doing what I was doing. I've been like that ever since. By the time I was in my early twenties, I always trained more than anyone else. I sound like I'm boosting myself, but the only players I've worked alongside with anything like the same work ethic were John Terry and Didier Drogba.

Omid: Jimmy Floyd Hasselbaink always used to say you were by far the hardest trainer.

Frank: I genuinely wouldn't put myself at the top of the tree in loads of respects but, in terms of how I train, I knew I was up there.

Omid: When you were at West Ham, did your dad do extra training sessions with you?

Frank: He did, yeah. He'd tell me to do some extra sprints or to come in on days off. It became intrinsic to me to the point where

I became obsessed with my own game. I felt if I didn't do extra running or shooting then I was sure I'd fail in the next game.

Omid: What, were you superstitious?

Frank: Superstitious and slightly compulsive. I have learned to manage it now; if I see something that I think the team need to implement by Saturday, I will calmly spend the week working out how I can make it happen. As a player, I used to drive home from training thinking, 'How can I push myself tomorrow to be better than I was today?' I'd think the same thing every single day, to the point where it was quite tiring. When I retired from football I didn't miss playing. It was a massive release from twenty-one years of putting pressure on myself. Of course I had an amazing time playing, but my work ethic was always in overdrive. For example, my dad wanted me to wear running shoes with spikes on the soles when I was at West Ham, but I used to hide them because I knew the other players would take the mickey out of me. When I came to Chelsea, Dad said I wasn't quick enough and so I'd put the spikes on after training a few times a week. Dad thought it would make me lighter on my feet. I had to go around the back of Harlington [Chelsea's former training ground] so that Didier or Jimmy Floyd didn't see me running in spikes. After my first year at the club, I realized the fear of being too slow was all in my head.

Omid: But why running shoes with spikes? Did they represent something for you – were they some sort of symbol?

Frank: They were a symbol of what I wasn't and what I felt I should be.

Omid: That's amazing. And your overall dedication paid off: you were very fit, you were known as the 'box-to-box' midfielder and your skills weren't compromised. I mean, you scored so many brilliant free kicks.

Frank: Thank you. When I was at Chelsea, I often stayed behind with Didier to practise. Didier would get Ray Wilkins, God bless him, to kick balls for us and set up cones that we could dribble around. Or I'd practise with Franco [Gianfranco Zola], who was the absolute master of free kicks.

Omid: Apparently Ross Barkley is now being tutored by Gianfranco.

Frank: I could never do what Franco did.

Omid: He had a special technique, but so did you. You used to hit the ball hard and flat. I remember an amazing one in the FA Cup against Ipswich.

Frank: People sometimes talked about how I scored a lot of deflections, but that was usually because I got my shots away quickly and on target and if it went in, then great.

Omid: Is it a skill to try to get the ball in off a defender's arse?

Frank: It just happened naturally. If I tried to claim it as a skill, it'd be a step too far! You have to practise constantly and then make the best of the situation you find yourself in. Didier texts me about it now, joking about the hours we spent trying to perfect free kicks.

Omid: In the end a lot of the goals you scored were with one touch and then bang, back of the net.

Frank: You're right. I couldn't do what Franco did, which was to beat three players and hit the ball into the top corner of the net. My best bet was to touch and shoot. That sounds big-headed, but I mean it in quite a humble way; I just became really obsessed with scoring goals.

Omid: You scored 211 goals for Chelsea, which is unbelievable for a midfielder. Did you start out as a striker?

Frank: I was always midfield. I didn't initially have the energy or stamina to get from box to box, but all that running in spikes forced me to get faster and fitter.

Omid: How did you feel at Villa when you scored the two goals that made you Chelsea's all-time record goalscorer? I remember watching it on TV and getting very emotional about it.

Frank: Villa was a proper goosebump moment. There are a few goosebump moments when I look back, and Villa was definitely one of them – alongside scoring against Bolton to win the League in 2005 and winning the Champions League in 2012. A lot of memorable moments are, of course, team moments, but Villa was more of an individual thing. I felt incredible afterwards. I always thought I'd wanted to reach that milestone at Stamford Bridge, but it was actually better doing it at Villa because of the away fans. It was perfect.

✪   ✪   ✪

Omid: Now that you are a manager, who do you get advice from?

Frank: I speak to my dad fairly regularly. He wasn't a manager, but he had plenty of experience as a coach. We also clash in our football philosophies so the conversation can sometimes be difficult. My dad is old-school; he likes to get the ball forward. If we have a game where we are trying to play but the other team stop us, I know Dad will ring me when I'm driving home to tell me that the team needs to play longer balls.

I speak to Harry sometimes. I speak regularly with Jody [Morris, assistant manager of Derby and former Chelsea player] and Chris Jones [Derby's first-team fitness coach]. I try to be as open-minded and forward-thinking as I can. I don't want to exist in a bubble where I think I know everything.

Omid: So Frank Senior is still a big influence. I've heard of players taking advice from other managers – managers who have not necessarily managed them as players. Did you talk to any Premier League managers?

Frank: In my year off, I spent three days at Manchester City's training ground, shadowing Pep Guardiola. It was amazing to watch him work. His energy is off the scale. When you sit in his office, with its white boards on the wall analysing the teams they're about to play, you can't help but be impressed by his attention to detail. He was generous enough to give me ninety minutes of his time. He even carried on talking when someone knocked on the door and said he had other stuff to do! When I watched City train I could see why he's such a brilliant manger.

Omid: It sounds like you were totally open to learning about management.

Frank: Absolutely, though for the most part I've been learning on the job. The big thing for me has been managing a team; I had to draw on my own experience with managers I'd worked with as a player.

Omid: As a Chelsea fan, I noticed that José Mourinho seemed to make you a more confident player. Did he have a certain way of managing you that you've been able to draw on?

Frank: José was as impactful as any manager I worked with. All he did was be himself. He strolled in with a confidence I'd never seen before in football. At meetings he'd say things like, 'We're going to win the League this year. We're going to take fifteen points from our first five games.' Then there's the famous story in which we were naked in the shower and he told me that I was the best player in the world. At the time I felt far from the best player in the world and I don't think he thought I was either. It was similar to the way Harry had talked me up at the fans' forum years earlier; it was a masterpiece of management because it unlocked something in me.

Omid: He knew you needed it.

Frank: Yeah, he did. I think a lot of it was very natural. He was always... himself. That's what really influenced me – his day-to-day confidence and persona. I was probably impressionable; I was twenty-five and ready for someone like him to come along and drag me up another notch or two. People ask what Mourinho did, and so much of it was down to his personality. Plus tactics. Organization. He was definitely forward-thinking for the time. Not only for me, but also for the team.

Omid: Would you say that his approach to you was mostly positive?

Frank: Yes, he hardly ever told me off. He gave me a dressing-down no more than a few times. He once got upset when I tried to shoot from a free kick when I should have crossed; he mentioned it at training the next day, but he never really came for me. He was selective in that respect, which I now realize is how you need to be. There are some players I have to be harsh with and others I have to be gentler with.

Omid: Because some of them are more sensitive?

Frank: Some of the players are *very* sensitive. It's changed since the early days of my career. The modern player is, I think, is even more sensitive to criticism. I'm not sure why. It's not just an age thing either. I find that some of the older players at Derby are the most sensitive. The young ones, who've come through academies, are used to endless video analysis of the way they played. They accept being told what they did wrong at the weekend and they quickly move on. But some of the older players don't like being made to watch their mistakes. So you have to be very careful.

Omid: I know you're very thorough; have you had to read loads of psychology books?

Frank: I have actually. Again, I'm learning on the job and drawing from my own experience. So José was a positive force for me, but when André Villas-Boas became manager there was conflict between us straight away. I pretty quickly felt he wanted to make the team younger and had pinpointed myself, Ashley Cole and Didier as older players that weren't pivotal to the team. My security on the team was very compromised very quickly.

AVB pulled me off at half-time against Manchester United, which was a big move because I'd never really been brought off at half-time. Anyone can be pulled off, so I didn't think *that* much of it. But then I didn't play for ten games on the trot. He didn't really communicate with me either. OK, I get that; the manager can't talk to every player all the time. That's not the way it goes. But to flip from José telling me I was the best in the world to not being played was a shock.

We'd developed this thing at Chelsea where everyone shook everyone's hand in the morning and maintained eye contact; it was a habit we learned from the African boys, who basically taught us not to be so uptight and British! When AVB dropped me, we no longer shook hands; there was a stand-off between us. It was stupid.

Anyway, he called me in one day and said, 'I don't like the way you've been playing. You've been letting us down on the left side. You and Ashley are not doing this or that.'

I said, 'OK, fine.'

He said, 'And I have to say to you, I know the story about José telling you that you were the best player in the world. I'm not the type of manager that's going to give you bullshit like that.'

I walked out not understanding why he'd felt the need to make that point. It felt like AVB was trying to transmit José's personality. He wasn't being genuine. José is quite an arrogant, confident man, but he is always true to himself. I am actually fond of AVB now and have no axe to grind – it just made me realize how you can say something critical to a player in an off-hand way and it can really affect the player.

We've got players at Derby who need confidence but who equally need to be told how to improve their game and be given a little jolt.

Omid: Are you able to do that?

Frank: Yeah. But I've had a few big moments; when we lost 4-1 to Aston Villa, I really lost my temper with a player in the dressing room. In front of everyone. I don't think it's the worst thing; I felt it needed to be done because we'd had a bad run and we'd played terribly. I think the players needed to see me lose my temper. It was a genuine reaction to my disappointment.

Omid: What you said about the shaking hands is very interesting because I wanted to ask you about the impact of Dicky Attenborough [the late director and Chelsea life president, who served on the club's board from 1969 to 1982] at Chelsea. He used to say that in the 1970s and 1980s film stars were role models, but from the 1990s onwards it switched to footballers. He claimed that he took you and John Terry under his wing and proclaimed you 'real gentlemen'. What kind of impact did he have on you and John?

Frank: John and I both adored him. I don't know how you couldn't. He was one of the biggest gentlemen I've ever met. He would come down to the dressing room and chat to us about how he wanted us to behave as Chelsea players. Whatever he said was gold and you listened to every word. John and I were involved in a few incidents in our early days at Chelsea; we were young kids going out and making mistakes. Richard Attenborough saw that we were actually decent lads, but he wanted to make sure we didn't carry on making those kinds of mistakes.

Omid: Did he tell you off?

Frank: No, but Ken Bates did. A few times. Richard didn't need to. He was an incredible man. It wasn't just because of him, but John and I tried to create an atmosphere at Chelsea where there was huge mutual respect between the players, and a proper work ethic. Football was changing when we were there; there was an influx of players from all over the world, which absolutely made the Premier League a better place to be.

John had watched Dennis Wise lead the dressing room and John took it to the next level. If you came to play for Chelsea, you had to behave and train in a certain way. John was backed up by me, by Didier, Petr Čech and Ashley Cole. Once the respect and work ethic were imprinted on the players, the dressing room pretty much ran itself.

Omid: Didier has said that Fernando Torres didn't really do well at Chelsea because he was overawed by all the characters in the dressing room.

Frank: It's quite possible. I felt for Fernando because Anelka, Drogba and Malouda were scoring a lot of goals at that time, so Torres had been parachuted into a successful team for a British-record transfer fee of £50 million and he might well have felt left out. The dressing room wasn't an aggressive environment, but there were some big personalities and he probably found it hard to mix in.

Omid: Would the French- or Spanish-speaking players talk amongst themselves?

Frank: Yes, and you have to be aware of that not going too far. But it's not only about language; we all sat on different tables when I played for England. It's a pattern that the manager has to break.

⚽ ⚽ ⚽

Omid: I'd like to ask you about some specific moments in games, ones that I've returned to in my head over the years. In 2006, in the Champions League game at the Camp Nou that ended up 2-2, you chipped the keeper. Did you mean to do that?

Frank: Yes! I thought I'd give it a go. What did I have to lose? A lot of the best moments in sport happen like that.

Omid: Six years later, in the Champions League semi-final, you made an incredible pass to Ramires at the Camp Nou that made it 2-2 at half-time. Was that instinctive?

Frank: Pure instinct. We were outnumbered by Barcelona and I hadn't played a full pass till that moment. I edged the ball and I think Messi came around, I kind of half-shoved him off and made my only pass. Sometimes those ones are made slightly easier by having nothing else on.

Omid: But did you see Ramires make that run?

Frank: Yeah. Sometimes you feel the player running, but I used to turn my head a lot in the game.

Omid: What was said at half-time? It was a dramatic first half, with John being sent off.

Frank: We'd had a lovely little boost just before half-time, when Ramires scored from my pass. Robbie [Di Matteo, manager at the time] was really positive. He said we could hang on to the game. But then the second half was terrible. In footballing terms, it was horrible. Firstly, we were nervous because the game was on such a knife edge and we could so easily have lost this massive game. Secondly, the game was physically and mentally tiring because when you play Barcelona all you can think about is losing the ball to Messi! Messi fights and fights. He never gives up.

Omid: But we beat Barcelona, and Chelsea went on to win the Champions League! So I have to ask – and it's a big question – what felt better, getting A* for your GCSE Latin or winning the Champions League?

Frank: The Champions League. Just. No, definitely! I get asked about learning Latin a lot, but I can hardly remember it now. At school, I was just quite diligent and I wanted to please my teachers. I was never a classic A* student.

Omid: Oh come on, you have 12 GCSEs at A or A* and you have a really impressive IQ!

Frank: Well, yeah, but…

Omid: What is your IQ?

Frank: 150-something.

Omid: That's outrageous! A genius is 151. That puts you in the top 0.5 per cent of the world's population. How did you find out?

Frank: We did the test at the training ground when John had taken a kick in the head at Arsenal. The club doctor said, 'We need to test everyone, because the next time anyone gets kicked we need to have something to judge them against.' I didn't think much of it and I came out with a high score.

Omid: You come from a working-class background, but you had a middle-class education.

Frank: Both true.

Omid: We had a player at Chelsea called Patrick Bamford who I once watched train and he was a machine. But he was also very softly spoken and very middle-class. Do you think there's a bias against middle-class players? Have you seen middle-class talent that's been flipped aside? And could that have happened to you if you didn't have that famous dad?

Frank: It's a really good question. My story was slightly skewed by my dad's involvement. There were those accusations of nepotism at West Ham. And I was aware of my private education, yes.

Omid: Did you ever get that from other players? Did Jamie Carragher ever say, 'Look at you with your silver spoon' or similar?

Frank: No; the main thing with Carragher was the north–south divide, the Liverpool–Chelsea divide. He's a proud Scouser and so we had some conflict because of that.

Omid: Did he feel that you were trying to poach Stevie Gerrard?

Frank: Stevie and I were put up against each other by the fans and the press. And I would always look to see how well Stevie was doing because I wanted to do better at Chelsea. But the minute we came together with England we'd have been crazy to continue that 'battle'. The only benefit was if we both played well and won games. We could have worked harder at our relationship back then, but we're much closer now. We text and keep in touch.

Omid: Did you enjoy playing for England?

Frank: It's complicated. I remember when Hernán Crespo was at Chelsea all those years ago. and every time Argentina played he was chomping at the bit to go home and play. Argentina's players live all over the world and they pine for their country, so when they go home there's this really positive, patriotic feeling. Whereas most England players play in England and are up against each other week in, week out.

Omid: Do you watch the current England team and feel slightly envious?

Frank: It certainly makes you consider where we may have gone slightly wrong. I was on my pro-licence course last week and we were talking about what a brilliant job Gareth Southgate has done, how his players all work together and how he's bringing the young players up. When I played for England, there was no England philosophy. I played for Fabio Capello, an Italian, and Sven-Göran Eriksson, a Swede. It's a cliché, I know, but I think Gareth really *feels* it. Plus the Germans, Spanish and French teams were miles ahead of us. Not any more. We've caught up.

Omid: Is it true that you didn't watch England for a couple of years?

Frank: I didn't. They bored me. When I was playing in America, I retired from England and I'd only watch the major tournaments, not the qualifiers. Now I watch every game again!

Omid: I have to ask you, how upset were you when your goal against Germany was disallowed at the 2010 World Cup?

Frank: At least it forced FIFA to introduce goal-line technology! On a personal level, I've comes to terms with it. When it happened I felt so angry and frustrated because it would have changed the game. It's the main question I am asked when I travel around the world. The goal that I never scored as opposed to goals I did score.

But the truth is that I never scored in a World Cup, which is a regret.

Omid: How difficult was it to play in a World Cup?

Frank: Very tough. I didn't like being away from home for a long time. South Africa in 2010 was difficult. It should have been fun, but it wasn't. Part of Gareth's brilliance was changing the tone at the Russian World Cup. He's got a young squad and he opened up to the media. Let them in. He worked hard at his relationship with the media. He knows how quickly the press can turn after a bad game.

Omid: You mentioned disliking being away from home during big tournaments – I assume because you missed your family. How much does having a happy family life impact on the way you play?

Frank: It certainly had an impact on me. I had a tough time when I was twenty-nine. I lost my mum and I was in the middle of splitting up with my ex-girlfriend.

Omid: At the same time?

Frank: Yes, which was tough on me personally. Strangely, the year after I lost my mum, I had one of my best seasons. It was really weird how that worked.

Omid: You lost your mum in 2008 and had a good season in 2009–10?

Frank: Yeah. And after I split up from my girlfriend, I was living alone. Two of my mates moved in with me, which isn't really conducive to being a professional athlete. And some of the things we were getting up to – going out, sitting up too late… But I had a really good year, scored a lot of goals, important goals. Then I met Christine [née Bleakley] and was so happy for the latter years of my career, from 2010 onwards. If you aren't happy at home it can be a deal breaker. I'm lucky to have grown up in a very sound family unit, with a lot of love from my mum and football knowledge from my dad. So I was quite secure. But I know not everybody has that. A lot of young players come from a working-class environment and we don't know their stories. It can be difficult for them emotionally, in terms of knowing who to trust and a million other things.

Omid: We touched on this earlier, but do you always try to be aware of what's going on behind the scenes with the players?

Frank: I try to be aware. We do a wellness test, which is a more physical than mental assessment. For example, how well has the player been sleeping? And then we can have a meeting with the player and see what we need to work on.

Omid: Do you ever give players marital or relationship advice?

Frank: A couple of situations have arisen this year with players who have issues at home and I've given advice when I've felt that I was in a good position to do so. I think it helped, but I can't be completely sure.

Omid: That's proper man-management. Can you tell when players aren't listening? Do you ever say, 'Oi! Hello? You there?' in training or meetings?

Frank: Yeah, I do.

Omid: Do you ever ban phones? I know that Southampton's manager does. He also switches off the Wi-Fi.

Frank: I don't. There are rules: no phones in the dressing room pre-game or the meeting rooms. If you've got a phone with you then it has to be on silent and no one can sit staring at their device. But in the modern day you also have to be careful of saying 'No phones anywhere' because players rely on them. I remember Capello absolutely hammering Emile Heskey for looking at his phone. He did it in front of everyone, which I didn't think was the right way to deal with it. That incident has stayed with me; I don't want to be that kind of manager. All the players were on edge afterwards, which is not productive.

The World Cup in South Africa was a challenge because Capello was so tough. He would walk past you in a corridor and you'd immediately think you were doing something wrong. Having said that, I quite liked the fact that he was being genuine. That's who he is. It's the way he works. Which is why I liked Mourinho.

◊   ◊   ◊

Omid: Now, as a comedian, the next question interests me greatly. How important was having a laugh when you were a player – and even now that you're a manager?

Frank: It is a big part of it. I've thought about this a lot this year because it's easy to forget. It's a really highly driven, competitive world that we live in and, as a manager, I'm planning ahead pretty much every day of the week. So to factor in how can we make the players laugh or have a down moment is huge. Absolutely huge. I can lose sight of that if I'm not careful. It's not just about laughing, but being less intense about everything all the time. We'll tell the lads to have a day off or organize a go-karting trip. I don't really like go-karting, but most of the players do. You see them bond and mess around and relax. At Chelsea we used to have a lot of laughs – as captain, John was pivotal to that.

Omid: I can attest to his sense of humour. I did a thing with him for Chelsea TV once and he was a great improviser, making out he was really sensitive about jokes around his name, as we hid all the Terry's Chocolate Orange boxes from sight.

Frank: A really good laugh. The combination of John and Billy McCulloch, the Chelsea physio, was crazy. We used to get Billy to do things on Chelsea TV and to mess around generally. We had a really great dressing room with people who enjoyed laughing at themselves. A bit of pranking and having a joke was crucial to building the team spirit.

Omid: I'm going to tell you a quick story now that you might find interesting. When we won the League with Antonio Conte, they asked me to do some stand-up at the end of the season and Ray told me to just go for it. I made a joke that I adored John Terry so much I'd made love to a poster of him more than I had my own wife. And when Chelsea won the League, my wife asked, 'Why is there a poster of John Terry above the bed and why are there so many holes in it?' That joke went down well. I then teased John and Gary Cahill. As I was turning my attention to the younger players, I could see John watching me.

I asked Eden Hazard if he was thinking of becoming a manager in the future. He said he didn't know. Or an actor. He said no. I said, 'But it's a Chelsea tradition. Vinnie Jones was in *Snatched* and Frank Leboeuf was in *The Theory of Everything*.' Eden said, 'No, no, just football.' I said, 'But last year you played the role of someone who couldn't play football at all.' And there was a massive laugh. John called me over and said, 'What are you doing? You can have a go at me and Gary, but don't have a go at him. We don't want to lose him, just take it easy on him. That's enough.'

Frank: That's why John was a much better club captain than me. He's a born leader. He had everyone's numbers in his phone whereas I wasn't so communicative at that point. He always had their backs, so I'm not at all surprised by that story.

Omid: I loved the fact that John protected Eden.

Frank: I love that too. He was always protecting the players in one way or another.

Omid: Did he ever say anything to you during the game?

Frank: No, John and I had an ultimate respect thing. He might tell me that my training was a joke though! I remember being injured once and when I came back to training John said, 'You don't realize how much you brought training up today.' I was pushing thirty, thirty-one at the time, so I wasn't a baby. He always seemed to choose the right moments to say those little things that meant a lot. We were good together because John was often the fist-pumping type whereas I was subtler.

Omid: What did you chat about in the dressing room or over lunch? Did the players discuss cultural events, like the latest hit film or what was going on in politics?

Frank: Not so much. But if there was a big political issue it would probably pop up.

Omid: Do your players ever discuss a divisive, toxic issue like Brexit? Or would you put the kibosh on it?

Frank: Actually I would encourage them to speak about it. If it wasn't quite so toxic I'd call a meeting and say, 'Right, instead of a meeting about football, lads, let's talk about Brexit.' Just to surprise them. I'd love that.

Omid: Really?

Frank: I think that sort of stuff's brilliant. It might be a dead room with everyone silent and you'd have to say, 'Let's go back to football.' But I'm interested in politics. When I was playing, not too many of my teammates were interested. Most of them were into computer games. I imagine most footballers would still rather chat about computer games than Brexit.

I started writing the children's books when I was thirty because I used to get bored on the team coach when everyone was on their computers. I wanted to use my time more constructively and test myself.

Omid: Are there about fourteen books now?

Frank: There are twenty! They are pretty short stories and I really enjoyed the process, but I'm done now. I had ideas for the first five books and was shocked when a publisher wanted to publish them. I loved doing something different because when you live in the football bubble you can easily go through your life slightly on autopilot. Work, training, home, training.

Omid: I'd like to return to politics for a moment. Do you have any political aspirations?

Frank: None. I don't envy any prime minister. Their job is so, so difficult. Especially in the modern world, where everything is so divisive and we all have to love or hate something. I think it would be so hard to manage that.

Omid: You played for the most metropolitan football club on the planet. If we were to go into a Brexit 'no deal' situation, how is that going to affect you as a manager? Does that mean you can't sign European players?

Frank: I don't know. It's a worry.

Omid: How many foreign players have you got in the squad at Derby?

Frank: Not that many. We are a very British-based squad. Off the top of my head, two or three.

Omid: Would a hard Brexit mean if you fancy a player from France, for example, that you couldn't have him?

Frank: It could do. I think it might work differently at the top end, but possibly not for the smaller clubs. The influx of foreign players to the Premier League has done us a huge amount of good. I learned so much from Drogba and Zola, so to think of the door being shut to players like that in the future is terrible.

✧ ✧ ✧

Omid: Did you think you'd play for Chelsea for life?

Frank: I never thought I'd leave Chelsea to go to another club in England. But I'm delighted that I had a year at Man City. It's a great club with fans who've been through hard times, like Chelsea fans. The club has a fantastic structure and the new training ground is breathtaking. When I got to City I realized that I'd been on autopilot for the last few years at Chelsea. Every day was similar. When I arrived at City, I felt like the new kid at school and I was thirty-six! I didn't know who to say hello to. It was good to test myself a little bit.

Omid: You never even meant to play for City – you were just supposed to train with them.

Frank: Chelsea told me that I wasn't getting a new contract for the following season, which was disappointing to say the least. I didn't necessarily want a big send-off, but I'd have liked the choice. I ended up more or less leaving via the back door. I met up with people from New York City FC, which is part of the City Football Group, but their season didn't start for six months. So I was going to have six months off before pre-season started.

Christine and I went away on holiday and then I went to New York. The day that I signed for New York City, I got a call saying, 'Manuel Pellegrini [former City manager] wants to meet you, with the idea that you stay at City for four months until you move to New York.' Christine and I were sitting in our house in New York, having a few drinks. I didn't know what to do. I rang my dad and he said, 'Son, they're Premier League champions and they want you at thirty-six. What you've done at Chelsea is set in stone and it's not gonna change anything.' He was right; it was a nice feeling to be wanted. So I met Pellegrini and he set out his little vision of how the four months would pan out and I agreed to go to City. I had to cancel the holiday I'd booked!

I played pretty well for them. I scored on New Year's Day for us to go level on points with Chelsea. City wanted me to stay on for the rest of the year and I knew I was going to get some criticism in New York, but I couldn't turn them down. It ended up being a great year.

Omid: How did you feel when Pellegrini brought you on at seventy-eight minutes against Chelsea? Did you think you were going to play?

Frank: I wasn't sure. It was a weird one for me and it actually worked out perfectly in the end because it was a draw and the Chelsea fans were incredible.

Omid: They gave you a big reception, didn't they?

Frank: Massive. And in the end Chelsea went on to win the League, so I didn't affect anything too negatively. I'd rather have had a more positive exit from Chelsea, but I'm over that now.

Omid: Did José tell you?

Frank: Yeah, he pulled me in and said, 'The club are not going to give you a new contract.' He said he'd fight for me, but I didn't think that was right. Young players were ready to come up. It can't have been easy for him because we were pretty close.

✿ ✿ ✿

Omid: As a former Chelsea player, do you have an opinion on the way a few Chelsea fans treated Raheem Sterling at Stamford Bridge? What is your feeling about racism in the Premier League?

Frank: Sadly it's something we all have to work on to get rid of. I think sometimes there's an undercurrent of racism and at other times it's hardcore racism. Both are obviously wrong and both have to be tackled.

Omid: Were you aware of it as a player?

Frank: I didn't hear fans say anything, but I remember playing in Madrid and the home fans taunting Ashley Cole. It was awful. We clearly can't be complacent about it and we can't make empty gestures. Which is why it's important for players to speak out.

Omid: On a slightly different note, are you aware of any Asian players coming through at Derby? For example, Leicester have got Hamza Choudhury.

Frank: I was trying to get him on loan last summer. He's a very good young player and a fantastic role model for the Asian community. I'm guessing the lack of Asian players is down to the lack of role models. You can't aspire to what you don't see. Maybe it will take an Asian player being really successful to bring more Asian players into the game.

Omid: Perhaps we should talk about something other than racism. I have a few more questions from Twitter. First up: do you have a favourite comedian?

Frank: I laughed and cried when I watched *Afterlife*, Ricky Gervais's Netflix series. If you have lost anyone, it absolutely hits home. At the same time, it makes you smile, which is genius. I loved it so, so much.

Omid: I'll pass that on to Ricky. He'll be very happy to hear it.

Frank: Do you know him? Of course you do! I met him once, quite a few years ago. The last person I saw doing stand-up was Jack Whitehall, because I know him a bit. Oh, and yourself, of course.

Omid: Thank you very much. Another Twitter question: do you have any regrets dating back to your football career?

Frank: I regret not having a successful tournament with England. At times I could have played better for them. I would rather not talk about regrets because where does it stop? We should have won more league titles at Chelsea. And on and on…

Omid: What was the best goal you've scored? The goal that is never talked about is the one you scored in the FA Cup semi-final against Spurs in 2012. You hit an amazing free kick in the eightieth minute that seems to be largely forgotten.

Frank: You're right, it is overlooked. It was the fifth goal, I think. Or the final one.

Omid: It was the fourth out of Chelsea's five.

Frank: Your memory! We won 5-1? The best goal I scored on a technical level was against Bayern Munich at home, in the Champions League quarter-finals. In terms of the goal that means the most, it was the Villa goal that we discussed earlier. The most emotional goal I scored was a penalty against Liverpool. My mum was really ill and [former Chelsea manager] Avram Grant said he wasn't going to play me. I begged him to let me play. And I scored a penalty. I then got subbed a few minutes before the end of the game and by the time I got to the dressing room I was ready to collapse. I've never been so exhausted in my life. Emotionally as well as physically.

Omid: I have a memory of you being utterly overwhelmed, but doing well to cover it up on the pitch.

Frank: I was gone. I was absolutely gone. I went home and opened up a beer with my dad but I couldn't get through more than half of it. I was a wreck.

Omid: Had you not really grieved for your mum before?

Frank: No, and I was extremely close to her. When she passed away I don't think my dad or I grieved until months later. I was living on my own, probably drinking a few too many and it hit me just at the point where everyone else was moving on. But the support I had at Chelsea was incredible. The whole squad turned up at mum's funeral.

Omid: All of them?

Frank: All of them. Just incredible support. Even squad members I didn't know very well. I remember seeing all the players coming into the church in their club suits, and I was like, 'Wow'. I was in floods of tears. The severity of it all hit me. And the fact that the players cared enough to come. They were another kind of family.

♢ ♢ ♢

Omid: I know this is a bit egotistical, but I just wanted to show you this on my phone. Are you aware of RoboKeeper? It's a robotic keeper that anticipates your moves.

Frank: Yeah, I've seen it.

Omid: So Messi took it sixteen times and couldn't score. I had one go and I scored. Here's the video.

Frank: Blimey! Right in the top corner. If you hadn't told me you'd scored, I'd have said you were going to mishit it.

Omid: I was a player in my time. I can play.

Frank: I'm impressed.

Omid: Does it make you miss scoring goals?

Frank: Nope. Not at all. I'm very happy being a manager.

Omid: And I'm very happy being a comedian. Although one day I'd love to manage a bunch of comedians. Just the younger ones, though. I think the older ones might get a bit sensitive when I showed them a video of themselves when they've been really crap. They don't appreciate that kind of thing, apparently.

Rachel
Riley

&

Rio
Ferdinand

Rachel: Are you glad social media didn't exist when you were a player?

Rio: I would have loved it! I'd have been opening people up every single week. Banter was a key part of my psyche as a kid. If you couldn't handle banter and the loudness and the voices, then you weren't in it. You wouldn't have made it. You certainly wouldn't have survived on my estate, 100 per cent.

New Era Global Sports Management, April 2019

Rachel Riley was born in Thorpe Bay, Essex, in 1986. She studied mathematics at Oxford and briefly considered working in the City before joining *Countdown* as their numbers expert in 2009. She co-presented *The Gadget Show* from 2013 to 2014 and, in 2016, *It's Not Rocket Science* and *Friday Night Football* on Sky Sports. In 2013, Riley appeared on *Strictly Come Dancing* with professional dancing partner Pasha Kovalev. She visits schools to encourage pupils

– especially girls – to embrace maths and science. She is also involved with Primary League Primary Stars, an initiative that helps children to develop their skills and ambition both on and off the pitch.

Rio Ferdinand was born in Camberwell, London, in 1978. He grew up in Peckham with an Irish mother and an Afro-Saint Lucian father. During his school years, he played football and took gymnastics, ballet and drama classes. A gifted athelete, he trained with Queens Park Rangers from the age of ten and at eleven was offered a scholarship to attend the Central School of Ballet in London. He joined West Ham's youth team in 1992 as a centre back and in 1995 signed for the senior team. He played for Leeds from 2000 to 2002, for Manchester United from 2002 to 2014 and for QPR from 2014 to 2015. He played eighty-one times for England between 1997 and 2011. While at Manchester United, he won the Premier League six times, the League Cup twice, the UEFA Champions League once and the FIFA Club World Cup once. In 2017, following the death of his wife, he presented the BBC One documentary *Rio Ferdinand: Being Mum and Dad*. He is a pundit for BT Sport.

⚽ ⚽ ⚽

Rio Ferdinand: Hiya. Nice to see you. When was the last time I saw you? Was it at United?

Rachel Riley: Yeah, I was probably waving at you.

Rio: How are you doing? You've been on the dancing show and everything, haven't you?

Rachel: Oh god. Have I not seen you since *Strictly*? Anyway, let's get going. I know you're a busy man. Do you know what this book is about?

Rio: Yeah, Gary Lineker gave me a briefing.

Rachel: There are so many things I want to talk to you about. We've got West Ham, United, England, knife crime, mental health, bereavement, punditry, getting into trouble, millions of businesses.

Rio: Ask me anything.

Rachel: Let's go right back to the beginning. What was it like growing up in Peckham?

Rio: They were the best days of my life. When I was a kid, Peckham had a bad reputation for violence and gangs, but I had the most fun times. A group of about eight of us all grew up together and we still meet up all the time for Sunday dinner or just to hang out with the kids. We sit there screaming, laughing about old times.

It's so mad how Peckham has been gentrified. My missus' best mate has just moved there and we went to see her and to have a bit of food in the place over the road from her flat. The menu was so fancy that I couldn't understand it!

Rachel: What does that level of change make you feel?

Rio: It's generally good; it brings a positive side to Peckham that was never there before. The only way to get out of there before was either by being a footballer or a rapper. And now people think it's a cool place to go and live.

Rachel: You grew up not only playing football, but also doing ballet, which I imagine was unusual back then.

Rio: Yeah. I got a scholarship to the Central School of Ballet in Clerkenwell. I represented Southwark in gymnastics at the London Youth Games and a scout approached my teacher, asking if I'd like to try ballet. I thought it would be an adventure; when I was ten or eleven, my mum and dad were very strict and didn't let me off the estate very often, so doing ballet was a chance to break free. Plus there were three boys from Peckham and a load of girls, which was great for me. I told my mates that I was going to dance school and they didn't ask any questions, so I didn't have to defend myself.

Rachel: My other half [Pasha Kovalev] is a ballroom dancer. When he was seven or eight, his mother took him to see a dance show and as soon as he saw all the women on stage, he thought 'yes please'. I have never understood why men who dance are teased; it's such a masculine thing to do.

Rio: The physical demands are massive. It's way harder than anyone thinks. It taught me discipline, application and dedication. I had to learn to balance and be super supple. I had to meet new people and get along with them. So many elements to ballet actually helped me become a footballer.

Rachel: When did football take over? You come from a footballing family – not just your brother Anton but also your cousin Les – so I assume it was always on the radar?

Rio: I didn't really know Les that well until he made it as a player because he lived in west London. I always played football with my mates on the estate and I trained with QPR when I was ten. So there was a period when I was doing ballet, football, gymnastics and a bit of drama at school. Eventually, when I was twelve or thirteen, my dad said, 'You're doing too much. You're going to burn out. You need to pick something.' Luckily enough, I chose football. I had to leave ballet school, which was really hard, but the right decision – I was never going to be a ballet dancer. Or a gymnast. Or an actor.

Rachel: As a Man United fan, I'm very glad you made that decision! You went on to play for West Ham, Leeds, Man United and QPR. When you look at the scores, which team do you look for first?

Rio: Man United. Always. I was there for thirteen years and I won a lot of trophies during that time. I came through the ranks at West Ham and I always look for their results straight after. And Leeds too.

Rachel: Did you watch your old West Ham boss Harry Redknapp on *I'm A Celebrity*?

Rio: I saw snippets of it on social media. He put everyone to shame, didn't he? The way he talked so emotionally about his missus showed just how much work a lot of men have got to do. He's a great, great fella. A man of the people.

Rachel: Did it tempt you to go into the jungle?

Rio: It looks as though the jungle is great fun, but I'm not sure I could make it through some of the challenges. I like my food too much.

Rachel: How about *Strictly*?

Rio: I'd probably win *Strictly* because I can dance. But I wouldn't do it. I haven't got the time. They're good shows, challenging shows. But I'm too busy as it is.

Rachel: Let's talk about Man United. What are your fondest memories?

Rio: Other than winning? The people. I spent more time with them than I did with my family. When I go back there it's just brilliant. Especially since Ole [Gunnar Solskjær] has taken over. I can't help smiling when I talk about Peckham and I'm the same with Man United. It's got so much history, whether it's the tragedy of the Munich air crash or all the great times. I remember doing a press conference after I'd signed my deal and someone asked what I wanted to get out of my time with the club. I said that all I wanted was to etch my name into the history of the club and be remembered for doing good things. Which meant winning. I was lucky; I think I achieved that.

Rachel: Has the club still got the same ethos about winning? Are players prepared to work their balls off to win?

Rio: The club has changed. Football has changed. There are players who sign to big clubs just to earn a big pay cheque, not because they care about winning everything they can possibly win. I could have got a lot more money if I'd signed for a club other than Man United. But I wanted to go to Man United to win. I had opportunities to leave for more money, but I couldn't walk away from the possibility of winning more trophies.

Rachel: Perhaps it's because players don't have to fight as hard for their success – for example, young players no longer have to clean senior players' boots. They can turn up at a club at the age of eighteen and be handed a Ferrari.

Rio: Frank Lampard and I speak a lot about this when we're together. In fact, a lot of the old players talk about it. Young footballers have no barriers or obstacles in the way. If everything is easy, the rewards aren't so great. You don't appreciate things as much. Of course, it's still a difficult journey to take, from youth to senior team, from squad to team. But the players aren't as robust because they are handed so much on a platter.

When kids play football today, they are ferried to and from training and to and from games. Their kits are all laid out for them. Their boots are cleaned for them. Nutritionally balanced food is waiting for them. When I was a kid, we had to look after the first team's kit. Clean their boots. Make sure everything was ready for them. We were disciplined. We respected the older players. Now you get a seventeen-year-old kid bowling about the place who hasn't yet played in the first team but is acting like he owns the place. I don't think that bodes well either for clubs or for football as a whole.

Rachel: I imagine that's the kind of thing your former teammate Ole is dealing with right now. What do you think of his appointment and what sort of challenges lie ahead of him?

Rio: I spoke very loudly and very publicly about my backing of Ole. He lost one game in seventeen. He's won trophies with the club. You should be rewarded for what you achieve. But now, after he's lost a few key games, people are saying he was given the job too quickly. Or that he's not the right man after all.

Rachel: I love Ole.

Rio: I do too. He's there for all the right reasons. But he's going to need time. For a start, he's inherited a bunch of players that he didn't sign.

259

Rachel: Do you think we've got a leader in the team?

Rio: Not at the moment. They need a centre back who is a leader. But it's hard. I don't think there are many available top, top centre halves. I was talking to someone the other day about all the centre halves in the England team during my era: me, Sol Campbell, John Terry, Jamie Carragher, Jonathan Woodgate, Ledley King, Gary Cahill, Joleon Lescott. Then Matty Upson and Gary Caldwell came in. Gareth Southgate in his later years. Ugo Ehiogu. That's a whole team of defenders and I've left a few out probably. You couldn't pick out eleven centre halves who could play for England now.

Rachel: Why do you think that's the case?

Rio: I don't know! Sometimes these things just go in cycles.

Rachel: You obviously had a great relationship with Nemanja Vidić when you played. Are you still in touch with him?

Rio: Yeah, I still chat to Vidić. Funny guy. He doesn't have much to say on text so you have to ring him. We've got a WhatsApp group of former Man U players and he's not part of that. There are loads of us. Patrice Evra. Fletch [Darren Fletcher]. Anderson. Danny Welbeck. Ashley Young. We destroy each other.

Rachel: Obviously you can say anything in that WhatsApp group, but as a pundit do you have to toe a certain line?

Rio: You've got to be honest. Say as you see. Don't be vindictive. Those are the rules I apply to punditry. If I go along with those rules, I don't have any problems. Of course, I've had the odd person ring me and say, 'Well, you could have warned me before you said that about me.' My answer is always the same: I would have said it to your face – I've said worse to your face – so, you know, relax.

Rachel: How did you take criticism? Did you see a lot of it yourself when you were playing?

Rio: I was too good to get any criticism, ha ha! Seriously, I used it as fuel. I don't understand players who get upset with it. If you're honest enough with yourself, you know when you get something wrong or when you could have done better. I don't particularly enjoy criticizing other players on telly and highlighting their mistakes by replaying them over and over, but it is what it is.

Rachel: Social media has made it much harder too.

Rio: Totally. You're always in the public glare. Back in the day, if you made a mistake you just had to hope a few people missed *Match of the Day.* Now that shit lives on for a long, long time.

Rachel: Are you glad social media didn't exist when you were a player?

Rio: I would have loved it! I'd have been opening people up every single week. Banter was a key part of my psyche as a kid. If you

261

couldn't handle banter and the loudness and the voices, then you weren't in it. You wouldn't have made it. You certainly wouldn't have survived on my estate, 100 per cent.

Rachel: Is that where your strength comes from? Because you've spoken out on social media about things like knife crime, Brexit and mental health. You're not afraid to stick your head above the parapet.

Rio: You've got to have a thick skin for social media. You know that yourself. If you haven't got a thick skin for social media then don't go on it. You've got to be willing to accept that most of the comments – especially with football because it's quite tribal – are going to be negative. I'd say to young players not to read the comments. Don't get drawn in. Post what you're going to post and don't worry about it. Because all the other people on there are trying to get a bite off you.

Rachel: Does any of it ever get through to you?

Rio: I'm sure players are now told from an early age how to deal with it, but it's always a learning curve. I was probably a bit of a guinea pig because I was an early adopter. For example, I learned very quickly never to go on there when I'd had a drink. But I swear I'd have loved it; if I was playing now, I'd be tearing people up before a game. Not even after a game. *Before* a game. I would make sure I was in someone's head before the game even started. I'd have been at them on social media. Not aggressively, just playfully. 'Oh,

I'm playing against team X or Y's number nine tomorrow. You better sleep well tonight, son.' Little niggly things just to get in their head.

Rachel: It must be hard for players not to engage with the comments. Especially for young men like Raheem Sterling who gets all kinds of abuse sent his way.

Rio: I don't think he looks at his comments very often. Raheem has grown into his own skin this last year. He has a similar mindset to me, I think: he uses any negativity as fuel. I used to store up negative comments and then use them to motivate me to train harder and play better.

Rachel: Are you talking about negative comments from the media or fans?

Rio: The media formed a caricature of me based on their uninformed assumptions. And people generally believe what they read. Which is why I got into social media so quickly; I wanted to write my own narrative. This is my story and I'm going to be the one to tell it. Both on and off the pitch. As I said, I answered anyone who was unfairly critical of me on the pitch.

Rachel: It was interesting to see how Gareth Southgate tried to have a different relationship with the press when he became England manager.

Rio: He was brilliant. He let the press have access to England players during the World Cup in Russia and it was a roaring success. You saw the positivity both on the pitch and in the press. Results help. Of course they do. England got to the latter stages of the tournament. I don't know if the relationship between England and the media would have been so positive if England had been knocked out a couple of games earlier. But it worked.

Rachel: In terms of the men who have managed you, would you say that Sir Alex is the best manager you've ever had?

Rio: That's an easy answer: yes.

Rachel: What is your relationship like now that you no longer play for him? Is he in your WhatsApp group?

Rio: No! He wouldn't join in even if we invited him. But I speak to him now more than when I played for him. There's always a barrier between a manager and a player. No matter how well a manager might get on with a player, he has to draw a line in his head. But I'm lucky; I can call Sir Alex as and when. He's so different to any other manager; he humanizes everything, he drives everything. Which is why players were willing to run through brick walls for him.

Rachel: You won a lot of trophies with Sir Alex. Was there a favourite?

Rio: The Champions League. But I hadn't won anything before I got to United, so when I first got there winning the Premier League was my holy grail. And then you start setting more targets.

Rachel: Remind me how you won your first league title?

Rio: It was the end of my first season, so May 2003. Leeds, the team I had left to join United, beat Arsenal away on 3 May, which meant that we had won the League.

Rachel: Where were you when Leeds won?

Rio: I was at home. The phone starting going mad. *Ping! Ping!* Giggs and the Nevilles. All the boys. They'd won the League before, so they knew what to do. They knew where to meet.

Rachel: Were you screaming with joy?

Rio: Pretty much. Oh my god, my first season at United and my first league title! I was running around with no socks on. Screaming the house down. The neighbours must have been concerned…

Rachel: Did the whole team go out in Manchester?

Rio: Leeds beat Arsenal on the Sunday and I must have been out four or five times that following week. Smashed. I left my credit card in a club one day, went to collect it and stayed in there. I never meant to. We played Everton away in the last game of the season and we beat them 2-1, with a Becks free kick and a van Nistelrooy penalty.

Rachel: How confident were you that you were going to beat Chelsea in Moscow to win?

Rio: I was scared. Not scared, but wary. Straight after the final, we were going away with England. If we lost, I'd have to see Ashley Cole, Joe Cole, John Terry, Frank Lampard. So the relief when we beat them on penalties was immense. There's something special about winning the Champions League too: loads of United players have won the League, but not that many have won in Europe. It's an exclusive club of people.

Rachel: What was it like watching those penalties?

Rio: It was bad. If Giggsy hadn't scored the winning penalty, I was next up. My legs were gone. Pat [Patrice Evra] didn't want to take one, so I reluctantly agreed to be the eighth taker. It doesn't matter how much you practise. It doesn't prepare your legs for taking a walk of that magnitude. It's crazy. So I was just fortunate that Edwin van der Sar saved Anelka's penalty.

Rachel: And you went off to join the England camp with your head held high. What's the difference between playing for club and country?

Rio: It's a great achievement to play for England. When you're a kid, it's all you think about. I didn't think about playing for a particular club; I wanted to play somewhere to win. That was it. But with England… you want to play for England. I wanted to be the best in my position, the best in my country. That was always a target. It was great to be able to achieve that and to do it so many times. But we just didn't have a team capable of winning. For whatever reason it was. Our team weren't able to get past the quarter-finals. I have great memories from playing at West Ham, Leeds and England. But not like the memories I had at Man United. Because the key factor was winning.

Rachel: The squad you played for in for England had some of the best players in the world at the time. How do you think they compare to the current England squad?

Rio: I think if you went man to man, our team was better. But individuals don't win trophies. You need a team. And I think Gareth Southgate has built a team. That's the difference. If we'd have had Gareth Southgate as manager we'd have done better.

Rachel: Did he feel like a leader when you were playing with him for England?

Rio: He felt like a student of the game. He was serious. You could see he was on a journey. He was very focused on what he was doing.

Rachel: So he's not a loud, bullish boss?

Rio: He's not like that. But I don't think he needs to be like that either. As I said, he was very much a student. And you can see that in his approach with the England team at the moment. You can see he studies a lot. I wasn't surprised when he became England manager.

✿ ✿ ✿

Rachel: You've got so much going on now you are retired: your restaurant, your clothing line, businesses, punditry. Was that always the plan?

Rio: I never wanted to be pigeonholed. It's why I did athletics, gymnastics, ballet, drama *and* football. I could never sit still as a kid. My mum was a really big advocate of being busy all the time. She didn't understand why anyone would stay at home being bored or feeling content with their lot. My mum was a grafter. My dad's a grafter. He used to go to work in east London then come back to south London to pick me up to go training in west London. After training he'd drop my mates off in Brixton and finally go home to Peckham. My mum was the same and it just filtered down to me.

Rachel: Is it hard to instil that kind of work ethic in your kids, given how easily they could be spoilt?

Rio: Me and [my fiancée] Kate talk about this all the time. We talk about it with our friends too. I don't have to work, but I go to work because I want my kids to see someone working. My parents worked for as long as they could, why wouldn't I do the same? It's tricky because we do all this to give our kids a better life and then we make it worse for them by giving them too much too soon. You just have to find a balance, but it's difficult sometimes. I've done my best to keep my ten- and twelve-year-old off Instagram for as long as possible – until they are the absolute minority and start looking like the weird kid in their class.

Rachel: You're absolutely right though; you have to protect their mental health.

Rio: It's so draining. It takes over your life. It's harder for my daughter, I think, because the idea of what a 'perfect' woman is meant to look like is almost unobtainable. All I can do is manage it. For example, I'll randomly take their phones off them and scroll through everything. At the same time, they've got to make their own mistakes. I can't control everything. All I can do is try not to spoil them too much and *show* them that a strong work ethic is important; my parents never talked to me about their work ethic, they just got on with it.

Rachel: Are you an embarrassing dad?

Rio: Oh yes! All I have to do is pick them up at school in fitness shorts and a T-shirt. Or walk through the school gates. Of course,

I wind them up sometimes and do exactly what they don't want me to do.

Rachel: They must be very aware as they get older that you live your life in the public eye. Everything is documented in the papers, even your wife's death at a terribly young age. I wondered why you decided to talk about your grief so openly – and eloquently – instead of hiding yourself and your family away?

Rio: It's a complicated answer. Sometimes you don't appreciate someone else's situation until you experience a tragedy in your own life. Everyone is so focused on what they're doing. Especially as a sportsman. I saw a lot of bad stuff when I was growing up – I went to the same school as Stephen Lawrence and that's just one story – but that's just how it was. After my wife died, I became much more emotionally open. I let things get to me a bit more.

To answer your question: my family comes first. Always. I had to decide if talking openly about my grief would be a positive thing for them. I came to the decision that yes, it would be. I was surprised how many people were touched by my honesty and were able to align their story with mine. From a male perspective, putting my emotions out there was a big deal. I think a lot of men would feel that being open would take away from their masculinity.

Rachel: Especially in the alpha-male world of football. Do you think football is becoming less macho?

Rio: I was like that though. I was that macho player! It wasn't so much about the masculinity – it was more about keeping the energy in the training room. The motto of football was very much 'leave your baggage at the door'. Come in here and play football. Deal with your emotional stuff later. If I saw that another player was upset, I wasn't one for mollycoddling them. We were playing to win and there was no time for hugs. If I was in a changing room with someone who was in tears, I'd think 'Man up!' But I've softened now. I'm more appreciative of other people's situations and what might be going on behind closed doors.

Rachel: Do you think players get more support now? Is it important for players like Danny Rose to talk about depression?

Rio: It's great that Danny can do that. A decade ago a player with depression would have been laughed at. He wouldn't have been bought by any manager. The general feeling would have been: 'You earn all that money and play in front of huge crowds and you're living the dream and you're… depressed?' It's changing slowly, but that's still the way a lot of people speak. There's work to be done, but we're headed in the right direction.

Rachel: Football has been under the cosh recently to combat mental-health issues, homophobia and racism—

Rio: Yes, but it can't combat any of those things.

Rachel: Do you think it has a responsibility to try?

Rio: All football can do is set the tone. But it can't change the narrative because society's a bigger machine than just football.

Rachel: But don't you think that it has to try?

Rio: Yes, but all the players would have to come together and form some kind of unified front against racism or homophobia. And I don't know how you can make that happen. For example, racism is the key subject at the moment. It's in the news. There have been some very good documentaries on racism, but I'm generally only seeing black people talking about it. Well, racism isn't just about black people. So why is it just black people who are talking about it? Why isn't there a racist man speaking? And telling us why he's like that. I'd make my kids watch that. You can't just talk about one aspect of racism on a programme. You have to give the full 360 picture to understand it all. Yes, football can be used as a tool but it hasn't been used in the right way, I don't think. Not yet.

Rachel: Did you feel as though black players who experienced racism were offered proper support when you were a player – for example, when John Terry allegedly racially abused your brother Anton on the pitch.

Rio: I wouldn't say so, no. If my mum was here today she'd tell you no, 100 per cent. If you look at what happened to my brother's career afterwards it's enough to tell you what happened.

Rachel: I seem to be asking a lot of negative questions. Let's get on to something positive. Although I did want to ask about speaking out against Brexit.

Rio: Like most other people, I'm frazzled by Brexit. I'll leave that to Gary Lineker to do that. The only thing I'd like to say on Brexit is, 'Just make a decision, please.'

✪ ✪ ✪

Rachel: You're always posting photos of yourself working out, often with some amusing comment beneath, on Instagram. Do you actually enjoy working out?

Rio: Yeah, I like going to the gym. I think it's the best way to start a day. When I don't go to the gym I'm lackadaisical and lethargic all day. I ran pretty much every day for twenty-five years and I don't run any more. I never used to go to the gym, but I've replaced running with the gym! I weigh twenty kilos more than when I played. It's mad.

Rachel: You were training really hard at one point to get your professional boxing licence.

Rio: That was the hardest thing I've ever done in my life. But I'll only do something that's going to hurt me if there's a goal at the end of it. If I've got something to reach, I'll do it. I wouldn't have tried to become a professional boxer if I didn't think it was attainable.

Rachel: Why were you refused the licence?

Rio: Very sadly a professional boxer died from his injuries a few weeks before my application went in. If I'd become a professional boxer there would have been a lot of press attention and if, god forbid, something happened to me, the British Boxing Board of Control would have been in a difficult position. It's totally understandable. I've got no bad blood with anyone. It was probably a sign – someone saying, 'listen, chill.' But it was the hardest five, six months of my life, man. I was training five days a week for two and a half, three hours at times.

Rachel: Was it harder than football training?

Rio: Football didn't come close. Plus I was going to the Olympic training camp in Sheffield and sparring twice a week.

Rachel: Did you get used to getting hit in the face?

Rio: That was the best bit! How mad is that? I know, I know. But, you don't feel it because of the adrenaline. And then on the way home in the car, you suddenly feel it. The inside of your mouth is all cut up... It was weird. I just fell in love with it and I was desperate to do it. But that's life. I moved on.

Rachel: What's the next challenge?

Rio: I'm a long way from wanting to do another challenge! But I don't regret having a go at boxing. I'm happy being a pundit and coming in here and chatting to some of the players and managers we look after. I mentor about ten young players, which takes up a fair bit of time.

Rachel: What does the mentoring involve?

Rio: A lot of WhatsApp messages! Before, you had to regularly meet up with players, but I can now form a relationship with a young player via WhatsApp and meet up occasionally. I will talk to him about his attitude on the pitch or any issues he's having generally.

Rachel: Would you consider a career in coaching?

Rio: I was doing my coaching badges, but I've had to focus on my kids in the past couple of years. I was 100 per cent going to do it, but it had to go on the back burner.

Rachel: I think you'd be good at it.

Rio: I'd like to think so, but everyone thinks they're going to be a good coach! I've watched Roy Keane and then Frank Lampard and Stevie Gerrard go into it. You have to think you're going to be great because you have to believe in yourself. And it's not just about tactics; you've got to be a social worker too. The social side – by which I mean man-management – is so important and yet some people don't really think about it ahead of taking on a coaching job. The two best managers at the moment – Guardiola and Klopp – have an emotional connection to their players. Their players will run through brick walls for them, in the same way that players were willing to do with Sir Alex.

Rachel: You would think that footballers who'd played for Sir Alex would potentially make great managers, but it doesn't necessarily work that way if you think of Keane or Mark Hughes. Although obviously I'm hoping that Ole will be given some money over the summer and will stick it out.

Rio: Only time will tell. Look at David Moyes: he did an unbelievable job at Everton. What he did there was nothing short of a miracle. But then he went to United and it was a different kind of challenge. You need a huge personality to manage a club like United. You need to be able to come into a room and command the room straight away, to draw everyone to you. No disrespect to David Moyes, but he couldn't do it. It wasn't him. Sir Alex had an aura; people fed off his every word.

Rachel: There won't be another Sir Alex though. That era has gone.

Rio: Yeah, of course. It's hard for Ole because it's about the machine behind the club as well. United needs to be reconfigured and to go forward, like Liverpool in recent years. Liverpool has now got a formula that works for them and a manager to drive it. United needs to decide what its philosophy is, to work out which market they are in regarding potential players. They used to buy the world's best potential, from Rooney to Ronaldo, and keep them for ten years.

Rachel: If you were manager right now, as the 2018–19 season is coming to an end, what would you do?

Rio: Bloody hell! I would get rid of some big players to set the tone.

Rachel: Including Pogba?

Rio: I love Pogba. He could be doing more, but you could build a team around him. Or you could have done in the past. But if I was Ole now, I'd go in and move on certain players. I'd make it public. I'd explain why to the press. Bang. Bang. Bang. Bang.

Rachel: As a show of strength?

Rio: Yeah. And then everyone else knows. Do not fuck with me. At all. That's it. I would only want players who understand that work ethic, work rate and application on a daily basis is the key. Before I signed for Man United, at least half a dozen people would have written a dossier on my personality. Has he got the right work ethic? Does he want to learn? Is he humble? Is he reliable? Does he love football or is he a money-orientated person? Is he a happy bunny in the changing room? Does he add to the atmosphere or does he sometimes bring everyone down? All those questions, and more, would have been asked as part of Sir Alex's regime.

Rachel: It's interesting to think about who brings what to the changing room.

Rio: Robin van Persie is a prime example. The manager knew he was adding 100 per cent value from a football perspective. He was going to give us goals. The gaffer knew that he could win us the League. Which he did. He was at the top of his game, he'd been brilliant at Arsenal and he'd been to World Cups with Holland. He used to drive me into training because I was banned from driving at the time. He was eager to learn as much as he could about Man United's culture, about the winning mentality. He asked me endless bloody questions and I loved it. He wasn't just at the club for a few seasons to get a big pay day.

Rachel: Ole will have to be given the chance to buy his own versions of van Persie.

Rio: Of course. The club has to believe in Ole long term. You can't keep chopping and changing managers. Think of how much time Fergie got. He wasn't expected to turn the club around in one bloody season! Klopp has been at Liverpool since 2015 and he ain't won nothing yet. But he's been given time and you can see the progression.

⚽　⚽　⚽

Rio: You're not a Manc; how come you support United?

Rachel: My dad was United. He took me see Ipswich away in 1994, when I was eight. And then to the semi-final of the FA Cup when we played Oldham and Hughes—

Rio: Scored the volley.

Rachel: I was looking through my baby books recently for a TV show and I found a photo of myself in a cot, a couple of months old, surrounded by Man United teddy bears.

Rio: Strategic.

Rachel: I've been indoctrinated since I was born. What about your kids?

Rio: All Man United. I wished they were older so that they could have seen me play for United. They didn't really get to appreciate the time I was there at all, although I've got wicked photos of them on the pitch as toddlers.

Rachel: But they don't remember?

Rio: Only vaguely. But they couldn't fully appreciate it.

Rachel: How often do you go back to Old Trafford?

Rio: For work. As a pundit. And for the odd testimonial. But I don't really enjoy them any more because I normally get injured.

They need to play those games for us old players on smaller pitches. Whenever I play on the full-size pitch, I can't move for days and days!

Rachel: It'd be great to see you back at Old Trafford as manager one day.

Rio: We'll see. Maybe one day...

Wretch 32 & Ian Wright

Wretch: Did you feel calm after games?

Ian: No! When I was at the peak of my career, I could score a couple of really good goals for Arsenal but then give the ball away a few times and it would literally kill me for the week.

Allen & Unwin, April 2019

Wretch 32 [pronounced 'three two'] was born Jermaine Scott Sinclair in Tottenham, London, in 1985. When he was growing up, his mother called him 'Wretch', Jamaican slang for 'skinny'. His uncle is the activist Stafford Scott, who co-founded the Broadwater Farm Defence Campaign in 1985.

Wretch was a member of the grime collective Combination Chain Gang before forming The Movement with Ghetts, Scorcher and Mercston. He released his first single, 'Traktor', in 2011, followed by his major-label debut album, *Black and White*. His 2016 album, *Growing Over Life*, was a widely acclaimed breakthrough. He released *FR32* in 2017. Wretch won BBC 1Xtra's Best Hip Hop award in 2006,

Official Mixtape Awards' Most Street Heat in 2009 and BET Best International Act in 2012.

Ian Wright was born in south London in 1963. During his teens, Wright had trials at Southend United and Brighton before playing for Sunday league clubs. He signed as a semi-professional for Greenwich Borough in 1985, was spotted by a Crystal Palace scout and signed for Palace in August that year, just before turning twenty-two. He played for Arsenal from 1991 to 1998, scoring 128 goals in 221 appearances. In 1998 he moved to West Ham, then a year later to Celtic and in 2000 to Burnley. He scored nine goals in thirty-three appearances for England. He was a first-team coach for MK Dons in the 2012–13 season. He has worked for Talksport, Absolute Radio and BBC Radio 5 Live's *606*. He has enjoyed a varied television career, including hosting his own chat show, *Friday Night's All Wright*, and appearing as a pundit on *Match of the Day* and *BT Sport*.

✪　✪　✪

Ian Wright: I'm going to sit on the arm of this sofa until someone shouts, 'Come off the arm of the chair!' I sit on the arms of chairs and sofas all the time now just because I can. I've never seen the arm of a chair or sofa break; it was something our mums and grandmothers used to say to kids to show power!

Wretch 32: My mum was exactly the same, man…

Ian: I'm still doing all the things I couldn't do as a kid. I can't stop buying bikes because I didn't have one as a kid. When all the boys who lived on my block were away on their bikes, I'd have to play football. My brother was a little bit older, so he didn't want to hang around with me. Now, when I'm riding my bike – or my motor-bikes – I feel the freedom that I was desperate for as a kid. But I needed to practise my football as well, so it's all part of the story.

Wretch: Come off the arm of the chair right now! I'm joking, bro. My mum used to leave the plastic on the sofa and chairs.

Ian: When I was younger, you'd go to black people's houses and there was plastic *everywhere*. The video machine has a crochet blanket on it. It was an ornament. And people always had blue fish. To show off.

Wretch: I remember the blue fish!

Ian: You weren't allowed in the front room.

Wretch: A whole room that was not for use.

Ian: When I went to white friends' houses, they were hanging out in their front rooms! Anyway, what's happening, Wretch? How's it going in the studio?

Wretch: I've finished the new album. But I've got way too many songs; I can't stop writing, man. I might go back and tweak a chorus, but I'll stop soon.

Ian: Where do the lyrics come from?

Wretch: This is the easiest way to explain it to you: if someone passes you a ball, you automatically flick it up. It's intuitive for you. It's your thing. If I hear a beat, no matter if it's one minute or ten minutes, there will never be a day that I don't respond to it.

Ian: How did you know you could write lyrics? Did you read loads of books at school?

Wretch: Nah! I hated reading. It was a punishment. If I was in trouble at school or at home, I'd be sent to my room to finish a book. I'd read the back cover and ten pages of the book. And then I could at least pretend to mum that I'd read it. She certainly hadn't read it, so she couldn't say anything!

Ian: No wonder you hated books. Once when my young daughters were naughty, I told them to go and read in their rooms. My missus pulled me up straight away and said, 'You can't tell them that reading is a punishment!' She was right; kids will stop reading if they associate books with punishment.

I used to try and write songs when I was younger. I thought the song had to rhyme and follow a certain format. My brother used to laugh at how shit my lyrics were. It's a skill I have admired for ever.

I interviewed Lionel Richie and he said that the lyrics really started to flow when his first girlfriend blew him out. He told me that you can't really be a great writer until your heart is broken.

Wretch: That's a sick way of putting it. I know that I store all my feelings up. If something affected me in, say, 2010, I can go back to that place in my head and tap into that emotion as I'm writing. Writing is more therapy than anything else. It's like a soundtrack to a specific feeling; sometimes I don't know how much a certain event has affected me until I listen back to a song. I always feel so much better after I've written a song like that.

Ian: It's probably like me going to the gym. I had to find something to replace the adrenaline rush of football, and after a session at the gym I always feel calmer.

Wretch: Did you feel calm after games?

Ian: No! When I was at the peak of my career, I could score a couple of really good goals for Arsenal but then give the ball away a few times and it would literally kill me for the week. Even if we won. I was aiming for perfection on all fronts. There was no other way for me to play.

Wretch: It might have been different when you were playing, but don't you think that footballers now who seek perfection get killed for it? I'm thinking particularly of Ronaldo.

Ian: I know his reputation has since been called into question with last year's rape allegation, but you could see how *totally* driven he is in the [2015] documentary about his life. He's driven by the fact that people used to tease him when he was younger about being a tramp. His shoes had holes in them. His dad was an alcoholic. Where you look at where he is now, I can't for the life of me understand why people don't understand his story. He's not arrogant, he's simply totally dedicated to being the best. You have to respect the journey Ronaldo is on. He could clock off now, knowing that his family will be financially comfortable for generations to come. But he's got more to prove.

Wretch: He's under pressure all the time to win and then he puts extra pressure on himself.

Ian: The pressure on the Ronaldos, the Messis, the Zidanes and the Neymars of this world is off the scale.

Wretch: I love Ronaldo's passion. Do you remember when he got injured during Euro 2016? He came off but, instead of sitting down, he stood on the touchline, shouting encouragement.

Ian: And when Portugal won the game, the man's emotion just blasted out of him. It was pure and raw exhilaration. Ronaldo had this expression on his face that reminded me of Wes Morgan's when Leicester won the Premier League in 2016. He knew that what Leicester did would never be repeated. There's this brief moment, a fraction of a second, where Wes closes his eyes. It was the moment he fully appreciated all the hard work the team had done to get to that point.

In the lead-up to Arsenal winning the Premier League in 1998, I saw what Tony Adams went through in terms of his alcoholism. There were times when he nearly died. Wenger had to sort him out during his first full season as manager. To cut a long story short, when Tony scored that last goal to make it 4-2 against Everton, his head went back briefly and he closed his eyes. Those are the moments I look for. Especially when the player has just won the World Cup or the Champions League or the League, because it's pure and cannot be rehearsed.

Wretch: When I was ten or eleven, we won a football tournament. It was the one game that my dad came to watch. The other team were crying. My dad was quiet. When we got home he said to me, 'You're not going to make it as a footballer. The other team were crying because it meant so much to them. They needed to win, you don't need to win.' At first, I was thinking, 'Oh shut up, we won, be happy for me.' But then I got it. Football wasn't going to be my thing.

Ian: That was very insightful of your dad. You're lucky he came to a game; my dad didn't see me play until he watched me on the television. I started playing football at eight and I literally couldn't contain myself when I lost. Learning how to deal with losing was a constant battle for me, even when I started playing for Arsenal. George Graham used to talk about being as gracious in defeat as in victory. From the age of nine, all the way through Sunday-morning football and non-league football, I found it very difficult to deal with losing. When I was younger, because of the way my mum and stepdad were, I always felt that playing football was about people liking me. I had to keep winning or no one would like me. I learned how to lose when I turned professional, but I don't like it even now. If Arsenal are on the television and they're losing, I never get to the point where the referee blows the whistle. I leave the room. Do something else and come back.

Wretch: Are you just that way about Arsenal?

Ian: Arsenal is my love. People think it's only because I played for them, but I grew up on the same estate as David Rocastle and we went to the same primary school. When I was nineteen and still doing foolishness on the street, David – who was four years younger – used to meet me on the bridge and say, 'I'm playing against lads at Arsenal who are not as good as you. You need to focus on football.' He might have been younger than me, but he was ahead of me. I started supporting Arsenal when he signed for the youth team in 1982. Not just me; the *whole estate* started supporting Arsenal! It was massive for someone from our estate to be playing for Arsenal. Palace fans think that I've forgotten them, but it was always Arsenal. I've always had a problem with Arsenal losing, and now of course I have to talk about it on television!

Wretch: And you have to talk about it in a measured way. You can't be too emotional.

Ian: The emotions around football will never leave me. I will always be emotional. When I watch a sad film, I just burst into tears. I'm always close to tears.

Wretch: Were you like that when you were younger?

Ian: Yeah, man. If my mum cried, I'd instantly burst into tears.

Wretch: And then someone asks how you are – that's more tears!

Ian: I don't know why, but when I was a kid I just cried so much. I won't ever stop crying. I love crying! I got a surprise Father's Day card from my son Bradley and I couldn't stop blubbing. But my kids mean the world to me. When I was younger, I didn't think I'd ever get to the point of fathering kids who would be inspired by me. Bradley wrote in his card that all his mates wanted to be a superhero and he just wanted to be Ian Wright. Oh man, I'll be in tears again if I keep talking about this.

Wretch: I don't think you fully understand that generations of young black kids supported certain teams because of certain players. I was born in Tottenham and my dad is a Tottenham supporter. The day I saw you play, I was Arsenal. My dad could not believe it. But I was like, 'This could be my uncle.' Never underestimate the power of representation, man. Never.

Ian: Exactly. And we should all be looking after each other. For example, I've got this new television show in which I talk to young

English footballers. I chat to Jesse Lingard in the first episode and I referred to the theory Stormzy raises in his book – about how we're just not wired to deal with the constant comments and interactions in social media. I asked Jesse how he deals with it because I know for a fact that I wouldn't be able to.

I respect Stormzy so much and, as you just said, it's all about representation. There is all this talk about racism amongst football fans at the moment and we all need to come together and talk about it, intelligently and calmly. Black people, white people, old people, young people. Everyone. It could be amazing. But the idea of that kind of wide dialogue becoming a reality is so threatening for some people.

Did you read that article in the *Players' Tribune* by Kyle Korver [in which the white American basketball player brutally questions his conditioned reaction to the arrest of his black teammate]? That's what needs to happen. If I talk about Raheem specifically or racism in general, no matter how placidly, the first reaction will inevitably be, 'Oh fuck, here we go again.' I always say that you need a white man to talk about it as well. We need people like Kyle Korver standing up and telling his story so that white people understand. He writes about how he stands with his teammates but looks like the other guy. About the privilege he is granted based on the colour of his skin. About how he can 'fade into the crowd any time I want'. I like the way he signed the piece off, by saying that it's the responsibility of 'anyone on the privileged end of those inequalities to help make things right.' Hang on, I'll read out the rest to you: 'So if you don't want to know anything about me, outside of basketball, then listen – I get it. But if you do want to know something. Know *I believe that*... And if you're claiming my name, or likeness, for your own cause, in any way... know that about me. Know that I believe this matters.'

Wretch: You are so right, man. And yet – somehow – the responsibility is still seen as ours.

✦ ✦ ✦

Ian: When you chose to support Arsenal instead of Tottenham, how did your mates react?

Wretch: My dad and my uncles were Tottenham fans. My older friends supported Liverpool because of John Barnes. We were at the age where we were undecided. Most people go with their dad's team. But they understood that I went with Arsenal because of you.

Ian: The great thing is that your dad was fine with you choosing your own team. That's unusual.

Wretch: Listen, man, I bought my son an Arsenal shirt. I didn't ask which team he was going to support. Because of what I did, I wasn't going to take a chance!

Ian: You've taken away his human rights! How old are your kids?

Wretch: My boy is now thirteen and my daughter is seven. When he was younger, I got him the Arsenal kit and I put the numbers three and two on his shirt and I let him pick the name. One year, we were in the shop and I asked him which name he wanted. He wanted his own name and... the number nine. He broke my heart, bro.

Ian: [laughing his head off]

Wretch: I was devastated! But I was also happy because he was being himself.

Ian: When I was playing, I used to find it weird seeing people walking around with 'Wright' on their shirts. I think people should always have their own names on their shirts.

Wretch: With the adidas retro kits coming back, you're going to see your name everywhere! When we were kids, we used to buy our Arsenal kits from the market. They cost £20. They only had XL. But I wanted that kit so badly. When I asked my mum for the money, she was shocked by the price.

Ian: And it wasn't even your size!

Wretch: Finally, she gave me the £20. The next step was to try and persuade her to pay for the name on the back. There was a place that did it for £2 or £3 a letter. She didn't have the money to pay for six letters. So we got a permanent market and drew an eight on the back and wrote 'Wright' across the top.

Ian: Stop, man. Give me a moment. The tears are coming again.

Wretch: But that's how important you were. How important certain players are in your life.

Ian: It's true. I could watch Pogba or Özil all day. They are *artists*. Before them it was Zidane and Platini. When you watch them live they are magicians.

Wretch: Pogba is incredible.

Ian: I will defend him to the end. And think of how many black kids he's inspired around the world. I'm always so pleased to see Paul after a Man United game. But the abuse I get in the press and from fans…

Wretch: As a former Arsenal player chatting to a Man United player?

Ian: Yes. But I think that kind of attitude is slowly changing. I appreciate Pogba as a player, not because I secretly support United. I watch Juventus because I want to see Ronaldo, not because I love Juventus. And who doesn't love Messi? Who? The old guard have got to be moved on. They don't get it. I don't love basketball but I still read Kyle Korver's article. We have to open our minds.

Wretch: I always get stick because it's impossible for me to hate Tottenham. I'm from Tottenham. My whole family supports Tottenham. Any time I hear the word 'Tottenham' it warms my heart. No one understands that.

Ian: I've never disliked Tottenham. Glenn Hoddle was my man when I was going through my adolescent years. Clive Allen. Mitchell Thomas was one of my best mates and he played left back for Tottenham. I was so close to joining Tottenham from Palace – they were going to sign me or Paul Stewart and they chose him. There was no better feeling than scoring against Tottenham and to this day I am proud of my record of scoring against them. The day I signed for Arsenal, I was talking to Rocky [David Rocastle] till 3 a.m. about what it means to score against Tottenham and to beat them. That feeling never leaves you.

Equally, I met Dele Alli when he was sixteen and still playing for MK Dons and I don't care about him playing for Tottenham now. Good for him. I know what it means to Dele to be in the semi-final of the Champions League and so I'm happy for him. Spurs are being really ambitious under serious financial constraints. They've got an unbelievable stadium now. If they could win the Champions League, it would be like Leicester winning the League. How could you begrudge them?

⚽ ⚽ ⚽

Wretch: How much do you miss playing football?

Ian: You never lose that feeling of wanting to score a goal. My last game was with Burnley. As we were waiting to find out if they'd been promoted, it literally hit me. I'm not playing again. It was hard. I drove back to London on my own, thinking, 'It's over.' Halfway down the motorway the Burnley manager called me and tried to get me to stay. He nearly twisted my arm. But I'd made the decision. For months afterwards, I had serious withdrawal symptoms on Saturdays. All these games were about to kick off and I wasn't playing. My body was ready to go. Endorphins were being released. It's why a lot of those guys get depressed when they stop playing. I tried to get the same feeling from playing golf, but it was nowhere near as exciting as football. I'll never get over not being able to play another game of football on a professional level. I'll never get over the fact that I've retired. I always thought I'd retire at Arsenal, but that didn't happen in the end.

Even though I'm not a great drinker, when I stopped playing I was starting to go down that road because I was trying to fill a void. Working in television helped. Presenting *Friday Night's All Wright* was a cool thing to do. I was interviewing people like Will Smith and Denzel Washington. I gave Beyoncé her first gold disc when she was in… what's that little group called that she used to be in?

Wretch: Little group! You mean Destiny's Child. They were a big deal, man!

Ian: I know, I know! I just forget their name. I gave them their first gold disc. It was a great buzz meeting all those people, but it was nowhere near the same as football. I missed the crowd. The fans. When we played away from home, I used to get a lot of stick because in their minds I was this raw black footballer. But the Arsenal fans were always, always in my corner. The home fans would be booing me every time I touched the ball and the away fans would be singing my name over and over. You'd know they were fighting for you. As soon as I scored, I'd run over to them as a way of thanking them. A billion pounds could not replace that feeling. There is just no way of replicating it.

Wretch: It's funny you should say that because there's a question I always ask when I start work with a young artist: if money didn't exist, would you still be here today? Would you have turned up to every session if you weren't being paid?

Ian: When I first signed to Palace, I couldn't believe they were paying me to play. Steve Coppell gave me £100 for expenses in the first week and I was embarrassed, bro! It felt like a weed deal. I'd never really been paid to play football before.

Wretch: Had you given up the idea of ever being a professional footballer?

Ian: Pretty much. I was used to playing on a Sunday morning, scoring four or five goals and thinking that I was decent, but not good enough to go pro. I just loved playing. I loved scoring. I was scoring so frequently on a Saturday and Sunday that I used to practise other ways of scoring, like making the ball come off the woodwork and go into the goal. And then I went straight from

Sunday-morning football to Crystal Palace in the Second Division and I started to do the same with their first team. Even when I was at Arsenal, I'd do whatever I felt like doing. That's why I'd chip the goalkeeper so often. When I was younger, my teacher used to say that the best goals are those that the goalkeeper can't stop going in. When I scored those goals, I'd watch the game on television and it was the best feeling in the world when the camera zoomed in to the goalkeeper's baffled face!

Wretch: What else did that teacher tell you about shooting?

Ian: When I was about eight, I used to try and blast the ball in. Through the goalkeeper. My teacher taught me to look for the space *around* the goalkeeper. He told me about Jimmy Greaves. Sometimes his goals didn't even hit the back of the net.

Wretch: Greavsie's goals were so soft, man.

Ian: So soft. The man was always so beautiful with his finishing. I always tried to do something special on the finish so that people would talk about it. No money in the world can bring those feelings back. It's a great question you ask young musicians. What do they say?

Wretch: Some people are honest: they do it for the money.

Ian: You can tell when people are being honest. Or not. I've seen it with footballers. On the one hand, you can't do a job just for the money and think it's going to last for ever. Your heart has to be in it. On the other hand, there are African players who are trying to reset generations of poverty; they want to earn enough to make sure their family is OK for generations to come. When I started to blast the goals in at Palace and then Arsenal, I'd go around to my mum's and it would be like the wedding scene in *The Godfather*. People would turn up with their gas bills or whatever and I couldn't say no.

Wretch: I argue with my missus about how much footballers are paid. She insists they are paid way too much, but their careers are short, they might have to move around the country from club to club and the Premier League is brutal. It properly batters your body.

Ian: The clubs earn enough money to pay their players well. It's demand and supply. And football is changing all the time. I remember Wenger saying we were going to see more free transfers and he was right; players are going to start running contracts down. You can only make proper money as a free agent. A club can sign a player for nothing, pay them a lump sum and a huge wage and still save money. But there will always be the risk of injury and then you've paid all this money for a player who can't play.

Some players are just more vulnerable to injury – Darren Anderton was one of the best players I ever played with, but he was always getting injured. Same with Daniel Sturridge; he was supposed to be one of the best and he's been so unlucky with injury. You watch him come off the bench and you can't help but think, 'What next?'

Wretch: I know the fans give players a hard time sometimes, but some things are out of your control.

Ian: What are your fans like? Some parts of the media like to think that grime has issues.

Wretch: The media likes to exaggerate. But there is always a fear that somebody could be stabbed at one of my shows, god forbid. Of course, that kind of thing could happen anywhere, but if it happens at your gig, you're on some kind of police list. Somebody got stabbed at a Roddy Ricch show in Brixton and they cancelled the rest of his tour. He's American and now he can't come to the UK to perform.

Ian: But creatively do you feel like the scene is closer now?

Wretch: Totally. Black music in the UK is pop music. We're the dominant music genre.

Ian: Music isn't tribal any more either.

Wretch: Back in 2010, 2011, there were only a handful of black artists that were acceptable to the mainstream. A typical festival line-up would have hardly any rappers – maybe only Tinie Tempah and me. The next year there would be us two plus Tinchy Stryder and Professor Green. For a long time, when I performed at a festival

I was on my own. I had to prove myself so that the following year there'd be twice the number of rappers performing. And then twice as many again the year after.

Ian: It's the only way. People don't realize how easy it is to shut black music down. It has to test well.

Wretch: I had to make sure it tested well. But it's all changed. Kids can listen to anything they like on Spotify or whatever and, as you said, music isn't tribal. People just want to listen to good music.

Ian: I think people have got to start thinking about collaborations. Like when Run-DMC and Aerosmith did 'Walk This Way'.

Wretch: Or Stomzy with Linkin Park. Or Lil Nas X with Billy Ray Cyrus.

Ian: Exactly, man!

Wretch: Ed Sheeran has been genius at that. He started off in the grime scene. In around 2010, when he was homeless and busking for a living, he came to London and was making songs with grime MCs. You can hear when he's rapping that he's the real deal.

Ian: And he was the first guest on *The Big Narstie Show*.

Wretch: I met Ed when he stopped me at a train station. I'd released my first album independently and he asked who had played the keyboards on track one. Fast-forward to his second album and he sampled those keys on a track called 'Nina'. My album only sold 3,000 copies max, but Ed knows his shit. And he put us on the credits and made sure we were paid royalties.

Ian: That's what I'm saying! That's how it should work. My missus is all over Ed. She knows he's doing it because he loves it, not because he wanted to make money.

Wretch: Ed's one of the good guys, man. He's one of those who'd do it for no money.

Ian: He does it because it's in him. He goes to ground between records and then comes back with something extraordinary. Wretch, when you're in the studio, how much pressure are you under?

Wretch: I just want every record I make to be better than the last one. I look at my albums as if they're one continuous album. When I say better, I mean I want to sound better, to rap better. It's not really about the success of the record because that's out of my control. When I listen back, I want to be able to hear that I've progressed.

Ian: What's it like when you've written a personal track and then it's out there and people are listening to it and singing the lyrics back to you at gigs? Whenever I see that at a gig, it makes me feel so emotional.

Wretch: I feel emotional too! If the day ever comes that I'm in the studio or on stage and I don't get that special feeling, I'll quit. For example, '6 Words' is about my kids. To be able to express my love for them in a song and for that song to then be top ten in the UK singles chart and to hear people sing it back at me – that's like you chipping the keeper. And to sing it at V Festival in front of thousands of people and to bring my kids out on stage…

Ian: I couldn't do that! I'd be way too emotional. I'd be crying so much that I wouldn't be able to sing.

Wretch: I wrote a song called 'Time' about my uncle dying. My mum called me to tell me that my uncle had had a stroke but that he was getting better. Then she called me again to say he hadn't made it. I went to the hospital to pick her and my auntie up. I dropped my auntie off and went back to my mum's, but she wanted to be on her own. I didn't want to go back to my house because no one was there, so I thought I might as well go down to the studio because I had a session booked.

I started playing chords. I was thinking about my cousin, my uncle's boy, not getting enough time with his dad. The lyrics to 'Time' just came pouring out: 'Time won't be on your side, like I am.' I burst into tears in the recording booth. I'd been trying to be the man of the family all afternoon and I couldn't take it any more.

Fast-forward to a small, intimate show that was set up for superfans on the day of the album's release. It was a tiny venue. I told my sisters to stay with my mum and to keep her at the back of the venue. I knew I was going to perform 'Time' and I knew how hard it would be if I could see her. What do my sisters do? Let her stand at the front of the stage, right in front of me. I put my hand out. She put her hand out. We were holding hands.

Ian: That's an amazing story…

Wretch: I don't think it will ever be easy to perform that song, man.

Ian: Did you have anyone or anything in mind when you were recording the new record?

Wretch: I was thinking about what society thinks when it looks in the mirror. I wanted to write about everything to do with that. Once I'd got nine moody songs, I needed a bit of colour for the last three.

Ian: Is there any Brexit business on there?

Wretch: Nah, I didn't do Brexit this time round. I did it the album before, when Brexit was new.

Ian: Brexit is always in the back of everyone's minds though. You can't avoid it.

Wretch: The rise of racism is no coincidence, man. You know why people voted for it.

Ian: They're the same people who voted for Trump. They feel ignored. They're misinformed.

Wretch: They're the go-back-to-your-country people.

Ian: It's like when I used to watch Millwall as a kid. They used to shout 'black bastard!' at some of the players and then turn to me and say, 'Not you, mate.'

Wretch: We need to stand together.

       ⚽   ⚽   ⚽

Wretch: My phone is buzzing like crazy, man. I'm so late! But before we wrap this up, I wanted to ask you one more question. Out of all the incredible moments you experienced in your footballing career, are you able to pick out one that you replay in your head again and again?

Ian: The first goal I scored for Crystal Palace against Man United in the FA Cup final in 1990. I still think about it now; it's easily the best moment of my football career.

This chat has been so inspiring, bro. I can't thank you enough.

Wretch: You are a legend, man. Thank *you*.

Amy
Raphael

&

Vivianne
Miedema

Amy: Do the Dutch fans expect the women's game to be the same as the men's?

Vivianne: It's never going to be the same game. People always talk about women's football being much slower than men's, but it's not the same. Like Federer v Nadal is a completely different game to Serena Williams v Maria Sharapova.

Vivianne Miedema's flat, St Albans, May 2019

Amy Raphael was born in London in 1967. In the early 1990s, she was features editor of *The Face* and then *ELLE* and, in the latter part of the decade, she was editor-at-large and sports editor of *Esquire*. Raphael has freelanced for all the UK broadsheets. She interviewed Steve McManaman and George Graham for the football anthology *Perfect Pitch* and co-wrote Steve Coogan's autobiography. She has written several other books, including Mike Leigh and Danny Boyle's official biographies and *Never Mind the Bollocks: Women Rewrite Rock* and its sequel, *A Seat at the Table*. She has interviewed dozens of musicans, actors, directors and footballers, including Gianluca Vialli,

Sven-Göran Eriksson, Juan Sebastián Verón, Alessandro Del Piero and Johan Cruyff.

Vivianne Miedema was born in Hoogeveen, Netherlands, in 1996. She signed for SC Heerenveen at fourteen and made her senior debut at fifteen, scoring seventy-eight goals in sixty-nine games. She played for Bayern Munich from 2014 until 2017, scoring thirty-five goals in sixty-one games. In 2014–15, Bayern went unbeaten all season and won the Bundesliga for the first time since 1976. They won it again the following season. In 2017, Miedema signed for Arsenal and scored twenty-six goals in thirty appearances. At the end of her first season, Arsenal won the FA WSL Cup and at the end of her second, the club won the League for the first time since 2012. She played for Holland's Under-15 team in 2010 and joined the senior team in 2013, for whom she has scored fifty-seven goals in sixty-eight games. Holland won the Women's Euros in 2017. At the end of the 2018–19 season, Miedema was awarded the PFA Women's Player of the Year and the London Football Awards Women's Player of the Year. During the Women's World Cup 2019, Miedema became the all-time top scorer for the Netherlands women's team.

◇ ◇ ◇

Amy Raphael: I brought this article that I wrote about Arsenal Ladies for *Esquire* in 1999 to show you. Having not read it for two decades, I was struck by several things: the players going to Burger King en route to an away game against Doncaster Belles; the players training at Highbury, Arsenal's old ground, on a Thursday night, running up and down the North Stand steps and sprinting along the touchlines, careful to avoid the pitch, while the costly floodlights were turned off; the players, who weren't paid a penny to play, feeling unsupported by the FA.

Vivianne Miedema: And that was just twenty years ago?

Amy: Yes. I realize you were only two when I wrote that piece, but there has at least been some progress: you are living in a lovely flat with your Arsenal teammate Lisa Evans that is paid for by the club; you are a professional footballer with a salary; Arsenal Women has its own scout, doctor and physio; you have a proper training ground; you probably don't eat Burger Kings on the way to a game.

Vivianne: We are lucky to live here, for sure. But it's only in the last couple of years that we've been told to keep an eye on what we eat; whenever I joined the national team, our coach would let us eat pretty much anything simply because we train so hard and burn off any unwanted calories. Obviously, we can't eat fish and chips every day, but it's fine once a week or a few times a month. But you're right, the general attitude to food and nutrition has really changed and we're expected to eat healthily most of the time. I eat a lot though, so it's lucky I train so hard.

Amy: You've been playing since you were a kid growing up in Hoogeveen, in the north-eastern Netherlands.

Vivianne: Yeah, since I was four or five. My dad used to play football, so I had to watch him every Saturday afternoon. He was a number ten and sometimes a number nine. He played for a terrible team, by the way. I played football with the local boys, who were all happy for me to do so. When I was fourteen, I signed to [the Dutch women's team] SC Heerenveen and made my senior debut at fifteen. I didn't really have a choice. It was football or nothing!

Amy: Your brother Lars, who plays in Holland, is several years younger than you; did your dad expect both of you to become players?

Vivianne: That seemed to be his aim. He loved the fact that I was playing football; he certainly didn't think that Lars, as a boy, would be the one to make it.

Amy: Was there a certain point, around the time you hit early adolescence and your period started, that you ever thought of giving up?

Vivianne: Never. I played with the same boys from the age of five to fifteen and they never had a problem with me playing.

Amy: My daughter, who's fourteen and who plays for a team in the Sussex League, played with the boys throughout primary school, but it became much harder when she went to secondary school. The boys are always on the field playing football, but the girls don't feel welcome to join in – it seems to be the same at other schools too.

Vivianne: It's a bit different in Holland, I think. We only had short breaks during the school day and no one played football. When I started going away with the national team, the older boys were full of questions when I returned: 'How was it? Did you have a good time? Who did you play?' They were curious rather than judgemental. I'm quite surprised to hear that it becomes tricky for girls here once they go to secondary school. It's quite weird.

Amy: Everyone becomes more self-conscious at secondary school, and of course hormones kick in.

Vivianne: The difference with girls becomes bigger at that age. Maybe they want to be like the rest of the girls. I was a tomboy at that age, but it didn't matter.

Amy: Did you always play as a forward?

Vivianne: I used to play as a ten. A creative midfielder. When I was seven and playing with the Under-15s, I was really small and I wasn't as physical as the other girls, so I had to play as a left-winger. It's only basically in the last four or five years that I've actually become a striker.

Amy: You're very much a team player with Arsenal, but have you always been greedy to score goals?

Vivianne: When I played with the boys, me and this other boy were the stars of the team – he made it to the First Division in Holland, although he's stopped playing now. One of us always scored, so I didn't feel any pressure to score. But even now I don't start a game for Arsenal thinking, 'I've got to score a goal.' Never.

Amy: Because it's all about the team winning?

Vivianne: That's always the main goal. You play to win titles as a team, not to win something individually.

Amy: Is that why you don't often celebrate when you score? Because you don't want to take all the glory?

Vivianne: If we're already 3-0 up and I score a fourth, I think it would be disrespectful to the opponent to celebrate as a crazy idiot.

Amy: I noticed you celebrated your spectacular goal against Brighton last week.

Vivianne: I do celebrate sometimes! I think it's OK if you score the first goal.

Amy: So you beat Brighton 4-0 to win the first WSL title since 2012 in front of a record crowd of 5,265. There was a great atmosphere at the ground, but tickets were only £3 for adults and £1 for kids, which is absurd when the game was so thrilling.

Vivianne: It was thrilling for us all to play at the Amex instead of Crawley Town FC, where Brighton Women usually play. It was brilliant of Brighton to do that. I think all women's clubs should get at least a few games in the biggest stadia next season. It's so good for women's football. I know the tickets are cheap, but we have to get the people into the grounds to see how well we play first.

Amy: Going back to your school years: once you started playing for SC Heerenveen's senior team at fifteen, did you miss lots of school?

Vivianne: For a while I tried to combine school and football. My school tried to support me and I stayed after school to catch up, but at a certain point it just didn't work any more. I was lucky; during my final year, another school opened that was for elite athletes. It was full of kids who did ice-skating, wrestling and other Winter Olympic sports. And me. I had training at 3 p.m., so I could go to school from 10 a.m. till 2 p.m. Or from 9 a.m. till 1 p.m. It was more flexible than a normal school and it was great for me. It made my life so much easier after years of running from school to training to school to games. I then had the freedom to go away with the national team because I could take Friday off.

Amy: You played your first senior game for Holland in September 2013, at the age of seventeen.

Vivianne: My first ever cap was away to Albania and we won 4-0. There were maybe 250 people in the stands. Our right back at the time was a mixed-race girl. All I can remember from the game is the people in the stadium – I won't call them fans – making monkey noises. My second cap was a better experience; we were playing Portugal and I came on in the last fifteen minutes and scored three goals.

Amy: Hang on a second. You mean the people in the stadium were making those noises throughout the game? Did none of the officials take any action?

Vivianne: I don't know. This sounds really bad, but it was my first game for Holland. I was really nervous and I was concentrating on playing. I was shocked, obviously, but I don't remember what happened or if anyone tried to stop the noises. The girl was upset about it afterwards, but she was also brushing it off by saying, 'With all due respect, we were playing in Albania.' It's a sin that it happens in football, but I don't know what we could have done apart from stopping the game. You have to punish the people who behave in that way, but as players it's hard to know what to do apart from speak out against racism.

Amy: Do you think racism is as prevalent among fans of women's football as it is in men's?

Vivianne: I've been thinking about that. I don't think so. Not in England at least. It's a very different atmosphere at women's games – people tend to bring their families. There are a lot of young kids. Since that night in Albania, I have never been witness to any racism at games. I think there were only men allowed in the stadium that night.

Amy: Only men? But that was less than a decade ago!

Vivianne: I actually can't remember one woman in the stands. The 'fans' who were there were just hooligans. T-shirts off, drinks in hand, looking for trouble. They were there to have a fight, not to enjoy the game. We are usually quite sheltered from that kind of behaviour because we play in front of families in countries like Portugal, Spain or England.

Amy: Since you started playing for Holland, how have attitudes to women's football changed there?

Vivianne: It changed massively after Holland not only hosted the Euros in 2017 but also won the tournament. Before, we used to get 7,000, maybe 8,000 fans in the stadia. The older generation didn't like women's football at all. It wasn't widely accepted. But once the Euros were held in Holland, you could see people's attitude slowly changing. And now if we play a stadium with a capacity of 35,000, it will sell out within half an hour.

Amy: Did the fact that the men's team were in decline, failing to qualify either for Euro 2016 or the World Cup 2018, help turn people's attention towards the women's team?

Vivianne: It really has helped us. The timing was perfect; people just jumped right into the women's game and our team became really big news. Even now, when I go back to Holland to play with the national team, I feel like we've really been accepted and people really care about our progress in competitions like the World Cup in France.

Amy: Do the Dutch fans expect the women's game to be the same as the men's? Obviously you've done better than the men in recent years, but there is no avoiding the fact that women's football isn't as physical as men's.

Vivianne: It's never going to be the same game. People always talk about women's football being much slower than men's, but it's not the same. I always refer people to other sports. Federer v Nadal is a completely different game to Serena Williams v Maria Sharapova. The difference doesn't just exist in football; it exists in every single sport there is.

At the same time, I do feel like the women's game is being held back by the old guard. Once they are no longer involved in football, things will change and everything will become very exciting. Playing in front of over 5,000 people in Brighton is a great example of the game's potential, but it's still just one step in the right direction. We have to be patient, but the change will come.

⚽ ⚽ ⚽

Amy: You signed for Bayern Munich in 2014 and won the Bundesliga with them in 2014–15 and again the following year. Pep Guardiola was managing the men's team during your time there; was there any cross-over?

Vivianne: No, not really. We didn't even train at the men's facilities. We hardly saw the men's team. Other than when we both won the League at the end of the 2015 season – we were unbeaten all season and won the Bundesliga for the first time since 1976. We had a big party together, which was really nice. We were integrated at the party and we went on the balcony with them to celebrate our respective titles. That was pretty good. In the three seasons I was at Bayern, you could see the changes that were starting to happen.

When I moved to Arsenal in 2017, the first thing I noticed was the fact that the women train on the same pitches as the men. Result! Obviously there are still things at Arsenal that need to be better, but I feel that the club is at least improving all the time and trying to make the set-up for the women as good as possible.

Amy: Lucy Bronze talks about how incredible it is to play for Lyon, who give the women the same access to facilities as the men.

Vivianne: I think Lyon is one of the only clubs in Europe who actually have parity at that level. They are really lucky that the club's president is totally into women's football. But the moment he leaves, you don't know what's going to happen – because it's literally just him supporting the girls with whatever they need. The rest of the club is not even really behind it. I'm really wondering what's going to happen when he actually leaves the club.

Amy: It takes one visionary to make it, but also one new president to—

Vivianne: Destroy everything he's built.

Amy: How do the set-ups for women's football in Holland, Germany and England compare?

Vivianne: The Dutch men's league has no money compared to the Bundesliga or the Premier League. And you see that reflected both in the youth teams and the women's teams. Arsenal has maybe £250 million to spend a season while Ajax, who are the biggest team in Holland, have only got £20 million to spend. What Ajax is doing – bringing the academy players through to the first team – is amazing. It's so good for Dutch football.

Amy: It's great for the national team, but Ajax's young star players get snapped up really quickly – like Frenkie de Jong going to Barcelona.

Vivianne: It's great for the players because they need to take the next step in their career and they can't do that in Holland because if they are at Ajax, they are already at the top. But that's just how football works at the moment. It's all about the money. The club that's got the most money gets the best players. And even then they are not guaranteed success. Look at PSG. They keep spending money and money, but they can't win anything.

Amy: It's hard not to be amused by PSG's 'misfortune'.

Vivianne: I love it, to be honest, because I think the amount of money that is flooding the top clubs isn't necessarily a good thing. I'm really happy that it's not like that in the women's game yet.

Amy: There's a kind of sweet spot for the women's game, where players have a decent salary and hear the roar of the crowd week in, week out, without ever becoming overpaid superstars who are mobbed everywhere they go.

Vivianne: I agree. I don't get bothered too much here, but the other week I was lying by the pool in Tenerife in a bikini and someone asked me for an autograph. I was clearly on holiday. I wasn't with Arsenal. It was quite unsettling. Having said that, I am used to being stopped all the time in Holland. In terms of what is the perceived pinnacle of the women's game, I don't understand people who are always saying, 'Oh yeah, we want women's football to be on the same level as men's football.' I don't want that, because men's football is not about football any more. It's about everything around that.

Amy: It's a huge business.

Vivianne: It *is* business. Obviously the players want to win the League or the Champions League or the World Cup, but the club itself is more about profit. There's plenty of room for improvement in the women's game, but at least it's *real.* We all play because it's *fun.* It's not like any of us women can play for twenty years and then never have to work again. We will all have to work after we've retired from football. But the game is still pure and real.

Amy: It wasn't so long ago that women weren't professional and therefore played for nothing.

Vivianne: At this level, we get paid enough to at least move abroad, and nor do we have to do a secondary job. So it is amazing.

Amy: Do you look at the men's wages and think, 'For fuck's sake, what's that about?' Football brings me a huge amount of pleasure, but players' wages are obscene.

Vivianne: I find it ridiculous that they get paid so much. It's not fair to anyone in this society. Everyone knows that football has changed. As I said, it would just be nice if women's football could make one more step in the right direction.

Amy: I read somewhere that you wanted men and women playing for the Dutch national team to be paid the same.

Vivianne: No. Before we won the Euros, some of the girls were actually struggling to pay rent at the end of the month. After the Euros, we knew it was the right time for us to try and get a better deal. We tried everything we could to get a better deal for the team, which we obviously did. You have to be very loud about those kind of demands. You have to say, 'This is what we want!' It made sense for some of the bigger players, so I was one of those who went to the Dutch FA, alongside [FC Barcelona player] Lieke Martens. We never demanded equal pay. It's just not realistic. But I think we've got a good understanding with the Association right now. They really support women's football. They know that they need us, they know that we need them. So we've made steps. We're happy with where we are right now and we also know that what we have right now still needs to develop into something bigger and better. But that's only going to happen once the game is developing as well.

Amy: As you say, it's not just about the money. Recognition is important too. How did you feel about winning the PFA Women's Player of the Year award? Congratulations, by the way.

Vivianne: Thank you! I was picked up in a taxi straight after the Brighton game. I was standing in a row with all the Liverpool players like Andy Robertson. They were all nice guys. I missed the party back in Brighton, but it's great to get that kind of recognition.

Amy: How do you feel about women being eligible for the Ballon d'Or for the first time this year?

Vivianne: If there are awards for men's football, there should be awards for women's football. It's quite simple, really!

Amy: And what did you think when Ada Hegerberg, the inaugural winner of the women's Ballon d'Or, was asked to twerk on stage?

Vivianne: I don't know. I think that we live in a world where anything anyone says is taken out of context. Obviously it wasn't the right moment for the presenter to ask Ada Hegerberg to twerk, but it's not the end of the world either.

Amy: Are you a feminist?

Vivianne: No, I wouldn't say so. I think it's really good that women now have more opportunities, that women stand up for themselves and that women's football is growing. In the end, if a woman can do something better than a man, then a woman should get paid for it instead of a man. That's how easy it is for me. I don't understand why gender or race are still being discussed. We are all the same.

Amy: I presume you mean that it's ridiculous sexism and racism still exist, not that we are talking about the issues involved in both?

Vivianne: Yeah. It is ridiculous that we still need to put energy into discussing sexism and racism. I am aware of being a role model, especially in Holland. We can help the women's game to be more widely accepted. But, at a certain point, it's better not to fight and instead to get on with it and make it normal. I think it's really sad

323

that racism exists or that a guy is seen as better than a woman. When I'm in the locker room, I don't care if I sit next to someone from Africa or Asia or next to a boy. They are all just people to me and I don't understand how anyone can think differently.

Amy: At least gender and race are out there in the open, being discussed. Alongside mental-health issues, thanks to players like Danny Rose. But there isn't a single high-profile gay footballer in the men's game in this country. It's different in the women's game, I think – in the sense that gay players don't have to hide their sexuality in the same way.

Vivianne: Two things. One: it depends how you are brought up. My family are liberal and it wouldn't have occurred to me to judge anyone. I just mixed in with everyone. But then I'd say that Holland is really forward-looking in terms of accepting people as they are. Two: it might be easier for players to come out once the old guard have gone. If one male player comes out, sees that the reaction is largely positive – which I really hope it would be – then others will follow. The moment will come. And we'll just need to make sure that everyone is ready for that.

⚽ ⚽ ⚽

Amy: Which footballers did you admire when you were growing up?

Vivianne: I'm a Feyenoord fan, so I love Robin van Persie. Dirk Kuyt. Amazing players. And big examples. I think we're really lucky to live in an era in which we get to see Messi play.

Amy: That second Messi goal against Liverpool in the first leg of the Champions League semi-final this year. Oh my god. What the hell?!

Vivianne: It was *quality*. For me, Messi is the better footballer and Ronaldo is probably the better athlete. But they're just both unreal. They have got so much quality. They win games for their teams.

Amy: They are both at the peak of their games and yet they still train hard and, in most games, give everything. You're obviously at the start of your career, but are you a grafter too?

Vivianne: I should say yes, but... no. I've obviously really suffered with some injuries in the last year and I haven't played a lot this season. I know my body and I know what I can't do, and staying on the pitch for another half-hour after training isn't good for me. I'm not fit enough. Once I'm on the pitch, I try to give everything I can. I've got the experience and the quality to lead on the pitch, but I can't stay for two hours after training.

Amy: I bet you were totally dedicated when you were growing up.

Vivianne: Definitely! I got back from school around 2 p.m., trained then played with my brother and my friends until dinner-time, and then again till 9 p.m. Every night. I was always outside, always playing football. If it was raining, I'd play in the house. My mum didn't really like that. I always had a ball under my arm. But this season I've had to focus on staying fit.

Amy: When I was watching you give everything in the game against Brighton, I wondered if at any point you were tempted to hold back in case you got injured before the World Cup.

Vivianne: Nah. To be fair, I've not even thought about the World Cup yet.

Amy: Really? Surely you're excited about it?

Vivianne: I've started to think about it in the last two or three days. But, before that, I was focusing on the job in hand, which was to win the League with Arsenal. Once we'd won, I started to switch my attention to the World Cup. But I could never hold back in a game, even with a huge tournament on the horizon. I give everything to Arsenal and, when the time comes, I'll do the same for Holland.

Amy: I might have a bet on Holland to win the World Cup.

Vivianne: Well… that's a bit optimistic. But you never know!

Amy: Feyenoord are your Dutch team, but do you support Arsenal as well?

Vivianne: When Robin van Persie moved to Arsenal in 2004, I became an Arsenal fan. And I love Liverpool too, so I followed both before moving to England. But I have a soft spot for Arsenal because I play for the club. I always want them to do well. Liverpool is an amazing club and the team is so exciting to watch.

Amy: Liverpool have got maximum team spirit. Do you enjoy being part of a team?

Vivianne: I've never been in a team that is as close as this Arsenal team. We've got such amazing girls on the team. One of the reasons I started playing football is because I love playing with other people. It was really hard when I was out injured earlier on this season because I missed being with the team. At the same time, it was good for me to be training on my own. I had to focus on myself. I had three full-on seasons at Munich and I went to the Euros with Holland. I didn't have any kind of break and I was really tired. I was tired of football. Of the physicality of it. It's such a demanding game.

Amy: Just to be sure, you mean tired of playing not tired of the game?

Vivianne: God, no! I love football. I watch Hong Kong against Shanghai. That's how much I love football. I was just really tired and I put football first all the time, so I forget there are other things in life. I went home a few times last year and it was great. So now I'm back in top form again and I love playing.

Amy: It sounds like you had to reset yourself, as it were.

Vivianne: That's a good way of putting it. I was just getting some fresh energy to face the rest of a long but exciting season.

Amy: You mentioned your time at Bayern Munich as being intense; were you looking for a move?

Vivianne: I wasn't actively looking, but I was open. I didn't resign my contract, so clubs knew I was thinking of moving. Loads of different clubs came in. PSG. Man City. Chelsea. Arsenal. I visited clubs, but none felt right till I went to Arsenal. It was an easy choice for me. I just knew.

Amy: Are you ever motivated by money? I'm not asking if you're greedy, but since the women's game doesn't pay so much, is it an issue when you're signing to a new club?

Vivianne: If I'd gone to France or China, I'd have been paid way more money. Arsenal really wanted me, so they did everything they could to get me, but I didn't make a choice based on money. I chose Arsenal because it was the best club for me. I'm really happy that I made that choice. But I understand that some players – especially in women's football – go to China to earn decent money. Especially older players who don't want to have to worry about getting a job as soon as they retire.

Amy: Do you have any kind of plan regarding the next five or so years?

Vivianne: To be honest, I've got no idea. I'm not really thinking about the future. I'm really happy at Arsenal right now. The English league is going to be the best league, so I don't really see any reason for me to move any time soon. I'm not going to say that I want to stay here for the rest of my career, because it doesn't mean anything and it very rarely happens. I might want to go to Australia at some point. I'm twenty-two, so I hopefully have another ten years in me.

Amy: Have you considered coaching in the future?

Vivianne: I finished my FA Level 2 this year. I will probably start doing my UEFA B coaching next year. So yeah, that's the long-term plan.

Amy: Or you could always continue your career as a writer. Tell us about your other life, as the writer of a series of books in which you are a comic-book hero?

Vivianne: A publishing company in Holland contacted me and asked if I wanted to become a role model by putting my name to a series of books. I loved the idea and jumped right on it! I Skype with the writer when she is writing a book as she doesn't know anything about football. It worked out pretty well.

✪　✪　✪

Amy: Do your parents and your brother come and watch you?

Vivianne: It's quite hard for Lars because he plays football too. But the whole family is coming over for the end-of-season party. My parents are driving over with my grandparents. My brother and his girlfriend are flying over. But they don't get to come over that often because they're just too busy.

Amy: Do you miss home?

Vivianne: Only my family and friends. And the cheese! I left home when I was fifteen, although I was only a forty-five-minute drive away. And I left properly when I moved to Munich at the age of seventeen. I do get homesick sometimes, but I have a good life here.

Amy: Has the Brexit palaver been slightly unsettling for you?

Vivianne: I'll think about it if it happens! The club have basically said that for everyone who's already here, in the country, not much will change. Can you imagine the Premier League without all its foreign players? It's ludicrous. The Scottish players at Arsenal don't know if Scotland is going to become independent and stay in Europe… it's one big mess. I don't want to get stressed about something that might never happen.

Amy: Let's move on from the hypothetical to reality. Well, to what I hope will become a reality. Do you think the World Cup in

France will change the perception of women's football? It finally has decent sponsorship and games are selling out.

Vivianne: I really hope so! England as a country has a huge passion for football and when it hosts the women's Euros in 2021, I think everything will change. Let's make France one big festival and take it from there.

David Lammy

&

Eric Dier

David: Do you roll with Ronaldo?

Eric: No, ha ha. I've got some questions for you, but you might find them a bit strange.

David: Go ahead. Ask me anything.

Eric: I would like to know your opinion on basic income.

Houses of Parliament, May 2019

David Lammy was born in Tottenham, London, in 1972 to Guyanese parents. At the age of ten, he was awarded a choral scholarship to sing at Peterborough Cathedral and to attend The King's School, Peterborough. He studied law at the School of Oriental and African Studies in London and was called to the Bar of England and Wales in 1994. He practised as a barrister in England and the United States before becoming the first black Briton to study a Masters in Law at Harvard Law School. He was first elected as the Labour MP for Tottenham in 2000 and served eight years as a minister in the Labour government from 2002 to 2010. As a prominent campaigner for social justice, Lammy has been outspoken about Windrush British citizens being granted British citizenship, fought for justice for the Grenfell families and, in 2017, published the Lammy Review about the treatment of Black, Asian and Minority Ethnic individuals in the UK's criminal justice system. He is an ambassador for Action Aid as well as being the patron of a number of charities in Tottenham. He is the author of *Out of the Ashes: Britain After the Riots* and *Tribes: How Our Need to Belong Can Make or Break the Good Society.*

Eric Dier was born in Cheltenham in 1994. He is grandson of Ted Croker, a former secretary of the Football Association and president of Cheltenham Town, great-nephew of Peter Croker, who played professionally for Charlton Athletic, and son of Jeremy Dier, a retired professional tennis player. The Dier family moved to Portugal when Eric was seven and, a year later, he started playing for Sporting CP's academy. He signed professional terms with Sporting in 2010 before going on loan to Everton in January 2011 and winning the Under-18 Premier League with them at the end of the 2011 season. In 2012, upon his return to Lisbon, he moved from Sporting's B team to the first team. In 2014, Dier joined Tottenham Hotspur for £4 million. In 2011, the midfielder – who can also play at centre back and right back – was called up to the England Under-18s and, in 2015, to the senior team. He was in the England squad for the 2018 World Cup and scored the decisive penalty against Colombia – the first time England had ever won a penalty shoot-out at a World Cup. Tottenham were runners-up of the 2018–19 UEFA Champions League.

⚽ ⚽ ⚽

David Lammy: Welcome to Parliament, Eric. Have you ever visited before?

Eric Dier: No, it's my first time.

David: Let's get going with our questions. I am curious to know what it was like for you to move to Portugal at a young age and to then come back to Britain as a twenty-year-old. Do you feel British or European?

Eric: Until I was seven, we lived in Cowfold, Sussex; my dad is from Brighton and my mum is from Cheltenham. When I was seven, we moved to Portugal and all my early memories are of living there and not in England. So, although my family is British, I look at Portugal as my home.

David: Did you come back to Britain very often?

Eric: No, not really. The time to come back would have been the summer holidays and we didn't want to leave Portugal when it's nice and hot. I've got a big family – my parents and five siblings – so we were happy to be together in Portugal.

David: What did your parents do? I know they were both heavily involved in sport.

Eric: My mum wasn't working at this point, and my dad worked in tennis. As he travelled all over the world for work, it didn't matter where we lived. My parents thought Portugal offered a better lifestyle given the size of our family. My mum then worked on Euro 2004, which was obviously held in Portugal. My family moved back to England in 2010 because my siblings were starting to go to university here and my mum started a new job.

David: When you say you're Portuguese, what do you mean?

Eric: I find it hard to explain. The best way of putting it is to say that I'm English but I'm from Portugal, if that makes sense! I had the chance to play for Portugal when I was younger but I never accepted it because my parents are English. My grandparents are English. It's very clear in my mind that I'm English. But, in terms of everything that I learned and the way I am as a person, I owe that to growing up in Portugal.

David: But what does that really mean? I don't mean in terms of Mediterranean clichés such as being hot-tempered or eating late at night, but rather in the sense of how that upbringing has defined you?

Eric: I'm a bit more open-minded towards different cultures and the way different people live. I speak fluent Portuguese and so was able to pick up Spanish. I can very easily adapt to any environment. I'm just as comfortable sitting with the South American or Belgian or English players at Tottenham.

David: Do you roll with Ronaldo?

Eric: No, ha ha. I've got some questions for you, but you might find them a bit strange.

David: Go ahead. Ask me anything.

Eric: I would like to know your opinion on basic income.

David: On a basic-income guarantee?

Eric: Yeah.

David: I like a basic-income guarantee a lot. I'll give you some context by telling you about my own background. My dad bought our house in Tottenham for £6,000 so, by the time he left when I was twelve, the mortgage was pretty low. But we grew up poor because there was only one income. And, in those days, coming from a broken home brought a certain degree of embarrassment. Shame even. At the same time, it wasn't a chaotic life and we all felt very loved. My mum did two or three jobs to make sure my four siblings and I didn't miss out on things. If there was a school trip, she would save up for it. I remember being really upset when I was ten or eleven because I wanted a pair of adidas Gazelles but my mother could only afford to buy me a pair of trainers from Tesco. We may never have had branded clothes, but the bottom line was that we had stability.

I travel around the country a lot and what I see today all over

England as well as in my constituency is people who really have no money. Their zero-hour contracts mean they can't plan. Their benefits change week to week. Their job changes week to week in terms of how many hours they can do. Their housing tenure is really challenging. They certainly don't own their own home. Not in London. They are actually very lucky if they're in council housing, which is now rare. They're probably living in a rented flat of some kind and they could be thrown out by the landlord at any point. Which means children have to move from one school to another. I see a lot of that.

I'm very keen to give people back the dignity of stability. And that's not about being wealthy. It's not about social mobility. It's simply about the dignity of a stable life. The minute you're able to plan, to save up, to have a holiday – the things that many of us take for granted – well-being and health improve.

For all of those reasons, I think it's no longer just about the minimum wage. Or the minimum hourly rate. It's about a basic income to survive on. In a world of huge inequality, that is the way to go.

I have a comfortable life with my wife's combined earnings. My children don't want for things. I am not living anywhere like the life I had as a child. But I haven't got as much money as you, Eric. How do you feel about inequality? And I don't ask with any judgement, I'm just interested why you asked that question.

Eric: I asked because the basic-income guarantee is something that another player and I have discussed a lot. And it's the first time I've ever spoken to a politician.

David: Do you agree or disagree with it?

Eric: I think I agree with it. At the beginning I wasn't so sure, but the more I read about it, the more I think it's the only fair way. The player and I were talking about the fear that technology will put people out of work and we were wondering if the basic-income guarantee could protect them from that happening.

David: This is leading to all sorts of questions that I've got for you. But first of all, do I fear technology taking our jobs? It's happening already. The pace of technological change is huge. I sometimes worry that the political class is not being as honest with the population as they need to be about the kind of skills it now takes to get ahead in society. There is a group of jobs that are truly global and which pay truly global incomes. They range from being a global entrepreneur to being a heart surgeon to being a footballer. There are then a set of careers with high-level skills. Again, they command competitive salaries. And then there's a whole range of things that were done by human beings that artificial intelligence is now doing, and we will continue to see those jobs go. Now, it's not that new jobs don't arrive, but you need skills to do those jobs.

That is the reality, but I'm not sure how much people fully understand it. And I certainly don't think that we are doing well enough. And it lies behind some – but not all – of the Brexit noise. We're not doing well enough in huge tracts of central England, northern towns, seaside towns, areas where there is a scarcity of well-paid work that enables people to get on the ladder. So yes, absolutely, in those circumstances you've got to have a basic income for people.

Eric: Is London out of touch with the rest of the country?

David: Well, it depends whose London you are talking about. I'm not sure my constituents feel out of touch. In an age of identity politics we tend to talk about ethnic minorities in one box, white working-class in another. But they're all working class. And then, of course, there is a liberal elite who probably do tend to be out of touch. But what I think really divides is what I call an 'asset class'. People like my parents who were able to buy a house years ago that is now worth a lot of money. They have a comfortable income as a consequence of owning either a house or having a pension. And then everyone else – the people who live in other parts of the country where property hasn't seen huge appreciation – have no prospect of making that kind of money. I think those are the sorts of divides that are emerging.

But let's go back to equality. I would like to push you a bit more, if I may, on the context of your questions. What was your exposure to poverty when you were growing up?

Eric: If my parents hadn't had six kids, they would have been comfortable. We were never missing anything, but my parents didn't spoil us. If I wanted a specific pair of trainers, my dad would make me wait for them or not let me have them at all. They worked very hard and we went to good schools.

David: What kind of 'good school'? Do you mean private school?

Eric: I went to private school in Portugal for about two years. It was one of the best schools in Lisbon. When I was thirteen and started living in the Sporting Lisbon Academy, I went to a Portuguese school, which was completely at the opposite end of the spectrum. It was enlightening for me. I went from a school where kids had drivers taking them to school to a regular school where every kid walked or got the bus. So I experienced both extremes really.

David: Did you make friends on both sides of the tracks?

Eric: Absolutely. But the friendships I made at the Sporting Academy were really strong because sixty of us got the bus to school every day. So we had this togetherness from the start. I still have friends from that school who come to visit me in London and who I visit in various countries.

David: How educated do you feel? It's actually a personal question because my thirteen-year-old son is in the Development Squad at an elite football club. He desperately wants to be a footballer. He's a defender, probably a bit like Sol Campbell back in the day in the sense of build and play.

Eric: You might have to edit that, seeing as Sol went from Tottenham to Arsenal!

David: But I wonder if my son can pursue football *and* an education. I'm hoping you can help me out with this. The thought of you and your fellow footballers sitting around talking about basic income definitely puts me at ease a bit!

Eric: Football and education is a topic that I've come across a lot and I definitely have an opinion on it, but it's very tough. I think there's a complete misconception between footballers as they really are and what people think of footballers. I'm very lucky at Tottenham because I'm surrounded by people who are bright and curious about the world. But if we're talking specifically about education, I stopped going to school when I was sixteen. My focus was entirely on football. But you don't know if you're actually going to make it until you sign to a club and start playing for the senior team. After perhaps ten games you can be pretty sure that you're going to make a career in football. You have to keep working hard, training hard, try not to get injured. If you do that, you can make a career for the rest of your life.

David: Hang on a minute, Eric. That's not quite right, is it? You said 'for the rest of your life'. Do you mean up to thirty?

Eric: Sorry, I meant till you're thirty-five. The rest of your footballing life! But I had a belief when I was sixteen; I was pretty sure I could make it.

David: And you know by the age of sixteen that you are going to devote the first part of your adult life to football, right? One of the things I've seen in life, Eric, is that most people are generalists. I am definitely a generalist. I know a little about a lot of things.

343

Actually, as I've got older, I've become a little bit expert in some things. Particularly in public life. People tend to think of me when they think of tough domestic urban knife crime, gang crime and so on. But I like to know a little about a lot of things. However, some people are specialists. They become seriously expert at one thing and they make a trade out of it. They make a career out of it. And it feels to me like football requires you from a very early age to completely commit to it. You were committed to football, but other boys – and girls – become distracted by girls or boys at the age of fifteen or sixteen. Their focus shifts away from football. They start going to parties. The young players that make it are the ones who are most single-minded about their football. They are not generalists, they are specialists. They only want to pursue football.

Eric: The gaffer [Mauricio Pochettino] likes to use the word 'craft'. He says football is a craft.

David: Craft. Yes. Very good.

Eric: A craftsman has to take care of his craft. He has to look after it and work on it. So when you start to go out and get interested in girls, it's a pivotal time.

David: What age is that in Portugal?

Eric: Fourteen or fifteen. But I was completely obsessed. I had nothing else on my mind.

David: With girls?

Eric: No! With football. I was this obsessed: I lived at the Academy but my parents lived only an hour away. It would have been too much to go backwards and forwards during the week, but I could have easily gone home at weekends. However, we had a lot of African players from New Guinea and a lot of players from the north of Portugal who couldn't easily go home at weekends. If they weren't going home, neither was I. If they were suffering, I was going to suffer too. Because no one was going to suffer more than me, or be more dedicated. That was my mindset.

David: Wow. That says something about your character.

Eric: Yeah. So that was my mindset even when I was living at the Academy. I was just completely obsessed. When I was growing up, there were players around me who were better than me. Some of them still play, some don't. But it wasn't about their talent. I genuinely believe that success in football is about 10 per cent talent and 90 per cent hard work. And dedication. And giving 100 per cent every single day.

I had a best friend who played with me at Sporting from the age of eight until fourteen, fifteen. And then he wasn't wanted at Sporting any more and he went to play at other clubs, but they all let him go. He called me two or three times to discuss what he should do. It was extremely difficult for him, but he's a smart boy with a fantastic family. He realized that he needed to put football aside and focus on his studies. He went to university and now he works in Lisbon.

David: That is brutal. Especially for a boy of only fifteen or sixteen.

Eric: It really is. I would have found that kind of rejection incredibly hard to take. It's a very difficult decision to make and I think a lot of parents are delusional about their kids. They think their son is going to be the next Ronaldo, the next Messi. The most important thing for a parent to be is supportive until a decision has to be made: continue with football or leave it behind and continue your education or pursue another job. But try to make that decision sooner rather than later because I've seen guys in their early twenties realize they can't make it as a footballer and, by that time, they've missed out on other opportunities in life. I'm not talking about your son here, by the way. I'm talking about those choices in a very general way.

Didn't you leave home at a young age? I've done my research: you got a scholarship to sing at Peterborough Cathedral and to attend The King's School in Peterborough.

David: I'm glad you raised that. I sang every day for three or four years as a chorister. Once you practise something day in day out and it takes over your life and you become *really* good at it, you understand what excellence feels like. I always think it's a shame when I meet people who clearly haven't had the opportunity to experience that. It's about finessing a craft, as Pochettino would say. Once you've discovered that excellence, you can apply it to other things. You know what it takes, whether it's making the effort to write a speech that takes people with you in a persuasive way or writing a book. So the opportunity I had between the ages of ten and thirteen to really hone something has resonated through my adult life. Now, I haven't gone on to become a professional musician, even though there was a bit of me that wanted to become a young Michael Jackson at a certain point. But I am still using my voice, I just moved a few shades in a different direction.

What about you? You painted this picture of yourself as obsessed with football. Has that obsession remained now that you're in your mid-twenties?

Eric: It really has; I play football with my friends on the beach or in someone's garden every summer. I've never lost the enjoyment I had as a kid. But there are more distractions now than when I was a fifteen-year-old whose mates were dating and partying. All these opportunities arise to do this and that. A couple of years ago, I was having a chat with the gaffer in his office. He has a football on his desk to remind him that football is the priority. Football is number one. And my dad always said to me, growing up, 'If you take care of football, football will take care of you.' And that's the mentality I've always kept.

David: What did your dad mean by that?

Eric: If I focus on football, if I dedicate myself to it, then it will look after me.

David: A sort of philosophy. And can you apply that when you're injured, as you have been this season?

Eric: I can try! This year has been very tough for me. I'd never really been injured before and it was worse because it wasn't an injury, it was an illness. I would have preferred a football injury to acute appendicitis. With an injury you can work hard to get better, but you have no control over illness. I'm twenty-five now but I was twenty-four when my appendix burst, and it completely threw me. And then I kept picking up viruses afterwards because my immune system was compromised. I'd start training and I'd get ill again. I'd get better, get ill.

David: When you say it was a bad time, how bad exactly? Were you depressed?

Eric: No, I wasn't depressed. I tried to put it in context. I wasn't injured once in my first four and a half years at Spurs, so I was extremely lucky for a long time. My football wasn't on the ropes. I was just extremely frustrated.

David: I understand. Do you have another question for me?

Eric: I do, yes. Your father left you when you were twelve. I've heard lots of people say that being raised in a single-parent household was their downfall. Equally I've heard lots of people say it gave them drive and made them successful. Why do you think that is? I haven't asked the question very well.

David: Actually, you've asked the question very well. I don't know if I've got all of the answers, but there are definitely some things that come together. I happen to believe that in life that you are handed a suitcase with some clothes in, but no one gets all the clothes. You open the suitcase and life is in part about making the best of the clothes that you've got, right? In my suitcase I was handed a very, very wonderful woman that was my mother. A formidable, amazing, wonderful mother. And I say that because it was self-evident that she would sacrifice everything for me. She was the absolute opposite of lazy. Which is why to some extent she died quite young, at sixty-eight. As I have already said, she worked three jobs because she didn't want us to go without. She could be quite tough. She really believed in education. She left school at about fourteen to raise her brothers and sisters because her own mother died young. So she put a lot of effort into her children getting what she didn't get. And she was great. And she was my best friend growing up. I talked to her about everything. I might not have entirely lucked out on my father, although he had his strengths as well. But I definitely did on my mother. So that helped.

I was also precocious as a child. My wife and I talk about this a lot; as young people we both had adult friends. An example of this is the wonderful English teacher who taught me A level. Brenda Pinder was a fantastic teacher of Shakespeare and an amazing socialist. We became great friends. When I was applying to the Labour Party to become a Member of Parliament, I knew that she'd be really proud. I sent her the application form and she sent it back covered with red marks. I became friends with people who taught me at primary and secondary school and at university. I became friends with the local priest. Those friendships were important because I had a chance to watch adults fuck up and I knew not to make those mistakes myself.

Eric: Were you the youngest child?

David: My sister is younger than me, but I'm the second-youngest. My oldest brother is now sixty. I knew a lot of older kids who often got into trouble with the police, who were really struggling. Second-generation immigrants who were born in Britain, struggling with the expectations society had of them, from teachers to the police. This was in the mid-1980s, around the time of the first riots in Tottenham. I remember growing up and one of the biggest things I feared was going to prison. Please god, not me. Just anything but… Please god, I don't want that life.

Neither did I want a life as hard as my mother's had been. By the time I was twelve, thirteen, I was working in McDonald's, in KFC, in a warehouse and, later, as a security guard. I had to work to buy the things I wanted. To buy those Gazelle trainers. I worked alongside people for whom those jobs were permanent, and I was determined not to have to live that life. And I say that absolutely without judgement. But I wanted my life to be more. I wanted a job where every day is different.

You asked about single mums: my mum gave me an education and the chance to do better than she did. I was lucky. She was supportive of my ambition. And I need to be clear about that. I had a wonderful mother, wonderful teachers, wonderful mentors. Wonderful people who were determined to see this young black kid from Tottenham make it. And I guess I was receptive to that. Tell me who helped you to make it.

Eric: Primarily I would have to thank my family. My parents and my brothers and sisters. I have a very strong mum and dad. My brothers and sisters are incredible. They never let me get too big-headed. What did you feel about moving away from home? How old did you say you were?

David: I was eleven.

Eric: Wow, that's young. Did your siblings move away from home as well or was it just you?

David: Just me.

Eric: Yes, I was the only one who moved. Not being around my brothers and sisters when I was growing up is my biggest regret. I missed out on a lot with my brothers especially. From thirteen to twenty, I missed a lot. That's one of the things that has been most difficult for me. But, since then…

David: Hang on. You can't just skip over that. When you say it was difficult, what exactly do you mean? For example, do you look back on family photos with a sense of loss?

Eric: No, not family photos. But you can't just take time off for important family events when you're a footballer. So I missed my sister's wedding because I had a game. I don't regret missing my sister's wedding for the game because what else could I do? I couldn't not turn up for the game. But, over time, those things become hard. It was hard for me to be close to my brothers when I was at the Sporting Academy. We're extremely close now; one of my little brothers lives with me, and my other little brother lived with me until he went to Australia. Now I feel we've made up for that time. But there were times when I feel like our relationship was very superficial.

David: OK, I understand.

Eric: Simply because I wasn't there in the day-to-day. I've never really spoken about this, and my brothers don't even really know this, but a couple of years ago I found it extremely difficult to be in the position I was in. It's what I mean when I talk about the perception of footballers and people not understanding the dynamics involved. You're twenty years old and you're suddenly earning a lot of money, and your older sisters are still trying to find their way. I played for England when I was twenty, twenty-one, and my brothers didn't know what they wanted to do with their lives, which is normal at that age.

David: That must have been quite lonely.

Eric: It was, yes. It bothered me a lot. That period was probably the most difficult time for me. When I started to become successful and my brothers and sisters were still trying to find their feet.

David: When you say 'bothered', what does that mean? How exactly did it bother you?

Eric: I felt guilty. My brothers and sisters are extremely driven and hard-working as well. But football happens early and it can happen quickly. So I could be retired by thirty-five and they could be at the peak of their careers or certainly on the way up.

David: Do you think it bothered them?

Eric: Not as much as it bothered me. My siblings were never jealous.

David: In my own family it isn't about wealth and millions.

Eric: No, but it's not just that. It's fame. It's success.

David: For me it's status and a degree of profile, fame, whatever. I became a Member of Parliament very young, at twenty-seven, and I often felt quite isolated and exposed. When I arrived in Parliament, I'd never been to Westminster before in my life, but everyone knew who I was. I'd won a by-election. I was young, black and I could hear people: 'Oh, David Lammy. Look, it's David Lammy.' I didn't know who the hell they were so I felt incredibly exposed. I couldn't fart without it being in the newspapers.

I could see some of my friends thinking, 'God, what am I doing? He's an MP at twenty-seven and I've barely worked out what I want to do with my life.' And it's hard with your family too because you're learning your craft in those early years and you're putting in the hours. You don't do much hanging around and chilling. It might be different with football, but even when you are with family and loved ones, you're not entirely there because there's so much going on in your head.

My wife says when I became a father I didn't have any trouble taking on the responsibility because I'd already taken on the responsibility of Tottenham and my constituents, who needed a good MP. In that sense, I found fatherhood a breeze in comparison to becoming a Member of Parliament. So I think I sense some of what you're saying. Although obviously it's a bit different. Do you worry about life after thirty-five?

Eric: Not yet. I'm a big basketball fan and I like what Kobe Bryant said when he retired: 'If basketball is the greatest thing I'll ever do I'll be disappointed.' I hope my mentality will be the same. I certainly don't want to spend my post-football years being nostalgic. I want to always be looking forward. I don't really think about when I'm going to retire, but I might well stay in football in some capacity or another.

✪ ✪ ✪

David: You took the bold and intrepid and courageous step of tweeting your support of the People's Vote in March. I'm one of Parliament's ambassadors for a People's Vote, but tell me what you think about Europe and Brexit as someone who is British but from Portugal.

Eric: I was born in the UK and accepted in Portugal and I'm very grateful for that. When I go back to Portugal, it feels like going home. I tweeted 'People's Vote' when Theresa May was on her second or third attempt at getting the deal through. My little brother is very outspoken and he is always asking why I don't tweet my opinions. But it goes back to what you were saying earlier about knowing a little about a lot of things. I'm like that. So I wouldn't want to speak out about things I don't fully understand.

David: I think it's great that you tweeted 'People's Vote'.

Eric: I'm doing an Open University course in social science and I'm writing an essay at the moment about the 2011 London riots. My mum told me yesterday that you'd written a book called *Out of the Ashes* about the riots.

David: If you like, I'll go to my office and get you a copy before you go. How wonderful that you're doing an OU course. How long have you been doing it?

Eric: I'm at the end of my first year.

David: Are you actually getting through the work?

Eric: Yeah, because you can set your own pace.

David: Have you got any sense that the Open University are aware that it's you doing their course?

Eric: Yeah, they know because I have a tutor who I speak to on the phone.

David: Why did you pick social science?

Eric: It's just what interests me the most. I wasn't going to say anything about it because I like to keep it private, but I wanted to ask you about the London riots.

David: And what is the question of the essay you're writing?

Eric: 'If the radical perspective on riots is poverty, unemployment and inequality, what is the conservative perspective?'

David: Great. I love it.

Eric: I have to argue both sides.

David: Right. If I wasn't a Member of Parliament I would love to be a teacher. I'd love particularly to teach sixth-formers or university students. So I would say that all riots on the whole take a spark. That spark is usually a perceived act of injustice on behalf of the authority. The authority is usually the police. And it usually comes off the back of many years of perceived micro-aggressions or a profound sense of injustice. 'Stop and search' being the usual spark in most developed countries where riots occur.

And, of course, behind that you can examine poverty, inequality, lack of resources, lack of youth provision. Think, for example, of some parts of America – of downtown Chicago or Detroit – and what happens particularly to black urban communities if significant parts of the population have been put in prison over many, many years. You get a tipping point that can, of course, cause the underbelly of a riot. And years of grievance in relation to the state. But I don't know how radical that interpretation is.

Eric: I don't know why they use the word radical. It seems a bit unfair.

David: I suppose it's to create a contrast. The conservative perspective, I guess, is that the riot is a breakdown of social order. That it is a kind of anarchy. It would focus on the looting. If you look back at the 2011 riots, you will find politicians using emotive words like 'feral'. And police saying they've 'never seen this scale or kind of aggression'. So the conservative idea is that this is more about public order and a breakdown in order, and less of an examination of the underlying reasons for that breakdown in order.

It might be that it was simply about poor policing. But actually the truth of the riot, I suspect, is these underlying injustices that have been allowed to go on for way too long. And, in the end, most people don't riot if they've got a job. Most people don't riot if they own a home. Most people don't riot—

Eric: If they're happy.

David: If they have a happy future and some prospects. Something to look forward to. They riot if they haven't got a stake in society.

And that's the phrase I kept coming back to in my book. What does it mean to have a stake in society? And how is it that we've created – not just in this country, but in lots of the developed world – people with no stake in society? And what happens when you have no stake in society? And since I wrote that book, we're also seeing a bunch of charlatans telling people that the reason you don't have a stake in society is because of the liberal elite down in London or because immigrants came and took your job. Or, if it's from a left perspective, it's because of the super-rich. The perspectives can come from different places, but a whole bunch of narratives start creeping in to explain why you haven't got that stake, and I think we're now getting into a period that's going to be very rocky indeed.

Eric: Has Tottenham recovered from the riots?

David: I wish I could say that the underlying reasons that led up to the riots had all been dealt with. But they haven't been dealt with by any stretch. However, there was a particular spark for the 2011 riots: Tottenham resident Mark Duggan was shot dead by police officers. I pray to God that something like that doesn't happen in my constituency again. I do think people recognize that tearing up and smashing up your own community is a bad idea, but I can't say Tottenham has recovered. I mean, it's recovered from the riots. But that's a slightly separate question to what are the ingredients that led up to it. And obviously people like myself and Tottenham Hotspur are doing all we can to try and amend it.

Eric: How important is Tottenham Hotspur in Tottenham?

David: The club is really good at partnering with charities, the local authority and others that can bring a lot of money and other things into the constituency. I am very glad that the club didn't move to the Olympic Park. I was really clear in my mind that whatever people feel about football and the huge amount of money, it represents excellence for my constituents. Football is an elite sport. And that is very, very precious. We haven't got a university or the BBC headquarters or a big international company in Tottenham. What we have is Tottenham Hotspur.

Eric: Are you excited about the new stadium?

David: Very. It's amazing. State of the art. It's absolutely a destination. It's a catalyst for regeneration. And I don't want that to be top-down. I want it to be grassroots. I want it to take local people with it. And there are tensions, particularly with all the housing issues in London. But it's an amazing stadium and it looks like it's lifting the fortunes of the team as well. I think being in the Champions League final is absolutely amazing. I remember growing up with Tottenham in the age of Glenn Hoddle, Ossie Ardiles, Ricky Villa and Garth Crooks, and just winning the FA Cup was a big deal for us. And if we were to win the Champions League, I can't tell you how important it would be for my constituents. This has been an incredible season for English football.

Eric: Yeah, this has been the most exciting season, pretty much since England reached the semi-finals of the World Cup.

David: It's strange to think that four English teams are in the two European finals against the backdrop of Brexit. It's been a great season, as you say, but also a deeply unpleasant one in terms of racism. We should talk about that too.

Eric: Yeah, I'd like to talk about that. I have a problem with it.

David: Go on.

Eric: I think it's misleading for people to talk about racism in football. It's about racism in society. My experience of football is that the players all respect one another, regardless of their background or heritage. I've asked foreign players if they have ever felt discriminated against in the dressing room and they've all said 'never'. Of course, there will be players who have experienced racist attitudes from other players, but I've never witnessed it. And the same goes for women's football. I've never seen a male footballer be disrespectful towards women's football.

I think one of the greatest things about football is the diversity within a team. At Tottenham I'm sharing a dressing room with players from South Korea, Kenya, Belgium, France, Spain, Argentina, Colombia. That's the beautiful thing about football. It brings people together in a way that I don't think anything else does.

David: I guess people are talking about the way football is regulated. I have some contact with black footballers old and new and they tell me about the racism that they get from fans and ask whether football is doing enough to deal with that. Now, you're right, that is society. In the stadium. But I guess they might be raising the question of how seriously that racism is being taken by FIFA, UEFA, the FA?

There is most definitely an issue. For example, Chris Hughton is a great, great guy. A model human being. A fantastic manager. I'm fond of Brighton and thank goodness they stayed up, but now that he's been sacked, there are no black managers in the Premier League. Not a single one. And that's where the football comes in. What do you think?

Eric: I agree with everything you've just said. I'm not denying there is racism in football, but I don't think football can be made responsible for a wider societal problem. It's a global problem.

David: Where do you stand on fans' tribalism?

Eric: That's a tricky one! When we played Dortmund at home, I was so impressed by their fans. They supported their team throughout the ninety minutes, even when they were down by three goals. They paid no attention to the Tottenham fans, they were just right behind their team.

David: The thing is that football fans are so invested in the history of their team and the pride they feel in their team's success. It's a

361

distraction from everyday life. Life can be tough for lots of people so it's no surprise that they invest so much in football. Because perhaps what's outside the stadium hasn't always been so great, right? Which is why I think it can get quite tribal.

Eric: Even school football or Sunday league football can provide a welcome distraction. Plus it helps you work in a team environment. It makes you sociable. It helps you speak up. It can be easier to integrate. Football can give kids so much. And adults. It's about togetherness. When we play football, we're all the same. Everyone's equal. Talking of speaking up, what do you think of Raheem doing so?

David: I think he has touched on a millennial zeitgeist. What he talks about is something that a younger generation can understand, white or black. He's been really clever at showing the unfairness of the media in relation to some of the discourse, narrative and coverage of him and other young black players.

It leads to a wider conversation about how people are judged. For example, Boris Johnson seems to be able to get away with absolute murder in public life. Stuff that I could never get away with. Stuff that a female colleague couldn't get away with. We'd be crucified. He is given a free ride because he's a public school boy.

Raheem's been really good at showing the way that language is used to talk about him and other players. I'm afraid that language is deeply racist and these things have to be pointed out. Those right-wing tabloid headlines might sell newspapers, they might create a narrative, but they have to be challenged.

There are broader issues about how football is challenging society. Your teammate Danny Rose has raised the issue of depression. But I don't personally comment that much now about racism in football because I spend so much time having to talk about issues in wider society.

Eric: It's interesting that racism isn't so rife in other sports. Anthony Joshua is a national treasure. Jessica Ennis. Mo Farah. They are celebrated as the face of sports in England.

David: This is a discussion that I've had before. I was recently raising some big issues on behalf of UK basketball, which is a really important game in constituencies like mine. It doesn't, I don't think, get its fair share of investment. So some of this is about where is the money going. Some of it's about challenging some of the stereotypes and the cost of these sports. Take sailing. The Greig City Academy in Haringey is a huge, wonderful school. It takes as many of its kids sailing as it can, but it's a sport that requires lots of funds, lots of resource and is not generally accessible to kids in constituencies like mine.

Sport can only benefit from diversity. When Tessa Jowell was Secretary of State for Culture and I was her Culture Minister, she told me how the atmosphere changed during the entire run of the 2012 Olympics. At the start there's swimming, sailing and archery and the Olympic village feels quite white. Then the athletes turn up, the diversity hits the roof and the whole atmosphere changes. And it's because it's suddenly much more mixed.

These are big questions for sport generally. But clearly there are issues of money and access and investment in particular sports that in the end will define how grassroots sport brings on elite professionals like yourself.

Listen, Eric. I could sit here and talk to you all day, but I'm running really late for an interview with a journalist who wants to talk to me about the marijuana laws.

Eric: What's your take on that?

David: Briefly: the war on drugs hasn't worked. A young black guy caught smoking a joint as he walks down Tottenham High Road is far more likely to be stopped and searched than someone doing the same at, say, Oxford University. My instinct tells me this is unfair. And in the end, when I look at knife crime and gang crime, it's not actually about the knives and the gangs. There have always been gangs. Dickens was writing about gangs in Britain. It's about organized criminality and the organization particularly of cocaine around the world and into this country, where it is generally consumed by middle-class people. There are different rules for different people. I'm interested to find out how you can begin to change that. I'm interested to know if we should follow the Canadian model. But I'm not going to ask you what you think!

Eric: I really appreciate your time. It's been a privilege.

David: Thank you for coming. Good luck with your degree and on the pitch. I will be watching at the new stadium and hoping that there will be many victory parades down Tottenham High Road for my constituents to enjoy.

Acknowledgments

For going above and beyond:
Everyone in the book, who gave their time without hesitation; Brian Bilston; James Corden; Clare Drysdale (editorial director at Allen & Unwin); Joanne Glasbey; Bonnie Raphael Irvine; Gary Lineker; David Maddock; David Morrissey; Laura Padoan (spokesperson for refugees at UNHCR UK); Andy Prevezer; Dan Rookwood.

Huge thanks:
Akua Agyemfra, Charlotte Atyeo, Joe Bacon, Carol Bishop, Marie-Christine Bouchier, Roscoe Bowman, Jeanette Brennan, Rich Carr, Karen Cham, Lizzie Chapman, John Cross, Dan Davies, Oliver Durose, FlowSports, Simon Heggie, Emma Heyworth-Dunn, Kelly Hogarth, Flo Howard, Rebecca James, Jordan Johnson, Dylan Jones, Josh Kaile, KBJ Management, Simon Kuper, Caroline McAteer, Matt McCann, Ryan Mundy, Roger Pask, Carol Raphael, Alex Segal, Patricia Sergison, Ehsen Shah, Laura Sherlock, Alex Spillius, Kate Straker, Sarah Strickland, Becky Thomas, Lisa Thomas, Gemma Thompson, Jo Unwin and Jon Wilde.

Thank you also to Hope Street Hotel, Liverpool, for giving me a discounted bed for the night and to Virgin Trains for complimentary travel to Liverpool and Manchester.